Download Forms on Nolo.com

To download the forms, go to this book's companion page at:

 www.nolo.com/back-of-book/LEAR.html

Checking the companion page is also a good way
to stay informed on topics related to this book.

More Resources
from Nolo.com

 ### Legal Forms, Books, & Software

Hundreds of do-it-yourself products—all written in plain English,
approved, and updated by our in-house legal editors.

 ### Legal Articles

Get informed with thousands of free articles on everyday legal topics.
Our articles are accurate, up to date, and reader friendly.

 ### Find a Lawyer

Want to talk to a lawyer? Use Nolo to find a lawyer who can help
you with your case.

15th Edition

Leases & Rental Agreements

**Attorneys Ann O'Connell
& Janet Portman**

FIFTEENTH EDITION   AUGUST 2023

Book and Cover Design   SUSAN PUTNEY

Editor   JANET PORTMAN

Proofreading   IRENE BARNARD

Index   RICHARD GENOVA

Printing   SHERIDAN

ISSN: 1555-5291 (print)
ISSN: 2328-059X (online)

ISBN: 978-1-4133-3126-4 (pbk)
ISBN: 978-1-4133-3127-1 (ebook)

This book covers only United States law, unless it specifically states otherwise.

> **Please note**
>
> Accurate, plain-English legal information can help you solve many of your own legal problems. But this text is not a substitute for personalized advice from a knowledgeable lawyer. If you want the help of a trained professional— and we'll always point out situations in which we think that's a good idea— consult an attorney licensed to practice in your state.

MH Sub I, LLC dba Nolo, 909 N. Pacific Coast Hwy, 11th Fl, El Segundo, CA 90245.

About the Authors

Ann O'Connell is a legal editor at Nolo specializing in landlord-tenant and real estate law. She is a coauthor of *Nolo's Essential Guide to Buying Your First Home, Every Tenant's Legal Guide, Renters' Rights,* and *Every Landlord's Legal Guide.* Before joining Nolo, Ann was a freelance writer for other publications and law firms. She is a member of the bar in California, Nevada, and Colorado, where she is both an active attorney and a real estate broker. Ann has practiced in California and Colorado, and had her own firm in Colorado, where she focused on real estate, landlord-tenant, and small business law. Ann earned her B.A. from Boston College and her J.D. from UC Berkeley Law.

Janet Portman, an attorney and Nolo's Executive Editor, received undergraduate and graduate degrees from Stanford and a law degree from Santa Clara University. She is an expert on landlord-tenant law and the coauthor of *Every Tenant's Legal Guide, Renters' Rights, The California Landlord's Law Book: Rights & Responsibilities, Every Landlord's Legal Guide,* and *First-Time Landlord.*

Table of Contents

Your Lease and Rental Documents Companion

The month-to-month rental agreement or long-term lease that you and your tenant sign forms the contractual basis of your relationship. Taken together with federal, state, and local laws, it sets out almost all the legal and practical rules you and your tenant must follow, such as how many people may occupy the rental and for how long, the rent and deposit, and your (and your tenant's) repair and maintenance responsibilities.

We'll take you step by step through preparing a lease or rental agreement and the forms that supplement them. These forms include a rental application to help you choose the best tenants (and weed out the risky ones), and a landlord-tenant checklist to document the condition of the rental unit at the beginning and end of the tenancy (and avoid disputes over security deposits).

Fortunately, you don't need a lawyer to draft these important rental documents—just this book. Here's how we can help you:

State-specific legal information. We'll show you how to use the detailed state law charts in Appendix A to write legally compliant clauses. For example, the "State Security Deposit Rules" chart contains each state's rules on how much deposit you can charge, whether you need to keep the deposit in a separate account or pay interest on it, when you must return the deposit, and whether you're exempt from the rules based on the number of rental properties you own.

Where to find the forms. You'll find downloadable and customizable versions of the forms in this book on a companion page for this book on the Nolo website (see the box below for details).

To help you understand and complete the forms, we provide filled-out samples in the text.

> ⚠ CAUTION
>
> **Who shouldn't use our lease or rental agreement?** Don't use the forms in this book if you're renting out property that's subsidized by the government, or is a mobile home, hotel, or commercial property. Landlords who accept Section 8 vouchers will need to use the HUD addendum, which will add to the terms and conditions of the lease you draft using this product (the HUD terms will prevail in case of any inconsistencies). If you're renting out your condominium or townhouse, use these forms in conjunction with your homeowners' association CC&Rs (covenants, conditions, and restrictions).

> **Get Forms and More at This Book's Companion Page on Nolo.com**
>
> You'll find the lease, rental agreement, and all of the other forms in this book on its companion page on Nolo's website at:
>
> **www.nolo.com/back-of-book/LEAR.html**
>
> See Appendix B for a complete list of forms available on Nolo.com.

Other Helpful Nolo Titles and Online Information and Resources for Landlords

A lease or rental agreement is only one part of a landlord-tenant legal relationship. Nolo publishes several other books for landlords (most with legal forms and state-by-state information) that complement this book, including:

- *Every Landlord's Legal Guide.* A comprehensive explanation of landlord-tenant laws and the practical steps rental property owners can take to comply with them (while at the same time running an efficient and profitable business). It covers most key laws affecting landlords in all 50 states, including repair and maintenance responsibilities; liability for crime and environmental health hazards such as lead, mold, and bed bugs; rules and procedures for collecting and returning security deposits; antidiscrimination laws; privacy rules; employment laws affecting managers; tenants' rights to break a lease and leave early; how to resolve problems with tenants or begin the eviction process; issues such as meth labs; and more.
- *First-Time Landlord: Your Guide to Renting Out a Single-Family Home.* A starter guide for people who are renting out a house for the first time (or are considering doing so) and want a basic overview of the legal, practical, and financial issues involved, including estimating costs and profits, co-owning rental property with family, and managing rental income to maximize tax deductions.
- *Every Landlord's Guide to Managing Property.* Provides practical and legal advice for small-time landlords who manage property and tenants on the side. Includes do-it-yourself advice on handling day-to-day issues, such as nitty-gritty maintenance and conflicts with tenants regarding late rent, pets, and unauthorized occupants.
- *Every Landlord's Tax Deduction Guide.* A comprehensive explanation of deductions and other tax write-offs available to landlords, such as depreciation and insurance. Includes instructions for filling out Schedule E.
- For California landlords: *The California Landlord's Law Book: Rights & Responsibilities*, which contains all the information California landlords need to run their business; and *The California Landlord's Law Book: Evictions*, which takes you step-by-step through the court process of eviction.

You can order these landlord titles from Nolo's website (Nolo.com) or by phone (800-728-3555). You can also find Nolo books at bookstores and libraries.

The Nolo website has several online state-specific leases and other landlord forms for sale, lots of free information of interest to landlords, and 50-state charts of state laws, such as tenants' rights to withhold rent, eviction rules, restrictions on smoking in residential units, and small claims court limits. (Check out the "Landlords & Tenants" section at Nolo.com.) The "Legal Research" section on the Nolo website will also help you find federal and state laws that affect your property (look for the "Legal Research" link at the bottom of Nolo.com).

11 Tips for Being a Successful Landlord

1. **Don't rent to anyone before checking credit history, references, and background.** Haphazard screening often results in problem tenants who pay the rent late or not at all, trash your place, move in undesirable friends, or worse.

2. **Avoid illegal discrimination.** Comply with all federal, state, and local laws prohibiting discrimination on the basis of race or color, national origin, gender, age, familial status, disability, and other protected categories.

3. **Get all the important terms of the tenancy in writing.** Beginning with the rental application and lease or rental agreement, document your relationship with your tenants—including when and how you handle tenant complaints and repair problems, the amount of notice you must give to enter a tenant's apartment, and the like.

4. **Establish a clear, fair system of setting, collecting, holding, and returning security deposits.** Inspect and document the condition of the rental unit before the tenant moves in to avoid disputes over security deposits at move-out.

5. **Stay on top of repair and maintenance needs and make repairs when requested.** If the property is not kept in good repair, you'll alienate good tenants. And they might have the right to withhold rent, sue for injuries caused by defective conditions, or move out without notice.

6. **Don't let your tenants and property be easy marks for a criminal.** You could be liable for the tenant's injuries and losses.

7. **Respect your tenants' privacy.** Notify tenants whenever you plan to enter their rental unit, and provide at least 24 hours' notice (or the minimum amount required by state law).

8. **Disclose environmental hazards such as lead.** Landlords can be held liable for tenant health problems resulting from exposure to environmental poisons in the rental premises.

9. **Choose and supervise your manager carefully.** If a manager commits a crime or is incompetent, you could be held financially responsible. Do a thorough background check and clearly spell out the manager's duties.

10. **Purchase enough liability and other property insurance.** A well-designed insurance program can protect your rental property from losses caused by everything from fire and storms to burglary, vandalism, and personal injury and discrimination lawsuits.

11. **Try to resolve disputes with tenants without lawyers and lawsuits.** If you have a conflict with a tenant over rent, repairs, your access to the rental unit, noise, or some other issue that doesn't immediately warrant an eviction, meet with the tenant to see if the problem can be resolved informally. If that doesn't work, consider mediation by a neutral third party, often available at little or no cost from a publicly funded program. If your dispute involves money and all attempts to reach agreement fail, try small claims court, where you can represent yourself. Use it after a tenant moves out to collect unpaid rent or for property damage that the deposit can't cover.

Get a Little Help From Your Friends

Many landlords have discovered the value of belonging to a local or state association of rental property owners. These organizations range from small, volunteer-run groups to substantial city, county, or statewide organizations. Many offer a wide variety of services to members, including:

- legal information and updates through newsletters and seminars
- tenant-screening and credit check services
- training and practical advice on compliance with legal responsibilities
- a place to meet other rental property owners and exchange information and ideas, and
- referrals to professionals, including attorneys, accountants, maintenance firms, and property management companies.

If you can't find an association of rental property owners online, ask other landlords for references. You can also contact the National Apartment Association (www.naahq.org), a national organization whose members include many individual associations. Their website offers lots of free information, too.

1

Preparing a Lease or Rental Agreement

This chapter begins by explaining the differences between leases and rental agreements. You can use this information to decide which is right to use with your tenants. The chapter continues with step-by-step instructions on how to complete and customize your lease or rental agreement, taking into account important issues and legal considerations that we'll walk you through each step of the way.

 SEE AN EXPERT
The lease and rental agreement forms are legally sound as designed. If you change important terms or make major changes, however, you might affect a form's legal validity. Rather than take a chance, consider having an experienced landlord-tenant lawyer review your work.

Which Is Better, a Lease or a Rental Agreement?

One of the first decisions you need to make is whether to use a lease or a rental agreement. Often, your choice will depend on how long you want a tenant to stay, or whether you want the ability to raise the rent on relatively short notice. However, other factors come into play, so carefully read what follows before evaluating your own situation and making a decision.

Month-to-Month Rental Agreement

A written rental agreement establishes a tenancy for a short period of time. The law refers to these agreements as "periodic" or "month-to-month" tenancies, although it's often legally possible to base them on other time periods, as would be the case if the rent must be paid every two weeks. A month-to-month tenancy automatically renews each month—or other agreed-upon period— unless the landlord or tenant gives the other the proper amount of written notice (typically 30 days) to terminate the agreement.

Month-to-month rental agreements give landlords more flexibility than leases. You can increase the rent or change other terms of the tenancy on relatively short notice (subject to any restrictions of rent control laws or ordinances— see "Rent Control," below). And with proper notice, you can also end the tenancy at any time (again, subject to any rent control and eviction protection restrictions, anti-retaliation laws, and fair housing dictates). (Chapter 4 discusses notice requirements to change or end a rental agreement.) Not surprisingly, many landlords prefer to rent month to month, particularly in urban areas with tight rental markets where new tenants are usually easily found and rents are trending upwards.

On the flip side, a month-to-month tenancy almost guarantees more tenant turnover. Tenants who can legally move out with only 30 days' notice will be more inclined to leave than tenants who make a longer commitment (leaving before a lease is up carries financial risks). If you base your rental business strategy on seeking high-quality, long-term tenants, or if you live in an area where it's difficult to fill vacancies, you'll probably want tenants to commit for a longer period, such as a year. As discussed below, a fixed-term lease, especially when combined with tenant-friendly management policies, might encourage tenants to stay longer.

Fixed-Term Lease

A lease is a contract that obligates both you and the tenant for a set period of time—usually six months or a year, but sometimes longer. With a fixed-term lease, you can't raise the rent or change other terms of the tenancy until the lease runs out, unless the lease itself allows future changes or the tenant agrees in writing to the changes.

In addition, you usually can't prevail in an eviction lawsuit or even ask a tenant to move out before the lease term expires unless the tenant fails to pay the rent or violates another significant term of the lease or the law, such as repeatedly making too much noise or selling drugs on your property. This restriction can sometimes be problematic if you end up with a tenant you'd like to be rid of but don't have sufficient cause to evict.

Say, for example, that you wish to sell the property halfway into the lease term. The new owner usually purchases all the obligations of the previous owner, including the obligation to honor existing leases. The existence of long-term tenants—especially if the buyers want to occupy the property as their home—could be an obstacle to a sale (as would the presence of long-term tenants with a below-market rent). Of course, the opposite can be true: If you have good, long-term tenants paying a fair rent, the property might be very attractive to investment-property buyers.

At the end of the lease term, you have several options. You can:

- decline to renew the lease (except in areas where that's prohibited by state or local rent control)
- sign a new lease for a set period, or
- do nothing—which means, under the law of most states, that your lease will usually turn into a month-to-month tenancy if you continue to accept monthly rent from the tenant.

Although leases restrict your flexibility, there's often a big plus to having long-term tenants. Some tenants make a serious personal commitment when they enter into a long-term lease, in part because they think they'll be liable for several months' rent if they leave early. And people who plan to be with you over the long term are often more likely to respect your property and the rights of other tenants, making the management of your rental units easier and more pleasant.

You'll probably prefer to use leases in areas where there's a high vacancy rate or it's difficult to find tenants for one season of the year. For example, if you're renting near a college that is in session for only nine months a year, you're far better off with a year's lease. This is especially true if you have the market clout to charge a large deposit, so that a tenant who wants to leave early has an incentive to find someone to take over the tenancy.

Getting All the Rent Under a Lease Isn't a Sure Thing

In theory, tenants who sign a year-long lease will pay the rent 12 times. In reality, though, in the following situations you might not be able to collect the entire amount due under the lease when a tenant leaves early:

- **State law allows the tenant to leave.** Some state laws lay out situations in which tenants can leave their rentals before the lease ends and not owe additional rent. For example, a state might excuse a tenant who needs to move to a nursing home from liability for a broken lease.
- **Your shortcomings give tenants a legal reason to break the lease.** In most states, persistent and significant failures to keep the property habitable will justify an early move-out, as will repeated violations of tenant privacy.
- **Federal law gives a servicemember-tenant the right to leave.** Tenants in active military service are entitled to break a lease if required by their orders, as explained in "Special Rules for Active Military Tenants" in Chapter 4.
- **You haven't made reasonable efforts to rerent.** Tenants who leave without a legal reason are on the hook for the rent, but landlords in most states must make reasonable efforts to rerent. Once the place is rerented, the original tenant's obligation ends. If your property is attractive and easily rented, the original tenant might owe you no more than a month or two of rent—probably equal to their security deposit.

Finally, even tenants who leave without legal justification can often escape without paying the balance of the rent. It's usually a losing proposition to try to collect from a tenant who is either judgment-proof or long gone.

TIP

Always put your agreement in writing. Oral leases or rental agreements are perfectly legal for month-to-month tenancies and for leases of a year or less in most states. Even though oral agreements are easy and informal, it's never wise to use one. You can almost count on tenants claiming that you made, but didn't keep, certain oral promises—for example, to repaint the kitchen or to not increase the rent. Tenants might also forget what restrictions they agreed to, such as a no-subletting policy. And other issues—for example, how deposits can be used— probably weren't discussed at all. Especially dangerous is the fact that the parties might not accurately recall how long they intended the tenancy to last. If something goes wrong with an oral rental agreement or lease, you and your tenants are all too likely to end up in court, arguing over who said what to whom, when, and in what context.

Tips for Landlords Taking Over Rental Property

If you've recently bought (or inherited) rental property, you will likely be taking on tenants with existing rental agreements or leases. Be sure the last owner gives you copies of all tenant and property files, including leases and rental agreements, details on deposits (location and amounts, along with the deposits themselves), house rules, maintenance and repair records, and all other paperwork and records relevant to the property. If you want to change any of the terms of the lease or rental agreement, follow our advice in the first part of Chapter 4.

Instructions for Completing the Lease or Rental Agreement Form

This section explains each clause in the lease and rental agreement forms in this book, and how to fill in any blanks (in many cases, there will be nothing to fill in). When relevant, you'll need to check the state law charts in Appendix A to see whether your state has a specific rule that you'll need to enter, such as the amount of notice you give tenants before entering the rental property. Except for Clause 4, Term of the Tenancy, the lease and rental agreement forms are identical, covering the basic terms of the tenancy, such as the amount of rent and due date.

Check Your Local Laws

In some cities or counties, local ordinances or laws (particularly rent control and eviction protection laws) might apply to your rental business. In addition, these laws might affect the lease itself by requiring certain language or information to be in the document. We cannot list the requirements for every locality in the United States, but we can suggest that, to be extra careful, you take a moment to find out whether local laws affect your residential lease.

Fortunately, many cities and counties have placed their laws online. To find out whether your local government has done so, go to www. statelocalgov.net and look for your state and city. A useful source of city codes is www.municode. com. Or, simply call your local government offices, ask whether residential rentals are covered by local ordinances and, if so, where you can obtain a copy.

If local law varies from your state law—by imposing an interest requirement for security deposits, for example—be sure to follow the local rule. You might need to modify this lease accordingly.

How to Edit (or Add) a Lease or Rental Agreement Clause

You might want to change our lease and rental agreement forms in some situations, and the instructions suggest possible modifications for doing so, including how to prepare an attachment (see "How to Prepare an Attachment," below, for advice).

It's easy to make changes to the lease or rental agreement form by using the electronic versions available for download on the Nolo website—for example, if you want to:

- edit or add something to a clause
- delete a clause (for example, Clause 20 on tenant rules and regulations, if you don't have a separate set of these), or
- add a new clause.

If your additions or modifications are very slight, and can be done in the margins of the lease or rental agreement, you could instead enter them on the hard copy. If you do this, be sure that you and all tenants initial and date the insertions.

Be sure to renumber the clauses if you add or delete a clause. And if you make extensive changes on your own, you might wish to have your work reviewed by an experienced landlords' lawyer.

TIP

Don't be tempted to cram too many details into your lease or rental agreement. Instead, send new tenants a move-in letter that dovetails with your lease or rental agreement and highlights important terms of the tenancy—for example, how and where to report maintenance problems, procedures for returning security deposits, or special rules for use of a pool or laundry room. (See Chapter 3 for advice on preparing a move-in letter.)

You might be tempted to simply download the lease or rental agreement from the Nolo website and skip the detailed instructions. This would be a mistake. If there is one area of landlord-tenant law where details count, this is it. Make sure you really do have the information necessary to create a lease or a rental agreement that accurately reflects your business strategy and complies with all the laws of your state.

 FORM

Rental agreement and lease forms. The Month-to-Month Residential Rental Agreement and the Fixed-Term Residential Lease (in English and in Spanish) can be downloaded from the Nolo website; the link is in Appendix B. A filled-in sample rental agreement is shown at the end of this chapter.

Clause 1. Identification of Landlord and Tenant

> This Agreement is between _____
> _____ ("Tenant")
> and _____
> ("Landlord"). Each Tenant is jointly and severally liable for the payment of rent and performance of all other terms of this Agreement.

Every lease or rental agreement must identify the tenant and the landlord or property owner—usually called the "parties" to the agreement. The term "Agreement" (a synonym for "contract") refers to either the lease or the rental agreement.

Any competent adult—at least 18 years of age—may be a party to a lease or rental agreement. (Teenagers who are younger than age 18 and who have achieved legal adult status through court order, military service, or marriage may also be parties to a lease.)

Joint and several liability. The last sentence of Clause 1 states that if you have more than one tenant, they (the cotenants) are all "jointly and severally" liable (legally responsible) for paying rent and abiding by all the terms of the agreement. This essential bit of legalese simply means that each tenant is legally responsible for the whole rent and complying with the lease. This part of the clause gives you important rights; it means you can legally seek the entire rent from any one of the tenants should the others skip out or be unable to pay. A "jointly and severally liable" clause also gives you the right to evict all of the tenants even if just one has broken the terms of the lease—for example, by seriously damaging the property.

How to Fill in Clause 1

In the first blank, fill in the names of all tenants —all adults who will live in the rental, including both members of a married couple. This is a crucial step: By requiring signatures from everyone who lives in the unit, you emphasize your expectation that each individual is responsible for the rent, the use of the property, and all terms of the agreement. Also, make sure all tenants' names match their legal documents, such as a driver's license. You can set a reasonable limit on the number of people per rental unit. (See "How Many Tenants to Allow," below.)

In the second blank, list the names of all landlords or property owners who will be signing. If you're using a business name, enter your name, followed by your business name.

> **EXAMPLE:** Joe Smith, doing business as Apple Lane Apartments.

If more than one landlord or owner is signing (such as married property owners), you might want to put both names on the agreement if you each plan to actively participate in managing the property.

RELATED TOPIC

More on choosing tenants. Chapter 2 provides detailed advice on choosing tenants.

Clause 2. Identification of Premises

Subject to the terms and conditions set forth in this Agreement, Landlord rents to Tenant, for residential purposes only, the premises located at _____ ("the Premises").
Rental of the Premises also includes _____
_____ .
Rental of the Premises excludes _____
_____ .

Clause 2 identifies the street address of the property being rented (the premises) and provides details on extras such as furnishings and parking spaces. The words "for residential purposes only" are to prevent a tenant from using the property for a business that might affect your insurance or violate zoning laws, or that might burden other tenants or neighbors. Don't go overboard by enforcing this against people who work from home and whose activities don't negatively affect their neighbors or your property.

How to Fill in Clause 2

In the first blank, fill in the street address of the unit or house you are renting. Specify the apartment or building number, if any, as well as the city, state, and zip code.

In the second blank, add details on furnishings and appliances. If the rental unit has only a few basic furnishings, list them in the text of Clause 2.

> **EXAMPLE:** Double bed, night table, blue sofa, and round kitchen table and two matching chairs.

Home Businesses on Rental Property

According to the Small Business Administration, about 60% of businesses that have no employees are run from home. If a tenant wants you to modify Clause 2 to allow the operation of a business, you have some checking to do—even if you're inclined to say yes. For starters, you'll need to check local zoning laws for restrictions on home-based businesses, including the type of businesses allowed (if any), the amount of car and truck traffic the business can generate, outside signs, on-street parking, the number of employees, and the percentage of floor space devoted to the business. And if your rental is in a planned unit or a condominium development, check the CC&Rs of the homeowners' association.

You'll also want to find out if your insurance company requires a special policy to cover the potential liability of tenants' employees or guests. In many situations, a home office for occasional use will not be a problem. But if the tenant wants to operate a business that involves people and deliveries coming and going, such as a therapy practice, jewelry importer, or small business consulting firm, you should seriously consider expanding or increasing your coverage. You might also want to require that the tenant maintain certain types of liability insurance, so that you won't wind up paying if the tenant's business somehow results in an injury occurring on the rental property—for example, a business customer who trips and falls on the front steps.

Finally, be aware that if you allow a residence to be used as a commercial site, your property might need to meet the accessibility requirements of the federal Americans with Disabilities Act (ADA). For more information on the ADA, see www.ADA.gov or contact the U.S. Department of Justice, Disability Rights Section, Civil Rights Division, in Washington, D.C., at 800-514-0301.

 CAUTION
You might not be able to restrict a child care home business. A tenant who wants to operate a child care business in the rental might be entitled to do so, despite your general prohibition against businesses. In California and New York, for example, legislators and courts have declared a strong public policy in favor of home-based child care, in single-family homes or in multifamily settings, and have limited a landlord's ability to say no. (Cal. Health & Safety Code §§ 1597.40 and 1597.41; *Haberbaum v. Gotbaum*, 698 NYS 2d 406 (N.Y. City Civ. Ct. 1999).) If you're concerned about a tenant running a child care business in the apartment, check with your state's office of consumer protection (find yours at www.USA.gov) for information on laws that cover in-home child care in residential properties.

If you decide to allow a tenant to run a business from your rental property, you might want to provide details in Clause 24 (Additional Provisions) of your lease or rental agreement.

If the rental is fully furnished, it makes sense to attach a separate room-by-room list to the lease or rental agreement. In this case, simply write in something like this: "The rental unit is fully furnished. See Attachment 1, Addition to Clause 2, Identification of Premises, for a complete list of furnishings." Or you can provide information on furnishings on the Landlord-Tenant Checklist included in Chapter 3.

Also use line two to elaborate on other items that the rental includes (do so in the third blank of Clause 2). For example, if the rental includes a parking space, storage in the garage or basement, or access to other parts of the property, such as a gardening shed in the backyard or an on-site gym, include it in your description of the premises.

EXAMPLES:

Parking space #5 in underground garage

Open parking in lot on west side of building,

maximum 2 vehicles per unit (no motorhomes)

Storage unit #5 in basement

Storage space available on west side of garage

How to Prepare an Attachment

An attachment is simply a separate document with specific details relevant to a clause, such as a list of furnishings (Clause 2) or detailed rules and regulations (Clause 20). Every time you make an attachment, number and name it by referring to the relevant clause—for example, "Attachment 1, Addition to Clause 2, Identification of Premises," "Attachment 2, Addition to Clause 20, Tenant Rules and Regulations." Then, in the agreement itself, refer to the attachment by name, like this: "See 'Attachment 2, Addition to Clause 20, Tenant Rules and Regulations.'" Everyone signing the lease or rental agreement should sign and date each page of an attachment, and you should staple the attachment to all physical copies of the lease or rental agreement.

If your rules about parking or access to other areas of the property are quite detailed—for example, guest parking rules and gym use rules—you probably should include them in Clause 20 (Tenant Rules and Regulations) of the agreement.

If the rented premises will not include a particular part of the rental property that a tenant might reasonably assume is included, such as a garage or storage shed you wish to use yourself or rent to someone else, explicitly exclude it from your description of the premises. You can do this by entering details about the items that are excluded on the third blank.

Clause 3. Limits on Use and Occupancy

> The Premises are to be used only as a private residence for Tenant(s) listed in Clause 1 of this Agreement, and their minor children: _____ . Occupancy by guests for more than _____ is prohibited without Landlord's written consent and will be considered a breach of this Agreement.

Clause 3 specifies that the rental unit is the residence of the tenants and their minor children only. It lets the tenants know that they may not move anyone else in as a permanent resident without your consent. The value of this clause is that a tenant who tries to move in a relative or friend for a longer period has clearly violated a defined standard, which gives you grounds for eviction. (New York landlords, however, are subject to the "Roommate Law." See "How Many Tenants to Allow," below, for details.)

Clause 3 also allows you to set a time limit for guest stays. Even if you don't plan to strictly enforce restrictions on guests, this provision will be very handy if a tenant tries to move in a friend or relative for a month or two, calling that person a guest. It will give you the leverage you need to ask the guest to leave, request that the guest apply to become a tenant with an appropriate increase in rent, or, if necessary, evict the tenant for violating this clause.

How to Fill in Clause 3

In the first blank, have your tenant write the full name of all minors who will be living in the rental. In the second blank, fill in the number of days you allow guests to stay over a given time period without your consent.

How Many Tenants to Allow

Two kinds of laws affect the number of people who may live in a rental unit.

State and local health and safety codes typically set *maximum* limits on the number of tenants, based on the size of the unit and the number of bedrooms and bathrooms.

Even more important, the federal government has taken the lead in establishing *minimum* limits on the number of tenants, through passage of the Fair Housing Act (42 U.S.C. §§ 3601–3619, 3631) and by means of regulations from the Department of Housing and Urban Development (HUD). HUD generally considers a limit of two persons per bedroom a reasonable occupancy standard. Because the number of bedrooms isn't the only factor—the size of the bedrooms and configuration of the rental unit are also considered—the federal test has become known as the "two per bedroom plus" standard. States and localities can set their own occupancy standards as long as they are more generous than the federal government's—that is, by allowing more people per rental unit.

The Fair Housing Act is designed primarily to disallow illegal discrimination against families with children, but it also allows you to establish your own "reasonable" restrictions on the number of people per rental unit—as long as your policy is truly tied to health and safety needs. In addition, you can adopt standards that are driven by a legitimate business reason or necessity, such as the capacities of the plumbing or electrical systems. Your personal preferences (such as a desire to reduce wear and tear by limiting the number of occupants or to ensure a quiet, uncrowded environment for upscale tenants),

however, do not constitute a legitimate business reason. If your occupancy policy limits the number of tenants for any reason other than health, safety, and legitimate business needs, you risk charges that you are discriminating against families.

Figuring out whether your occupancy policy is legal is not always a simple matter. Furthermore, laws on occupancy limits often change. For more information, call HUD's Housing Discrimination Hotline at 800-669-9777, or check the HUD website at www.HUD.gov. Check your local and state housing authority for other occupancy standards that might affect your rental property. The HUD website includes contact information for these agencies.

> **TIP**
> **New York landlords should check out the state's "Roommate Law."** New York landlords must comply with the "Unlawful Restrictions on Occupancy" law, commonly known as the Roommate Law. (N.Y. Real Prop. § 235-f.) The Roommate Law prohibits New York landlords from limiting occupancy of a rental unit to just the tenant named on the lease or rental agreement. It permits tenants to share their rental units with their immediate family members, and, in many cases, with unrelated, nontenant occupants, too, so long as a tenant (or tenant's spouse) occupies the unit as a primary residence. The number of total occupants is still restricted, however, by local laws governing overcrowding.

We suggest you allow up to two consecutive weeks in any six-month period, but, of course, you might want to modify this based on your own preferences. For example, you could write in the blank, "two weeks in any six-month period."

! CAUTION

Don't discriminate against families with children. You can legally establish reasonable space-to-people ratios, but you cannot use overcrowding as an excuse for refusing to rent to tenants with children, especially if you would rent to the same number of adults. (See "How Many Tenants to Allow," above.) Discrimination against families with children is illegal, except in housing reserved for senior citizens only. Just as important as adopting a reasonable people-to-square-foot standard in the first place is the maintenance of a consistent occupancy policy. If you allow three adults to live in a two-bedroom apartment, you had better let a couple with a child live in the same type of unit, or you're leaving yourself open to charges of illegal discrimination.

Clause 4. Term of the Tenancy

This clause sets out the key difference between a lease and a rental agreement: how long a rent-paying tenant is entitled to stay. The early part of this chapter discusses the pros and cons of leases and rental agreements.

Lease Provision

> The term of the rental will begin on _____, and end on _____ .

This lease provision sets a definite date for the beginning and the expiration of the lease and obligates both the landlord and the tenant for a specific term.

Most leases run for one year, but you can designate a longer or shorter period if it makes sense for you and the tenant. A year is a common duration because it allows you to raise the rent at reasonably frequent intervals if market conditions allow. A long period—two, three, or even five years—can be appropriate, for example, if you're renting out your own house because you'll be away for an extended period or if you have agreed to allow tenants to make major repairs or remodel your property at their expense.

How to Fill in Clause 4 (Lease)

In the first blank, fill in the starting date—the date the tenant has the right to move in, such as the first of the month. This date is usually not the date that you and the tenant sign the lease. The signing date is simply the date that you're both bound to the terms of the lease. If the tenant moves in before the regular rental period—such as the middle of the month and you want rent due on the first of every month—you will need to prorate the rent for the first partial month as explained in Clause 5 (Payment of Rent).

In the second blank, fill in the expiration date. This is the date by which the tenant needs to move out if you or the tenant decide not to renew the lease for another period of time.

Rental Agreement Provision

> The rental will begin on _____, and continue on a month-to-month basis. Landlord may terminate the tenancy or modify the terms of this Agreement by giving the Tenant _____ days' written notice. Tenant may terminate the tenancy by giving the Landlord _____ days' written notice.

This rental agreement provides for a month-to-month tenancy. It specifies how much written notice you must give a tenant to change or end a tenancy, and how much notice the tenant must provide you before moving out. (Chapter 4 discusses changing or ending a month-to-month rental agreement.)

How to Fill in Clause 4 (Rental Agreement)

In the first blank, fill in the date the tenancy will begin—the date the tenant has the right to move in, such as the first of the month. This date usually isn't the date that you and the tenant sign. The signing date is simply the date that you're both bound to the terms of the rental agreement. If the tenant moves in before the regular rental period—such as the middle of the month, and you want rent due on the first of every month—you will need to prorate the rent for the first partial month as explained in Clause 5 (Payment of Rent).

In the next two blanks, fill in the amount of written notice you'll need to give tenants to end or change a tenancy and the amount of notice tenants must provide to end a tenancy. In most cases, to comply with the law of your state, this will be 30 days for both landlord and tenant. (See the "State Rules on Notice Required to Change or Terminate a Month-to-Month Tenancy" chart in Appendix A for a list of each state's notice requirements.)

Possible Modifications to Clause 4 (Rental Agreement)

This rental agreement is month-to-month, although you can change it to a different interval as long as you don't go below the minimum notice period required by your state's law. If your interval is lower, be aware that notice requirements to change or end a tenancy might also need to differ from those required for standard month-to-month rental agreements, because state law often requires that all key notice periods be the same.

RENT CONTROL

Rent control might limit your right to terminate or change the terms of a tenancy. Even a month-to-month tenancy can be limited by a rent control law. Check state or local rent control laws for details.

Clause 5. Payment of Rent

Regular monthly rent.

Tenant will pay to Landlord a monthly rent of $_____ , payable in advance on the first day of each month, except when that day falls on a weekend or legal holiday, in which case rent is due on the next business day. Rent will be paid as follows, or in another manner as Landlord designates from time to time:

Delivery of payment.

Rent will be paid:
- ☐ by mail, to _____
- ☐ in person, at _____
- ☐ electronically, to _____

Form of payment.

Landlord will accept payment the form of:
- ☐ cash
- ☐ personal check made payable to _____
- ☐ certified funds or money order made payable to _____
- ☐ credit or debit card
- ☐ other electronic funds transfer

Prorated first month's rent.

- ☐ On signing this Agreement, Tenant will pay to Landlord for the period of _____ through _____ the sum of $_____ as rent, payable in advance of the start of the tenancy.
- ☐ Upon move-in, Tenant will owe as rent the prorated rent specified above, plus one full month's rent in the amount designated above, for a total of $_____.

This clause provides details on the amount of rent and when, where, and how it's paid. It requires the tenant to pay rent monthly on the first day of the month, unless the first day falls on a weekend or a legal holiday, in which case rent is due on the next business day. (Extending the rent due date for holidays is legally required in some states and is a general rule in most.) Clause 5 also covers prorating rent if a tenant moves in before the regular rental period.

How to Fill in Clause 5

Regular monthly rent. In the first blank, state the amount of monthly rent. Unless your premises are subject to a local rent control ordinance, you can legally charge as much rent as you want (or, more practically speaking, as much as the market will bear).

Delivery of payment. Next, specify to whom and where the rent is to be paid. If you accept payment by mail (most common), list the specific person (such as yourself) to whom rent checks will be mailed. Be sure to include the exact address, including the building or office name and suite number. If the tenant will pay rent in person, add the address, such as your office or the manager's unit at the rental property. Note the hours when rent can be paid in person, such as 9 a.m. to 5 p.m. weekdays and 9 a.m. to noon on Saturdays.

CAUTION

California landlords should take special care to inform tenants of where and how rent is paid. State law (Cal. Civ. Code §§ 1962 and 1962.5) requires landlords to notify tenants (either in a separate writing or in a written rental agreement or lease) of the name and street address of the owner or manager responsible for collection of rent, how rent is to be paid, and who is available for services of notices. A landlord in California may not evict for nonpayment of any rent that came due during any period that the landlord wasn't in compliance with this requirement.

Form of payment. Note all the forms of payment you'll accept, such as personal check and electronic funds transfer, and to whom payment must be made. You can require that tenants pay rent only by check, or give them several options, such as personal check, money order, cashier's check, credit card, automatic credit card debit, or electronic funds transfer.

TIP

Looking for ways to ensure that rent payments are timely and reliable? Credit card and automatic debit are two common methods, especially for landlords with large numbers of rental units. If you accept credit cards, you must pay a fee—a percentage of the amount charged—for the privilege, but the cost could be worth it if accepting credit cards results in more on-time rent payments and less hassle for you and your tenants. In terms of automatic debit, you can get tenants' permission to have rent payments debited automatically each month from the tenants' bank accounts and transferred into your account.

CAUTION

Don't accept cash unless you have no choice. You face an increased risk of robbery if word gets out that you are taking in large amounts of cash. We recommend that you insist that rent be paid by check, money order, or credit card. If you do accept cash, be sure to provide a written, dated receipt stating the tenant's name and the amount of rent paid. Such a receipt is required by law in a few states, and it's a good idea everywhere. Also, check your state law for any other restrictions regarding cash payments. For example, California landlords cannot demand that rent be paid only in cash, unless a tenant has previously bounced a check and the landlord has given the tenant notice to that effect; in that event, the landlord can demand cash payments for no longer than three months. (Cal. Civ. Code § 1947.3.)

Prorated first month's rent. If the tenant moves in before the regular rental period—say in the middle of the month, and you want rent due on the first of every month—you can specify the prorated amount due for the first partial month. To figure out prorated rent, divide the monthly rent by 30 days and multiply by the number of days in the first (partial) rental period. That will avoid confusion about what you expect to be paid. Enter the move-in date, such as "June 21, 20xx," and the amount of prorated monthly rent.

> **EXAMPLE:** Meg rents an apartment for $2,100 per month, with rent due on the first of the month. She moves in on June 21, so she should pay ten days' prorated rent of $700 when she moves in. ($2,100 ÷ 30 = $70 x 10 days = $700.) Beginning with July 1, Meg's full $2,100 rent check is due on the first of the month.

You'll see two options for when the tenant will pay the prorated rent. The first option is for the tenant to pay the prorated amount at the time of signing the lease or rental agreement. The second option is for the tenant to pay the prorated rent plus the full amount of the first month's rent at move-in. Check the box next to the option that best applies to your situation.

If the tenant is moving in on the first of the month, you can ignore or delete this section of the clause.

Possible Modifications to Clause 5

Here are a few common ways to modify Clause 5.

Rent due date. You can establish a rent due date different from the first of the month, such as the day of the month on which the tenant moves in. For example, if the tenant moved in on July 10, rent would be due on that date, a system that saves the trouble of prorating the first month's rent.

Frequency of rent payments. You aren't legally required to have your tenant pay rent on a monthly basis. You can modify the clause and require that the rent be paid twice a month, each week, or by whatever schedule suits you.

Rent Control

"Rent control" is the common term for laws that regulate rent increases and usually also limit the situations in which landlords can terminate tenancies. Rent control also goes by the names "rent stabilization" and "rent regulation." Maryland, New Jersey, and New York allow cities and counties to enact local rent control ordinances.

Three states—California, Oregon, and New York—have state-wide rent control, and Washington, D.C. has district-wide rent control. Although rent control ordinances used to be found mostly in larger cities only (such as San Francisco, Los Angeles, New York City, and Newark), many smaller communities have now adopted some form of rent regulation.

Rent control laws usually regulate much more than rent. As mentioned above, many laws restrict the ability of owners to terminate tenancies (known as "just cause" eviction protections), and impose additional procedural steps when landlords terminate tenancies. Many laws also require landlords to disclose certain information in a lease or rental agreement—for example, the address of the local rent control board.

If you own rental property in an area subject to rent control, you should always have a current copy of the ordinance and any regulations interpreting it.

Check with your local rent control board or city manager's or mayor's office for more information on rent control, and modify our forms accordingly. If you're an Oregon landlord, consider contacting or joining a rental-related association, such as the Oregon Rental Housing Alliance or the Oregon Rental Housing Association, Inc., to stay on top of Oregon rent control developments.

Prorated first month's rent. You could make any other arrangement for collecting the prorated first month's rent. For example, you could have the tenant pay the prorated amount at move-in without requiring the payment of the first full month's rent at the same time. This might be a good option if the tenant is moving in early in the month and has a few weeks before the first of the next month.

RELATED TOPIC

See the following chapters for rent-related discussions:

- collecting deposits and potential problems with calling a deposit the "last month's rent": Clause 8, this chapter
- the value of highlighting your rent rules in a move-in letter to new tenants, and collecting the first month's rent: Chapter 3
- tenant's obligations to pay rent when breaking a lease: Chapter 4, and
- legal citations for state rent rules: Appendix A.

Clause 6. Late Charges

Because Landlord and Tenant agree that actual damages for late rent payments are very difficult or impossible to determine, Landlord and Tenant agree to the following:

- Tenant will pay Landlord a late charge if Tenant fails to pay the rent in full within _____ days after the date it is due.
- The late charge will be $_____, plus $_____ for each individual day that the rent continues to be unpaid. The total late charge for any one month will not exceed $_____.

Landlord does not waive the right to insist on payment of the rent in full on the date it is due.

In most states, you can charge a late fee if rent isn't paid on time. This clause spells out the details of your policy on late fees. Charging a late fee doesn't mean that you give up your right to insist that rent be paid on the due date. To bring this point home, Clause 6 states that you do not

waive the right to insist on full payment of the rent on the date it is due. A late fee is simply one way to compensate you for your losses that result from not being paid on time.

A few states have statutes that put precise limits on the amount of late fees or when they can be collected. (See the Late Fees column in the "State Rent Rules" chart in Appendix A before completing this clause.)

RENT CONTROL

Some rent control laws also regulate late fees. If you own rental units in a state or city with rent control, check the laws carefully.

Even if your state doesn't have specific rules restricting late fees, you are still bound by general legal principles that prohibit unreasonably high fees. Unless your state imposes more specific statutory rules on late fees, you should be on safe ground if you adhere to these principles:

- The total late charge should not exceed 4%–5% of the rent. That's $40 to $50 on a $1,000-per-month rental.
- Any late fee that increases each day the rent is late should be moderate and have an upper limit. A late charge that increases without a maximum could be considered interest charged at an illegal ("usurious") rate. Although state usury laws don't directly apply to late charges, judges often use these laws as one guideline in judging whether a particular provision is reasonable. Most states set the maximum interest rate that may be charged for a debt at about 10% to 12%. A late charge that would generally be acceptable for a monthly rent of $1,000 would be a charge of $10 if rent isn't paid by the end of the second business day after it's due, plus $5 for each additional day, up to a maximum of 5% of the monthly rental amount.

CAUTION

Don't try to disguise excessive late charges by giving a "discount" for early payment. One landlord we know concluded that he couldn't get away with charging a $100 late charge on an $850 rent payment, so, instead, he designed a rental agreement calling for a rent of $950 with a $100 discount if the rent wasn't more than three days late. Ingenious as this ploy sounds, it's unlikely to stand up in court, unless the discount for timely payment is modest. Giving a relatively large discount is, in effect, the same as charging an excessive late fee, and a judge is likely to see it as such.

How to Fill in Clause 6

In the first blank, specify how many days (if any) you will allow as a grace period before charging a late fee. You don't have to give a grace period, but many landlords don't charge a late fee until the rent is two or three days late. If you don't allow any grace period, simply remove "within _____ days after," so that the first bullet point reads "Tenant will pay Landlord a late charge if Tenant fails to pay the rent in full the date it is due."

In the second bullet point, the first blank is for entering the amount of your late charge when the grace period (if any) has expired. The second blank is for the amount that you'll charge for each additional day that the rent is late. The third blank is for the maximum total in late fees you'll charge.

Possible Modifications to Clause 6

If you decide not to charge a late fee (something we consider unwise), you can simply delete this clause, or write the words "N/A" or "Not Applicable" on it.

Clause 7. Returned Check and Other Bank Charges

If any check offered by Tenant to Landlord in payment of rent or any other amount due under this Agreement is returned for lack of sufficient funds, a "stop payment," or any other reason, Landlord will make a demand for payment and otherwise pursue remedies as allowed by law.

As with late charges, any bounced-check charges you demand must be reasonable. Some states regulate the amount you can charge; in the absence of such regulation, you should seek no more than the amount your bank charges you for a returned check, probably $25 to $35 per returned item, plus a few dollars for your trouble. Some states regulate the maximum amount you can charge. Check with your state consumer protection agency for any restrictions on bounced-check charges. A list of state consumer protection agencies is available at www.USA.gov.

TIP

Don't tolerate repeated bad checks. If a tenant habitually pays rent late or gives you bad checks, give written notice demanding that the tenant pay the rent or move within a few days. How long the tenant is allowed to stay depends on state law; in most places, it's about 3 to 15 days. In most instances, tenants who receive this kind of "pay rent or quit" notice pay up and reform their ways, and that's the end of it. But, if the tenant doesn't pay the rent (or move), you can file an eviction lawsuit. An alternative is to serve the tenant with a 30-day notice to change Clause 5 of the lease or rental agreement to require payment with a money order or a verified credit card transaction.

How to Fill in Clause 7

You don't need to add anything to this clause.

Clause 8. Security Deposit

> On signing this Agreement, Tenant will pay to Landlord the sum of $ _____ as a security deposit. Tenant may not, without Landlord's prior written consent, apply this security deposit to the last month's rent or to any other sum due under this Agreement. Within _____ after Tenant has vacated the Premises, returned the keys, and provided Landlord with a forwarding address, Landlord will return the deposit in full or give Tenant an itemized written statement of the reasons for, and the dollar amount of, any of the security deposit retained by Landlord, along with a check for any deposit balance.

Most landlords quite sensibly ask for a security deposit before entrusting hundreds of thousands of dollars' worth of real estate to a tenant. But it's easy to get into legal trouble over deposits, because they are strictly regulated by state law and, sometimes, also by city ordinance. The law of most states dictates how large a deposit you can require, how you can use it, when you must return it, and more. Several states and cities require you to put deposits in a separate account and pay interest on them.

The use and return of security deposits is a frequent source of disputes between landlords and tenants. To avoid confusion and legal hassles, this clause is clear on the subject, including:

- the dollar amount of the deposit
- the fact that the deposit may not be used for the last month's rent without your prior approval, and
- when the deposit will be returned, along with an itemized statement of deductions.

This section discusses the basic information you need to complete Clause 8. Check the "State Security Deposit Rules" chart in Appendix A for specific details that apply to your situation.

If, after reviewing these tables, you have any questions of what's allowed in your state, get a current copy of your state's security deposit statute or a summary from a landlords' association. In addition, be sure to check local ordinances in all areas where you own property. Cities, particularly those with rent control, might have additional rules on security deposits, such as a requirement that you pay interest on deposits.

Basic State Rules on Security Deposits

The general purpose of a security deposit is to give the landlord a source of funds if a tenant fails to pay the rent when it's due or doesn't pay for damage to the rental unit. Rent you collect in advance for the first month is not considered part of the security deposit. Specifically:

- Many states limit the amount you can collect to a maximum of one or two months' rent. The limit might be higher for furnished units.
- Several states and cities (particularly those with rent control) require landlords to pay interest, and specify the interest rate that must be paid and when payments must be made. Some states require you to put deposits in a separate account, sometimes called a "trust" account, rather than mixing the funds with personal or business accounts. In most locations, however, you don't have to pay tenants interest on deposits or put them in a separate bank account. In other words, you can put the money in your bank account and use it, as long as you have it available when the tenant moves out.
- When a tenant moves out, you have a set amount of time (usually from 14 to 30 days, depending on the state) to either return the tenant's entire deposit or provide an itemized statement of deductions and refund any deposit balance, including any required interest.

Don't Charge Nonrefundable Fees

State laws are often muddled on the subject of whether charging nonrefundable deposits and fees is legal. Some specifically allow landlords to collect a nonrefundable fee—such as for pets, cleaning, or redecorating—as long as this is clearly stated in the lease or rental agreement. In addition, most states allow landlords to charge prospective tenants a nonrefundable fee for the cost of a credit report and related screening fees (discussed in Chapter 3).

But many states—and this is clearly the trend—specifically prohibit nonrefundable fees. All such fees are legally considered security deposits, no matter what their label, and must be refundable. It's also illegal in many states to make the return of deposits contingent upon a tenant staying for a minimum period of time.

Generally, it's best to avoid the legal uncertainties and not try to collect any nonrefundable fees. In addition, most landlords have found that making all deposits refundable avoids many time-consuming arguments and even lawsuits with tenants. It's much simpler just to consider the expenses these fees cover as part of your overhead and figure them into the rent, raising it, if necessary.

If you have a specific concern about a particular tenant—for example, you're afraid a tenant's pet will damage the carpets or furniture—just ask for a higher security deposit (but do check your state's maximum). That way, you're covered if the pet causes damage, and if it doesn't, the tenant won't have to shell out unnecessarily.

If, despite our advice, you want to charge a nonrefundable fee, check your state's law to find what (if any) kinds of nonrefundable fees are allowed. Then, make sure your lease or rental agreement is clear on the subject.

- You can withhold all or part of the deposit to pay for:
  - unpaid rent
  - repairing damage to the premises (except for "ordinary wear and tear") caused by the tenant, a family member, or a guest
  - cleaning necessary to restore the rental unit to its condition at the beginning of the tenancy (over and above "ordinary wear and tear"), and
  - restoring or replacing rental unit property taken or damaged or destroyed by the tenant. States typically also allow you to use a deposit to cover the tenant's other obligations under the lease or rental agreement, which might include payment of utility charges.

The laws of many states set heavy penalties for violations of security deposit statutes. See Chapter 4 for a discussion of inspecting the rental unit and returning deposits when a tenant leaves.

How Much Deposit Should You Charge?

Normally, the best advice is to charge as much as the market will bear, within legal limits. The more the tenant has at stake, the better the chance your property will be respected. And, the larger the deposit, the more financial protection you'll have if a tenant leaves owing you rent or needing to do expensive repairs.

Market forces, however, often require accepting a deposit that's lower than the legal maximum. Your common sense and your business sense need to work together in setting security deposits. Here are a number of considerations to keep in mind:

Charge the full limit in high-risk situations: For example, where there's a lot of tenant turnover, or the tenant has a pet and you're concerned about damage, or the tenant's credit is shaky and you're worried about unpaid rent. In situations like these, you'll want as large a cushion as possible.

- **Consider the psychological advantage of a higher rent rather than a high deposit.** Many tenants would rather pay a slightly higher rent than an enormous deposit. Also, many acceptable, solvent tenants have a hard time coming up with several months' rent, especially when they're still awaiting the return of a previous security deposit.
- **Charge a bigger deposit for single-family homes.** Unlike multiunit residences, where close-by neighbors or a manager can spot, report, and quickly stop any destruction of the premises, the single-family home is somewhat of an island. The condition of the interior and even the exterior might be hard to assess, unless you live close by or can frequently check its condition. And, of course, the cost of repairing damage to a house is likely to be higher than for an apartment.
- **Gain a marketing advantage by allowing a deposit to be paid in installments.** If rentals are plentiful in your area, with comparable units renting at about the same price, you might gain a competitive edge by allowing tenants to pay the deposit in several installments, rather than one lump sum.

 TIP

Require renters' insurance as an alternative to a high security deposit. If you're worried about damage but don't think you can raise the deposit any higher, require renters' insurance. You can give your property an extra measure of protection by insisting that the tenant purchase renters' insurance, which might cover accidental damage done by the tenant or guests. (See the discussion of renters' insurance under Clause 15.)

Last Month's Rent

It's a common practice (but often unwise) to collect a sum of money called "last month's rent" from a tenant who's moving in. Landlords tend to treat this money as just another security deposit, and use it to cover not only the last month's rent, but also other expenses such as repairs or cleaning.

Problems can arise because some states restrict the use of money labeled as the "last month's rent" to its stated purpose: the rent for the tenant's last month of occupancy. If you use any of it to repair damage by the former tenant, you're violating the law. Also, using the "last month's rent" for cleaning and repairs could lead to a dispute with a tenant who feels that the last month's rent is taken care of and resents having to pay all or part of it. You would be better off if the tenant paid the last month's rent when it came due, leaving the entire security deposit available to cover any necessary cleaning and repairs.

Avoiding the term "last month's rent" also keeps things simpler if you raise the rent, but not the deposit, before the tenant's last month of occupancy. The problem arises when rent for the tenant's last month becomes due. Has the tenant already paid in full, or does the tenant owe more because the monthly rent is now higher? Legally, there's often no clear answer. In practice, it's a hassle you can easily avoid by not labeling any part of the security deposit "last month's rent."

Clause 8 of the form agreements makes it clear that the tenant may not apply the security deposit to the last month's rent without your prior written consent.

How to Fill in Clause 8

Once you know how much security deposit you can charge (see "State Security Deposit Rules" in Appendix A), fill in the amount in the first blank. Unless there's a lower limit, about two months is ideal. (See "How Much Deposit Should You Charge?" above.) It's never a good idea to charge less than one month's rent.

Next, fill in the time period when you will return the deposit, also using the chart "State Security Deposit Rules" in Appendix A. If your state doesn't have a statutory deadline for returning the deposit, 14 to 21 days is a reasonable time to return a tenant's deposit. (See the discussion of returning security deposits in Chapter 4.)

Possible Modifications to Clause 8

The laws of several states require you to give tenants written information on various aspects of the security deposit, including where you're holding the security deposit, interest payments, and the terms of and conditions under which you can withhold the security deposit. The "State Security Deposit Rules" chart in Appendix A gives you information on disclosures you might need to add to Clause 8.

Even if it's not required, you might want to provide additional details on security deposits in your lease or rental agreement. Here are optional clauses you can add to the end of Clause 8.

OPTIONAL CLAUSES

The security deposit will be held at: _____
(name and address of financial institution) .
Landlord will pay Tenant interest on all security deposits at the prevailing bank rate.

Landlord may withhold only that portion of Tenant's security deposit necessary to: (1) remedy any default by Tenant in the payment of rent; (2) repair damage to the Premises, except for ordinary wear and tear caused by Tenant or Tenant's guests; (3) clean the Premises, if necessary; and (4) compensate Landlord for any other losses as allowed by state law.

Disclose Shared Utility Arrangements

When you don't have separate gas and electric meters for each unit, or a tenant's meter serves any areas outside the tenant's unit (such as a water heater used in common with other tenants or even a lightbulb not under the tenant's control in a common area), you should disclose this in your lease or rental agreement. Simply add details to Clause 9. This type of disclosure is required by law in some states, and is fair in any case. The best solution is to put in a separate meter for the areas served outside the tenant's unit. If you don't do that, you should:

- pay for the utilities measured by the tenant's meter yourself by placing that utility in your name (and possibly upping the rent a little bit; do this before advertising the rental).
- reduce the tenant's rent to compensate for payment of utility usage outside of the tenant's unit (this will probably cost you more in the long run than if you added a new meter or simply paid for the utilities yourself), or
- sign a separate written agreement with the tenant, under which the tenant explicitly agrees to pay for others' utilities, too.

Clause 9. Utilities

Tenant will pay all utility charges, except for the following, which will be paid by Landlord:

_____
_____ .

This clause helps prevent misunderstandings as to who's responsible for paying utilities. Normally, landlords pay for garbage (and sometimes water, if there is a yard) to help make sure that the premises are well maintained. Tenants usually pay for other services, such as gas, electricity, cable TV, and internet access.

How to Fill in Clause 9

In the blank, fill in the utilities you—not the tenants—will be responsible for paying. If you won't be paying for any utilities, simply delete the last part of the clause so that the clause reads, "Tenant will pay all utility charges."

Clause 10. Prohibition of Assignment and Subletting

> Tenant will not sublet any part of the Premises or assign this Agreement without the prior written consent of Landlord. Violating this clause is grounds for terminating the tenancy.
>
> ☐ a. Tenant will not sublet or rent any part of the Premises for short-term stays of any duration, including but not limited to vacation rentals.
>
> ☐ b. Short-stay rentals are prohibited except as authorized by law. Any short-stay rental is expressly conditioned upon the Tenant's following all regulations, laws, and other requirements as a condition to offering a short-stay rental. Failure to follow all laws, ordinances, regulations, and other requirements, including any registration requirement, will be deemed a material, noncurable breach of this Agreement and will furnish cause for termination.

Clause 10 is an antisubletting clause, the breach of which is grounds for eviction. It prevents a tenant from, for example, subleasing during a vacation or renting out a room to someone without your permission.

Clause 10 is also designed to prevent assignments, a legal term that means your tenant transfers the entire tenancy to someone else. You need this clause to prevent your tenant from leaving in the middle of the month or lease term and moving in a replacement—maybe someone

you wouldn't choose to rent to—without your consent.

Should You Allow an Assignment or Subtenancy?

As a general rule, your best bet when tenants ask to assign the entire lease is to insist that the tenancy terminate and a new one begin—with the proposed "assignee" as the new tenant who (assuming you approve of the applicant) signs a new lease or rental agreement. This gives you the most direct legal relationship with the substitute.

You might, however, agree to an assignment in order to have a sure source of funds in the background (with an assignment, the original tenant remains responsible for the rent). This might come up if your original tenant is financially sound and trustworthy, but the proposed stand-in is less secure but acceptable otherwise. The hassle that comes with dealing with more than one person might be worth what you gain in keeping a sure and reliable source of funds on the hook.

In the same vein, when asked to approve of a sublet, most landlords will insist that the new resident become a full cotenant, so that the landlord has a direct legal relationship with the new resident.

By including Clause 10 in your lease or rental agreement, you have the option to decline the person your tenant proposes to take over the lease. Under the law of most states, however, you should realize that if a tenant who wishes to leave early provides you with another suitable tenant, you can't both unreasonably refuse to rent to this person and hold the tenant financially liable for breaking the lease. Typically, state law requires you to try to rerent the property reasonably quickly, and subtract any rent you receive from the amount the original tenant owed you for the remainder of the agreed-upon rental period. Lawyers call this the "mitigation-of-damages rule."

Subletting and Short-Term Stays (Airbnb)

Online businesses such as Airbnb act as clearing-houses for short-term, or short-stay rentals (less than 30 days). Tenants using these platforms sublet their rentals and pocket the rent, turning your property into a hotel. Landlords are universally opposed to this practice, though even they've jumped into the fray, taking regular rental property out of circulation in order to operate it solely as a short-term rental.

If you want to restrict tenants from running a short-term rental business, make it clear in your lease. First, however, check local law: Bowing to political pressure, many municipalities are changing their laws concerning short-stay tenancies, by requiring registration and limiting the number of short-stay days per year. It is possible that your locality has granted tenants the right to rent on Airbnb or other services under specific conditions and requirements.

How to Fill in Clause 10

After you've determined whether any local ordinances regulate short-term rentals, choose the appropriate alternative language for Clause 10. Alternate (a) flatly prohibits such rentals, while alternate (b) advises tenants that they must follow the short-term-stay law or risk termination of their tenancy.

 RESOURCE

For a related discussion of subleases, assignments, and the landlord's duty to mitigate damages, see Chapter 4.

Clause 11. Tenant's Maintenance Responsibilities

Tenant agrees to: (1) keep the Premises clean, sanitary, and in good condition and, upon termination of the tenancy, return the Premises to Landlord in a condition identical to that which existed when Tenant took occupancy, except for ordinary wear and tear; (2) immediately notify Landlord of any defects or dangerous conditions in and about the Premises of which Tenant becomes aware; and (3) reimburse Landlord, on demand by Landlord, for the cost of any repairs to the Premises, including Landlord's personal property therein, damaged by Tenant or Tenant's guests or business invitees through misuse or neglect.

Tenant has examined the Premises, including appliances, fixtures, carpets, drapes, and paint, and has found them to be in good, safe, and clean condition and repair, except as noted in the Landlord-Tenant Checklist.

Clause 11 makes the tenant responsible for keeping the rental premises clean and sanitary, and makes it clear that if the tenant damages the premises (for example, by breaking a window or scratching hardwood floors) or the landlord's personal property (for example, any furnishings included with the rental), it's the tenant's responsibility to pay for the damage.

It's the law in some states (and a wise practice in all) to notify tenants in writing of how to make complaint and repair requests. Clause 11 requires the tenant to alert you to defective or dangerous conditions.

Clause 11 also states that the tenant has examined the rental premises, including appliances, carpets, and paint, and found them to be safe and clean, except as noted in a separate form (the Landlord-Tenant Checklist, described in Chapter 4). Before the tenant moves in, you and

Ten Elements of a Good Maintenance and Repair System

As a general rule, landlords are legally required to offer livable premises when a tenant originally rents an apartment or rental unit, and to maintain the premises throughout the rental term. If rental property isn't maintained, the tenant might have the right to repair the problem and deduct the cost from the rent, withhold rent, sue for any injuries caused by defective conditions, or move out without notice. Your best defense against rent withholding hassles and other disputes with tenants is to establish and communicate a clear procedure for tenants to ask for repairs. You'll also want to routinely and thoroughly document all complaints, respond quickly when complaints are made, and schedule annual safety inspections. And, if you employ a manager or management company, make sure they fully accept and implement your guidelines.

Follow these steps to avoid maintenance and repair problems with tenants:

1. **Regularly look for dangerous conditions on the property and fix them promptly.** Reduce risk as much as possible—for example, by providing sufficient lighting in hallways, parking garages, and other common areas, strong locks on doors and windows, and safe stairs and handrails.

2. **Scrupulously comply with all public health and safety codes.** Your local building or housing authority and health or fire department can provide any information you need. Also, check state housing laws governing landlords' repair and maintenance responsibilities. (Appendix A includes citations for the major state laws affecting landlords. Check your statutes for headings such as "Landlord Obligations to Maintain Premises.")

3. **Clearly set out the tenant's responsibilities for repair and maintenance in your lease or rental agreement.** (See Clauses 11, 12, and 13 of the agreements in this chapter.)

4. **Use the written Landlord-Tenant Checklist form in Chapter 3 to check over the premises and fix any problems before new tenants move in.**

5. **Encourage tenants to immediately report plumbing, heating, weatherproofing, or other defects and safety or security problems.** They should report problems in the tenant's unit as well as in common areas like hallways and parking garages.

6. **Handle repairs (especially urgent ones, such as a broken door lock or lack of heat in winter) as soon as possible.** Notify the tenant by phone, text, or email and follow up in writing if repairs will take more than 48 hours, excluding weekends. Keep the tenant informed—for example, if you have problems scheduling a plumber, let your tenant know. For nonurgent repairs, be sure to give the tenant proper notice as required by state law. (See Clause 17 for details on notice required to enter rental premises.)

7. **Keep a written log of all tenant complaints, including those made orally.** Record your immediate and any follow-up responses (and subsequent tenant communications), with details as to how and when the problem was fixed, including reasons for any delay.

8. **Twice a year, give your tenants a checklist on which to report any potential safety hazards or problems you might have overlooked.** For example, low water pressure in the shower, peeling paint, or noisy neighbors. This is also a good time to remind tenants of their repair and maintenance responsibilities. Respond promptly and in writing to all repair requests, keeping copies for your records.

9. **Once a year, inspect all rental units for safety and maintenance problems, using the Landlord-Tenant Checklist as a guide.** Make sure smoke detectors, heating and plumbing systems, and major appliances are safe and in good working order. (Keep copies of the filled-in checklist.)

10. **Get a good liability insurance policy to cover injuries or losses suffered by others as the result of defective conditions on the property, and lawyers' bills for defending personal injury suits.**

the tenant should inspect the rental unit and fill out the Landlord-Tenant Checklist, describing what's in the unit and noting any problems. Doing so will help you avoid security deposit disputes when the tenant moves out.

Common Terms

Tenant. Someone who's signed a lease or a rental agreement, or who's gained the status of a tenant because the landlord has accepted that person's presence on the property or has accepted rent from the person.

Cotenants. Two or more tenants who rent the same property under the same lease or rental agreement, each 100% responsible for carrying out the agreement, including paying all the rent.

Subtenant. Someone who subleases (rents) all or part of the premises from a tenant and doesn't sign a lease or rental agreement with the landlord. A subtenant may either rent (sublet) an entire dwelling from a tenant who moves out temporarily—for example, for the summer—or rent one or more rooms from the tenant, who continues to live in the unit. The key to subtenant relationships is that the original tenant retains the primary relationship with the landlord and continues to exercise some control over the rental property, either by occupying part of the unit or by reserving the right to retake possession at a later date.

Assignment. The transfer by a tenant of all rights of tenancy to another tenant (the "assignee"). Unlike a subtenant, an assignee rents directly from the landlord. Unless released, the tenant remains responsible for the rent, like a guarantor.

Roommates. Two or more people, usually unrelated, living under the same roof and sharing rent and expenses. A roommate is usually a cotenant, but in some situations might be a subtenant.

How to Fill in Clause 11

You don't need to add anything to this clause.

RESOURCE

Comprehensive landlord law resource. Several times in this book, we recommend *Every Landlord's Legal Guide,* by Marcia Stewart, Janet Portman, and Ann O'Connell (Nolo). It's especially useful for its detailed discussion of landlords' and tenants' rights and responsibilities for repair and maintenance under state and local laws and judicial decisions. It provides practical advice on how to stay on top of repair and maintenance needs and minimize financial losses and legal problems with tenants. It discusses tenants' rights if you don't meet your legal responsibilities and the pros and cons of delegating repairs and maintenance to the tenant. *Every Landlord's Legal Guide* also includes chapters on landlords' liability for tenant injuries from defective housing conditions, such as a broken step or defective wiring; liability for environmental hazards such as asbestos and lead; and responsibility to provide secure premises and protect tenants from assault or criminal activities, such as drug dealing.

Clause 12. Repairs and Alterations by Tenant

a. Except as provided by law or as authorized by the prior written consent of Landlord, Tenant will not make any repairs or alterations to the Premises, including nailing holes in the walls or painting the rental unit.

b. Tenant will not, without Landlord's prior written consent, alter, rekey, or install any locks to the Premises or install or alter any security alarm system. Tenant will provide Landlord with a key or keys capable of unlocking all such rekeyed or new locks as well as instructions on how to disarm any altered or new security alarm system.

Clause 12 states that the tenant may not make alterations and repairs without your consent. This includes painting the unit or putting nails in the walls.

And, to make sure you can take advantage of your legal right of entry in an emergency situation, Clause 12 forbids the tenant from rekeying the locks or installing a security alarm system without your consent. If you do grant permission, make sure your tenant gives you duplicate keys, the name and phone number of the alarm company, and instructions on how to disarm the alarm system so that you can enter in case of emergency.

The "except as provided by law" language in Clause 12 is a reference to the fact that, in certain situations and in certain states, tenants have a narrowly defined right to alter or repair the premises, regardless of what you've said in the lease or rental agreement. Examples include:

- **Alterations by a person with a disability, such as lowering countertops for a tenant who uses a wheelchair.** Under the federal Fair Housing Act, persons with disabilities may modify a living space to the extent necessary to make the space safe and comfortable, as long as the modifications will not make the unit unacceptable to the next tenant, or if the tenant with a disability agrees to undo the modification when the tenant leaves. Even so, the tenant must first approach you with the request. (42 U.S.C. § 3604(f)(3)(A).)
- **Use of the "repair and deduct" procedure.** In most states, tenants have the right to repair defects or damage that makes the premises uninhabitable or substantially interferes with the tenant's safe use or enjoyment of the premises. The tenant must first notify you of the problem and give you a reasonable amount of time to fix it.
- **Installation of satellite dishes and antennas.** Federal law gives tenants limited rights to install wireless antennas and small satellite dishes. (47 C.F.R. § 1.4000.)

- **Specific alterations allowed by state statutes.** Some states allow tenants to install energy conservation measures (like removable interior storm windows) or burglary prevention devices without the landlord's prior consent. Check your state statutes or call your local rental property association for more information on these types of laws.

How to Fill in Clause 12

If you don't want the tenant to make any repairs without your permission, you don't need to add anything to this clause.

You might, however, want to go further and specifically prohibit certain repairs or alterations by adding details in Clause 24 (Additional Provisions). For example, you could make it clear that any "fixtures"—a legal term that describes any addition that's attached to the structure, such as bolted-in bookcases or built-in dishwashers—will become your property upon installation, and may not be removed by the tenant without your permission.

If you do authorize the tenant to make any repairs, provide enough detail so that the tenant knows exactly what is expected, how much repairs can cost, and who will pay. For example, if you allow the tenant to take over the repair of any broken windows, routine plumbing jobs, or landscaping, provide descriptions of and limits to the tasks.

CAUTION
Don't delegate to a tenant your responsibility for major maintenance of essential services. The duty to repair and maintain heating, plumbing, electrical, and structural systems (the roof, for example) is yours. Many courts have held that landlords cannot delegate to a tenant the responsibility for keeping the premises fit for habitation, fearing that the tenant will rarely be in the position, either practically or financially, to do the kinds of repairs needed to bring a structure up to par. Absent unusual circumstances, and even then only after carefully checking state law, it's a mistake to try to delegate this responsibility to the tenant.

Clause 13. Violating Laws and Causing Disturbances

> Tenant is entitled to quiet enjoyment of the Premises. Tenant and guests or invitees will not use the Premises or adjacent areas in such a way as to: (1) violate any law or ordinance, including laws prohibiting the use, possession, or sale of illegal drugs; (2) commit waste (severe property damage) or cause or tolerate a nuisance; or (3) annoy, disturb, inconvenience, or interfere with the quiet enjoyment and peace and quiet of any other tenant or nearby resident.

This type of clause is found in most leases and rental agreements. Although it contains some legal jargon, it's probably best to leave it as is, because courts have a lot of experience with these terms. As courts define it, the "covenant of quiet enjoyment" amounts to an implied promise that you will not act (or fail to act) in a way that interferes with or destroys the tenant's ability to use the rented premises.

Examples of landlord violations of the covenant of quiet enjoyment include:

- allowing garbage to pile up

Waste and Nuisance: What Are They?

In legalese, committing **waste** means causing severe damage—way beyond ordinary wear and tear—including a house or an apartment unit. Punching holes in walls, pulling out sinks and fixtures, and knocking down doors are examples of waste.

Nuisance means behavior that prevents neighbors from fully enjoying the use of their homes. Continuous loud noise and foul odors are examples of legal nuisances that could disturb nearby neighbors and affect their "quiet enjoyment" of the premises. So, too, is selling drugs or engaging in other illegal activities that greatly disturb neighbors.

- tolerating a major rodent infestation, or
- failing to control another tenant whose constant loud music makes it impossible for other tenants to sleep.

If you want to be able to enforce specific rules—for example, no loud music played after midnight—add them to Clause 20: Tenant Rules and Regulations, or to Clause 24: Additional Provisions.

How to Fill in Clause 13

You don't need to add anything to this clause.

How to Prevent Illegal Tenant Activity

You can take several practical steps to avoid trouble among your tenants and limit your exposure to lawsuits:

- Screen tenants carefully and choose tenants who are likely to be law-abiding and peaceful. (Chapter 2 recommends a comprehensive system for screening prospective tenants, including checking out references from past landlords and employers.)
- Establish a system to respond to tenants' complaints and concerns about other tenants, especially those involving drug dealing.
- Make it clear that you will not tolerate tenants' disruptive behavior. An explicit lease or rental agreement provision such as Clause 13, prohibiting drug dealing and illegal activity, is the most effective way to make this point. If a tenant does cause trouble, act swiftly. Some situations, such as drug dealing, call for prompt efforts to evict the troublemaker. Your failure to evict drug-dealing tenants can result in lawsuits from injured or annoyed tenants, and local, state, or federal authorities might levy stiff fines for allowing the illegal activity to continue. In extreme cases, you could actually lose your property to the government under public nuisance abatement laws and forfeiture laws.

Clause 14. Damage to the Premises

In the event the Premises are partially or totally damaged or destroyed by fire or other cause, the following will apply:

a. Premises totally damaged and destroyed. Landlord will have the option to: (1) repair such damage and restore the Premises, with this Agreement continuing in full force and effect, except that Tenant's rent will be abated while repairs are being made; or (2) give written notice to Tenant terminating this Agreement at any time within thirty (30) days after such damage, and specifying the termination date; in the event that Landlord gives such notice, this Agreement will expire and all of Tenant's rights pursuant to this Agreement will cease.

b. Premises partially damaged by fire or other cause. Landlord will attempt to repair such damage and restore the Premises within thirty (30) days after such damage. If only part of the Premises cannot be used, Tenant must pay rent only for the usable part, to be determined by Landlord. If Landlord is unable to complete repairs within thirty (30) days, this Agreement will expire and all of Tenant's rights pursuant to this Agreement will terminate at the option of either party. Whether the Premises are totally or partially destroyed will be decided by Landlord, in the exercise of its sole discretion.

c. In the event that Tenant, or Tenant's guests or invitees, in any way caused or contributed to the damage of the Premises, Landlord will have the right to terminate this Agreement at any time, and Tenant will be responsible for all losses, including, but not limited to, damage and repair costs as well as loss of rental income.

d. Landlord will not be required to repair or replace any property brought onto the Premises by Tenant.

This clause outlines what will happen if all or part of the premises is destroyed or damaged. Because there's no way of knowing the exact situation under which you might need to use this clause, it gives you a lot of flexibility: As the landlord, you'll have the option to try to repair or rebuild, or terminate the lease. If the tenant or tenant's guests damage or destroy your property, you'll be able to hold the tenant responsible.

How to Fill in Clause 14

You don't need to add anything to this clause.

Clause 15. Renters' Insurance

Tenant acknowledges that Landlord's property insurance policy will not cover damage to or loss of Tenant's personal property. Tenant will obtain a renters' insurance policy that will:

• reimburse Landlord for cost of fire or water damage caused by Tenant or Tenant's guests, and vandalism to the Premises
• indemnify Landlord against liability to third parties for any negligence on the part of Tenant, Tenant's guests, or invitees; and
• cover damage to Tenant's personal possessions to a minimum of $100,000.

Tenant will provide Landlord with proof of such policy by giving Landlord a certificate of insurance issued by the insurance company within fifteen (15) days of _____. The policy will name Landlord as an "additional insured." Tenant will provide Landlord with a certificate of insurance upon every renewal. Tenant will not allow such policy to expire during the rental term. Failure to obtain and maintain a renters' insurance policy will be treated as a material breach of this Agreement.

This clause requires the tenant to obtain a renters' insurance policy. The policy will insure the tenant's personal property, and the liability portion will cover loss or damage to your rental property caused by the tenant's carelessness.

Tenants must give you proof that they've purchased a policy within 15 days after the tenancy begins. Be sure to ask for it, and stay on top of any renewals.

This clause warns tenants that if they fail to buy and maintain a renters' policy, they will have materially breached the agreement. This will entitle you to terminate the tenancy if you wish.

Renters' Insurance

Renters' insurance covers losses to the tenant's belongings as a result of fire or theft, as well as injury to other people or property damage caused by the tenant's negligence. Besides protecting the tenant from personal liability, renters' insurance benefits you, too: If damage caused by the tenant could be covered by either the tenant's insurance policy or yours, a claim made on the tenant's policy will affect the tenant's premiums, not yours. Renters' insurance won't cover intentional damage by the tenant.

Be advised that it might not be legal for you to require your tenants to carry renters' insurance (in particular, liability insurance). Judges in some states (including Oklahoma) have held that tenants are by implication coinsureds under the landlord's property policy, because their rent helps pay the landlord's premiums. The theory is that making tenants buy additional insurance duplicates the insurance that you (and the tenants, indirectly) already carry, and shouldn't be allowed.

Unfortunately, it's very hard to get a good handle on which states adopt this approach. Only Virginia has clear, statutory law on the subject: Virginia allows a landlord to require a tenant to pay for renters' insurance that's obtained by the landlord. However, if the landlord also requires a security deposit, the combined cost of the insurance premiums and the security deposit cannot exceed two months' rent. (Va. Code §§ 55.1-1206, 1208.) Oregon also regulates landlords' requirements for renters' insurance (Or. Rev. Stat. § 90.222.)

Landlords subject to rent control might not be able to require renters' insurance, because a court might consider the premiums to be a rent overcharge. Before requiring tenants to carry renters' insurance, you'll need to check with your agent or lawyer on the legality of such a requirement in your state or locality.

The average cost of renters' insurance is typically less than $20 or $30 per month, depending on the location and size of the rental unit and the value of the policyholder's possessions. Some carriers offer discounts for new policies to customers with existing policies, and additional discounts for tenants who don't smoke (smoking is a major cause of house fires) and who can demonstrate they have risk-reduction measures such as smoke alarms, safes, alarm systems, or double-bolt locks.

How to Fill in Clause 15

In the blank, enter the date that the tenancy will begin—refer back to the date you wrote into Clause 4. Keep in mind that this date might be different from the date you signed the agreement, and it might also be different from the date the tenant actually moves in.

If you decide to not require the tenant to obtain renters' insurance, delete this clause, and renumber the following clauses.

Clause 16. Pets

No animal may be kept on the Premises without Landlord's prior written consent, except animals needed by tenants who have a disability, as that term is understood by law, and under the following conditions: _____
_____
_____ .

This clause prevents tenants from keeping pets without your written permission. If you want, you can have a flat "no pets" rule, though many landlords report that pet-owning tenants tend to be more appreciative, stable, and responsible than the norm. At the least, the clause provides you with a legal mechanism that will keep your premises from being waist-deep in Irish wolfhounds. Without this sort of provision—particularly if you use a longer-term lease that can't be terminated early save for a clear violation of one of its provisions—there's little to prevent your tenant from keeping multiple, dangerous, or nonhousebroken pets, except for city ordinances prohibiting exotic animals, and animal cruelty laws.

You have the right to prohibit all pets (including pets of guests), or to restrict the types of pets or dog breeds you allow, with the exception of trained dogs and some other animals used by people who have a mental or physical disability, as that term is defined by law.

How to Fill in Clause 16

If you do not allow pets, simply delete the words "and: _____ under the following conditions: _____ _____."

If you allow pets, identify the type and number of pets in the first blank—for example, "one cat" or "one dog weighing less than 20 pounds." It's also wise to spell out your pet rules in the second blank.

EXAMPLE:

Tenant must keep the grounds and adjacent street free of all animal waste. Tenant's pet must be well-behaved, on a leash when outside Tenant's exclusive rented premises, and under Tenant's control at all times. Pet must not pose a threat or apparent threat to the safety of other tenants, their guests, or other people on or near the Premises.

Your tenant rules and regulations document is another possible place to spell out your pet rules—in which case, add this language in the second blank: Tenant must comply with pet rules included in the Tenant Rules and Regulations (Clause 20) attached to this agreement.

Should You Require a Separate Security Deposit for Pets?

Some landlords allow pets but require the tenant to pay a separate deposit to cover any damage caused by the pet. The laws of a few states specifically allow separate, nonrefundable pet deposits. In others, charging a designated pet deposit is legal only if the total amount you charge for all deposits doesn't exceed the state maximum for deposits. (See Clause 8 for details on security deposits.)

Even where allowed, separate pet deposits can often be a bad idea, because they limit how you can use that part of the security deposit. For example, if the pet is well-behaved but the tenant trashes your unit, you can't use the pet portion of the deposit to clean up after the human. If you want to protect your property from damage done by a pet, you're probably better off charging a slightly higher rent or security deposit to start with (assuming you're not restricted by rent control or the upper security deposit limits).

If your tenant is a person with a disability and has a trained service animal, you cannot charge a separate pet deposit—service animals are not considered pets. But what about tenants with assistance animals—animals that provide emotional support and comfort or companionship? If your tenant is a person with a disability (as defined by law), you cannot charge a separate pet deposit if the tenant can demonstrate that the assistance animal provides some form of benefit that enables the tenant to live safely and equally on the premises.

Clause 17. Landlord's Right to Access

Landlord or Landlord's agents may enter the Premises in the event of an emergency, to make repairs or improvements, or to show the Premises to prospective buyers or tenants. Landlord may also enter the Premises to conduct an annual inspection to check for safety or maintenance problems. Except in cases of emergency, Tenant's abandonment of the Premises, court order, or where it is impractical to do so, Landlord will give Tenant _____ notice before entering.

Because you have a legal duty to keep the premises safe and habitable, as a practical matter you must monitor the property. For this reason, many states have access laws specifying the circumstances under which landlords may legally enter rented premises. Most access laws allow landlords to enter to make repairs, inspect the property, and show property to prospective tenants and purchasers. (See "General Rules of Entry," below.) State access laws typically specify the amount of notice required for such entry—usually 24 hours (unless it is impractical to do so—for example, in cases of emergency). A few states simply require the landlord to provide "reasonable" notice, often presumed to be 24 hours.

Clause 17 makes it clear to the tenant that you have a legal right of access to the property to make repairs or to show the premises for sale or rental, provided you give the tenant proper notice. (The chart "State Laws on Landlord's Access to Rental Property" in Appendix A provides details on a landlord's right to entry and notice requirements.)

How to Fill in Clause 17

In the blank, indicate the amount of notice you'll provide the tenant before entering—at least the minimum required in your state. If your state law simply requires "reasonable" notice or has no notice requirement, we suggest you provide at least 24 hours' notice.

General Rules of Entry

Except in cases of emergency, or where it is impractical to do so, you generally must enter only at reasonable times, and you must give at least the amount and type of notice required in your state.

Emergency. In all states, you can enter rental property to respond to a true emergency—such as a gas leak.

To make repairs or inspect the property. By law, many states allow you and your repair-person to enter the tenant's home to make necessary or agreed-upon repairs, decorations, alterations, or improvements, and to supply necessary or agreed-upon services—for example, when you need to fix a broken oven.

To show property. Most states with access laws allow a landlord to enter rented property to show it to prospective tenants or to prospective purchasers. (See Chapter 2 for advice on renting property that's still occupied.)

With the permission of the tenant. You can always enter rental property, even without notice, if the tenant agrees.

Entry after the tenant has moved out. To state the obvious, you may enter the premises after the tenant has completely moved out—regardless of whether the tenant left voluntarily after giving back the key or involuntarily as a result of an eviction lawsuit. In addition, if you reasonably believe the tenant has abandoned the property—that is, skipped out without giving any notice or returning the key—you may legally enter.

Clause 18. Extended Absences by Tenant

> Tenant will notify Landlord in advance if Tenant will be away from the Premises for _____ or more consecutive days. During such absence, Landlord may enter the Premises at times reasonably necessary to maintain the property and inspect for damage and needed repairs.

Several states give landlords the right to enter the rental during a tenant's extended absence, to maintain the property as necessary and to inspect for damage and needed repairs. Extended absence is often defined as seven days or more. For example, if you live in a cold-weather place and temperatures take a dive, it makes sense to check the pipes in rental units when the tenant is away in the winter.

While many states don't address this issue, either by statute or court decision, you should be on safe legal ground to enter rental property during a tenant's extended absence, as long as you have a genuine need to enter to protect the property from damage. You should enter only if something really needs to be done—that is, something tenants would do if they were home as part of their obligation to keep the property clean, safe, and in good repair.

To protect yourself, include Clause 18, which requires that the tenant notify you when they will be gone for an extended time and alerts the tenant of your intent to enter the premises during these times, if necessary.

How to Fill in Clause 18

In the blank, fill in the length of the tenant's expected absence that will trigger your tenant's duty to notify you. Ten or 14 days is common.

Clause 19. Possession of the Premises

> a. *Tenant's failure to take possession.* If, after signing this Agreement, Tenant fails to take possession of the Premises, Tenant will still be responsible for paying rent and complying with all other terms of this Agreement.
>
> b. *Landlord's failure to deliver possession.* If Landlord is unable to deliver possession of the Premises to Tenant for any reason not within Landlord's control, including, but not limited to, failure of prior occupants to vacate or partial or complete destruction of the Premises, Tenant will have the right to terminate this Agreement upon proper notice as required by law. In such event, Landlord's liability to Tenant will be limited to the return of all sums previously paid by Tenant to Landlord.

The first part of this clause (Part a) explains that a tenant who chooses not to move in (take possession) after signing the lease or rental agreement will still be required to pay rent and satisfy other conditions of the agreement. This doesn't mean, however, that you can sit back and expect to collect rent for the entire lease or rental agreement term. (As we explain in Chapter 4, in most states you must take reasonably prompt steps to rerent the premises, and you must credit the rent you collect against the first tenant's rent obligation.)

The second part of the clause (Part b) protects you if you're unable, for reasons beyond your control, to turn over possession after having signed the agreement or lease—for example, if a fire spreads from next door and destroys the premises. It limits your financial liability to the new tenant to the return of any prepaid rent and security deposits (the "sums previously paid," in the language of the clause).

(!) CAUTION

Clause 19 might not limit your liability if you cannot deliver possession because the old tenants are still on the premises—even when they are the subject of an eviction that you ultimately win. When a holdover tenant prevents the new tenant from moving in, landlords can be sued by the new tenant for not only the return of any prepaid rent and security deposits, but also for the costs of temporary housing, storage costs, and other losses. In some states, an attempt in the lease to limit the new tenant's recovery to the return of prepaid sums alone would not hold up in court. If disappointed new tenants sue you over their inability to move in, you'll want to be able to shift that financial liability to the holdover tenants. You'll have a stronger chance of doing this when the old tenants have given you written notice of their intent to move out. (See Clause 4, above, which requires written notice.)

How to Fill in Clause 19

You don't need to add anything to this clause.

Clause 20. Tenant Rules and Regulations

☐ Tenant acknowledges receipt of, and has read a copy of, Tenant Rules and Regulations, which are labeled Attachment_____ and attached to and incorporated into this Agreement by this reference. Tenant understands that serious or repeated violations of the rules may be grounds for termination.

Many landlords don't worry about detailed rules and regulations, especially when they rent single-family homes or duplexes. However, in larger buildings with many tenants, rules are usually important to control the use of common areas and equipment—both for the convenience, safety, and welfare of the tenants and as a way to protect your property from damage. Rules and regulations also help avoid confusion and misunderstandings about day-to-day issues such as garbage disposal, lost key charges, and parking rules.

When tenants break a rule or regulation, consider giving them a written warning to not engage in the behavior again, and keep a record of the tenant's violations. Depending on the circumstances, you might be able to terminate the tenancy of or evict a tenant who repeatedly or seriously violates your rules and regulations. Also, to avoid charges of illegal discrimination, make sure to apply the same rules, regulations, and consequences to all tenants.

What's Covered in Tenant Rules and Regulations

Tenant rules and regulations typically cover issues like:

- elevator safety and use
- pool rules
- garbage disposal and recycling
- vehicles and parking regulations—for example, restrictions of repairs on the premises or types of vehicles (such as no RVs)
- lockout and lost key charges
- if you allow pets, rules about where pets are allowed
- security systems
- details on what's considered excessive noise
- storage of bikes, baby strollers, and other equipment in halls, stairways, and other common areas
- directions for using items in the rental, such as how to use the fireplace
- use of the grounds and recreation areas
- maintenance of balconies and decks (for instance, no drying clothes on balconies)
- displaying signs in windows, and
- laundry room rules.

Some matters don't belong in your rules and regulations: Very important rules—such as a no-smoking policy or a prohibition on waterbeds—go directly into your lease or rental agreement. A rule is important enough to put in the lease or rental agreement if repeated (or even single) violations would justify a lease termination. (Most of the time, the consequence of run-of-the-mill rule-breaking isn't so dire.) Putting very important rules in your lease or rental agreement gives you the option to terminate a tenancy or evict a tenant who breaks the rule even just one time.

Because tenant rules and regulations are often lengthy and might be revised occasionally, we suggest you prepare a separate attachment. (See "How to Prepare an Attachment," above.) Be sure the rules and regulations (including any revisions) are dated on each page and signed or initialed by both you and the tenant.

How to Fill in Clause 20

If you have a document with tenant rules and regulations, check the box and attach it. Fill in the blank with the label you assign to the attachment. For example, if this is the first attachment referenced in the lease, you could call it Attachment A. If it's the second or third, label it "B," "C," and so on. Do the same if your rental is in a community with homeowners' association or condo rules. If you don't have a separate set of tenant rules and regulations, simply delete this clause (and renumber the remaining clauses).

Clause 21. Payment of Court Costs and Attorneys' Fees in a Lawsuit

> In any action or legal proceeding to enforce any part of this Agreement, the prevailing party ☐ will not / ☐ will recover reasonable attorneys' fees and court costs.

Many landlords assume that if they sue a tenant and win, the court will order the losing tenant to pay the landlord's court costs (filing fees, service of process charges, deposition costs, and so on) and attorneys' fees. This is not generally true. In most states, a court will order the losing tenant to pay your attorneys' fees only when a written agreement specifically provides for it, or if the law underlying the case calls for attorneys' fees to be paid.

If, however, you have an "attorneys' fees" clause in your lease, all this changes. If you hire a lawyer to bring a lawsuit and win, the judge will order your tenant to pay your costs and attorneys' fees. (In rare instances, a court will order the loser to pay costs and fees on its own, in the absence of a clause in the lease, if it finds that the behavior of the losing party was particularly egregious.)

But there's another important issue you need to know about: By law in many states, an attorneys' fees clause in a lease or a rental agreement works both ways, even if you haven't written it that way. That means that even when the lease states that only *you* are entitled to attorneys' fees if you win a lawsuit, your tenants will be entitled to collect their attorneys' fees from you if they prevail. The amount you would be ordered to pay would be whatever the judge decides is reasonable.

So, give some thought to whether you want to bind each of you to paying for the winner's costs and fees, especially if you live in a state that will read a "one-way" attorneys' fees clause as a two-way street. Remember, if you can't actually collect a judgment containing attorneys' fees from an evicted tenant (which often happens), the clause will not help you. But if the tenant prevails, you will be stuck paying the tenant's costs and fees. In addition, the presence of a two-way clause will make it far easier for a tenant to secure a willing lawyer for even a doubtful claim, because the source of the lawyer's fee (you, if you lose) will probably appear more financially solid than if the client were paying the bill.

If you intend to do all or most of your own legal work in any potential eviction or other lawsuit, you will almost surely be better off not to allow for attorneys' fees. Why? Because if the tenant wins, you'll have to pay the tenant's fees; but if you win, the tenant will owe you nothing, because you didn't hire an attorney. You can't even recover for the long hours you spent preparing for and handling the case. (In addition, it won't always be clear who "won" a lawsuit that gets settled before trial, as the great majority do. You'll need a settlement agreement that names you as the prevailing party, which can be hard to negotiate.)

Finally, be aware that attorneys' fees clauses only cover lawsuits concerning the meaning or implementation of the lease—such as a dispute about rent, security deposits, or your right to access. An attorneys' fees clause won't apply in a personal injury or discrimination lawsuit.

CAUTION
Check your state's laws about attorneys' fees clauses. Many states don't allow attorneys' fees requirements in leases and rental agreements. See "State Laws on Attorneys' Fees and Court Costs Clauses" in Appendix A for the rules in your state.

How to Fill in Clause 21

If you don't want to (or if it's illegal under your state's laws) allow for attorneys' fees, check the box before the words "will not" and delete or cross out the word "will."

If it's legal in your state, and you want to be entitled to attorneys' fees and costs if you win—and you're willing to risk paying them if you lose—check the box before the word "will" and delete or cross out the words "will not."

Disclosures of Hidden Defects

Landlords have a duty to warn tenants and others about naturally occurring dangers (such as loose soil) and human-made dangers (like low doorways or steep stairs) that are hidden or not obvious but that you know (or should know) about. Disclose hidden defects in Clause 22 of your lease or rental agreement, so that no one can ever claim that a tenant wasn't warned of a potentially dangerous condition. For example, if the building contains asbestos insulation that could be dangerous if anyone made a hole in the wall, disclose this to your tenants. If appropriate, also post warning signs near hazards, such as a ramp that's slippery when wet or a tree that drops entire strips of bark during windy weather.

While disclosure doesn't guarantee that you won't be legally liable, it will likely help (be sure your insurance protects you). Putting the tenant on notice that a problem exists will help prevent injuries and limit your liability should an injury occur from a defective condition in the rental unit or on the premises.

CAUTION
Some problems need to be fixed, not merely disclosed. Warning your tenants about a hidden defect doesn't absolve you of legal responsibility if the condition makes the dwelling uninhabitable or unreasonably dangerous. For example, you're courting liability if you rent an apartment with a gas heater that you know might blow up, even if you warn the tenant that the heater is faulty. Nor can you simply warn your tenants about prior crime on the premises and then fail to take reasonable measures (like installing dead bolts or an alarm system) to promote safety.

Clause 22. Disclosures

> Tenant acknowledges that Landlord has made the following disclosures regarding the premises:
> ☐ *Disclosure of Information on Lead-Based Paint and/or Lead-Based Paint Hazards*, and the booklet *Protect Your Family From Lead in Your Home.*
> ☐ Other disclosures: _____
> _____ .

Federal, state, or local laws might require you to make certain disclosures before a new tenant signs a lease or rental agreement or moves in.

Lead Disclosures

If your rental unit was built prior to 1978, before signing a lease or rental agreement you must tell new tenants about any known lead-based paint or lead-based paint hazards in the rental premises. This includes known hazards in both individual units and common areas, such as hallways, parking garages, or play areas. You must also give them an EPA pamphlet, *Protect Your Family From Lead in Your Home.* This is a requirement of the Residential Lead-Based Paint Hazard Reduction Act, commonly known as Title X (42 U.S.C. § 4852d), which is administered by the U.S. Environmental Protection Agency (EPA).

In addition, both you and the tenant must sign an EPA-approved form—*Disclosure of Information on Lead-Based Paint and/or Lead-Based Paint Hazards*—that will prove that you told your tenants what you know about these hazards on your premises. You must keep the disclosure form as part of your records for three years from the date of the start of the tenancy.

As discussed below, state laws on lead disclosure might also come into play.

FORM

Lead forms. You'll find copies of the *Disclosure of Information on Lead-Based Paint and/or Lead-Based Paint Hazards* form, and the EPA pamphlet *Protect Your Family From Lead in Your Home* (both in English and in Spanish) on the Nolo website; the link is included in Appendix B of this book.

CAUTION

Penalties are severe. In 2023, property owners who fail to comply with EPA regulations for disclosing lead-based paint hazards face penalties of up to $21,018 for each violation (24 C.F.R. § 30.65) and treble (triple) damages if a tenant is injured by your willful noncompliance. The fine amount tends to increase every year.

Rental Properties Exempt From Title X Regulations

Landlords who rent the following types of property aren't required to comply with federal lead disclosure requirements:

- housing built after January 1978
- housing certified lead-free by an accredited lead inspector
- lofts, efficiencies, and studios
- short-term vacation rentals of 100 days or less
- a single room rented in a residential dwelling
- housing designed for persons with disabilities, unless children younger than age six are present, and
- retirement communities (housing designed for seniors, where one or more tenant is at least 62 years old), unless children younger than age six are present.

RESOURCE

Lead disclosure forms, copies of Title X regulations, and background information on the evaluation and control of lead can be obtained by calling the National Lead Information Center at 800-424-LEAD, or checking www.epa.gov/lead.

Many states also prohibit the use of lead-based paint in residences, and require careful maintenance of existing lead-based building materials. Some states require property owners to disclose lead hazards to prospective tenants. If you are subject to a state statute, you must comply with it as well as federal law. Check with your state housing department or local office of the U.S. Department of Housing and Urban Development (www.HUD.gov) to find out if this applies to you.

Other Disclosures

Most states require at least a few other types of disclosures from landlords. For example, your state might require you to disclose known radon hazard risks, shared utility arrangements, or a history of bed bug problems. Local rent control ordinances often require disclosures, such as the name and address of the government agency or elected board that administers the ordinance. Some states require landlords to inform tenants of the name and address of the bank where their security deposit is being held. (Clause 8 covers security deposits; see "Required Landlord Disclosures" and "State Security Deposit Rules," in Appendix A.)

How to Fill in Clause 22

If your rental property was built before 1978, you must meet federal lead disclosure requirements, so check the first box and follow the advice above.

If you are legally required to make other disclosures as described above, check the second box and provide details in the blank space, adding pages as necessary.

Also, if there is a hidden (not obvious) problem with the property that could cause injury or substantially interfere with your tenant's safe enjoyment and use of the dwelling, and it's impossible or highly impractical to fix it, you are better off legally if you disclose the defective or dangerous condition before the tenant signs the lease. Examples include naturally occurring dangers, such as loose soil, and man-made dangers, such as steep stairs. (See "Disclosures of Hidden Defects," above, for more on the subject.)

Clause 23. Authority to Receive Legal Papers

The Landlord, any person managing the Premises, and anyone designated by the Landlord are authorized to accept service of process and receive other notices and demands, which may be delivered to:

☐ The Landlord, at the following address:

_____

_____

☐ The manager, at the following address:

_____

_____

☐ The following person, at the following address:

_____

_____

It's the law in many states, and a good idea in all, to give your tenants information about everyone whom you have authorized to receive notices and legal papers, such as a tenant's notice ending a tenancy or a tenant's court documents as part of an eviction defense. You might want to handle all of this yourself or delegate it to a manager or management company. Make sure the person you designate to receive legal papers is almost always available to receive tenant notices and legal papers. Also, keep your tenants up to date on any changes in this information.

How to Fill in Clause 23

Provide your name and street address or the name and address of someone you authorize to receive notices and legal papers on your behalf, such as a property manager.

Clause 24. Additional Provisions

Additional provisions are as follows: _____
_____ .

In this clause, you can list additional provisions or agreements that are unique to this tenancy, such as a provision that allows limited business use of the premises—for example, allowing piano lessons on weekdays only.

If you don't have separate tenant rules and regulations (see Clause 20, above), you can spell out a few rules under this clause—for example, how much you'll charge for a lost key, pool hours, or no-smoking rules.

How to Fill in Clause 24

List additional provisions or rules here or in an attachment. If you have no additional provisions, delete this clause or write "N/A" or "Not Applicable."

> **TIP**
> **You needn't put every small detail you want to communicate to the tenant into your lease or rental agreement.** Instead, prepare a welcoming, but no-nonsense, "move-in letter" that dovetails with the lease or rental agreement and highlights important terms of the tenancy—for example, how and where to report maintenance problems. You can also use a move-in letter to cover issues not included in the lease or rental agreement— for example, rules for use of a laundry room. (Chapter 3 covers move-in letters.)

> **CAUTION**
> **Don't include exculpatory ("If there's a problem, I'm not responsible") clauses or hold harmless ("If there's a problem, you are responsible") clauses.** Many form leases include provisions that attempt to absolve you in advance from responsibility for your legal misdeeds. For example, one lease form generated by a popular software package contains a broad provision stating that the landlord is not responsible for injuries to tenants and guests, even those caused intentionally. Many exculpatory clauses are blatantly illegal: If a tenant is injured because of a dangerous condition you failed to fix for an unreasonably long time, no boilerplate lease provision will protect you from civil—and possibly criminal—charges.

Clause 25. Validity of Each Part

If a court holds any portion of this Agreement to be invalid, its invalidity will not affect the validity or enforceability of any other provision of this Agreement.

This clause is known as a "savings" clause, and it's common in contracts of all kinds. It means that, in the unlikely event that one of the other clauses in the Agreement is found to be invalid by a court, the remainder of the Agreement will remain in force.

How to Fill in Clause 25

You don't need to add anything to this clause.

Clause 26. Grounds for Termination of Tenancy

The failure of Tenant or Tenant's guests or invitees to comply with any term of this Agreement, or the misrepresentation of any material fact on Tenant's rental application, is grounds for termination of the tenancy, with appropriate notice to the Tenant and procedures as required by law.

This clause states that any violation of the Agreement by the tenant, or by the tenant's business or social guests, is grounds for terminating the tenancy, according to the procedures established by your state or local laws. Making the tenant responsible for the actions of guests can be extremely important—for example, if you discover that the tenant's family or friends are dealing illegal drugs on the premises or have damaged the property. Clause 26 also tells tenants that if they made false statements on a rental application concerning an important fact—such as their rental and eviction—you may terminate the tenancy and evict if necessary.

How to Fill in Clause 26

You don't need to add anything to this clause.

Clause 27. Entire Agreement

> This document constitutes the entire Agreement between the parties, and no promises or representations, other than those contained here and those implied by law, have been made by Landlord or Tenant. Any modifications to this Agreement must be in writing, signed by Landlord and Tenant.

This clause establishes that the lease or rental agreement and any attachments (such as tenant rules and regulations) constitute the entire agreement between you and your tenant. It means that oral promises (by you or the tenant) to do something else with respect to any aspect of the rental are not binding. Any changes or additions must be in writing. For example, if your lease prohibits pets, and your tenant wants to get a dog and you agree, you should amend the Pets clause of the lease accordingly. This will help ensure that a casual conversation about pets, which the tenant misconstrues, doesn't lead the tenant to bringing in a dog without your permission. (Chapter 4 discusses how to modify signed rental agreements and leases.)

How to Fill in Clause 27

You don't need to add anything to this clause.

Instructions for Signing the Lease or Rental Agreement

After all terms are final, you're ready to sign. If you're signing paper versions, make two copies of the lease or rental agreement, including all attachments. (If you're signing electronically, see "Signing the Lease or Rental Agreement Electronically," below.) You and each tenant should sign both copies in the space at the end. Include your signature, street address, phone number, and email, or that of the person you authorize as your agent, such as a property manager. There's also space for the tenants' signatures and phone numbers. Again, as stressed in Clause 1, make sure all adults living in the rental unit, including both members of a married couple, sign the lease or rental agreement. And check that tenants' names and signatures match their driver's licenses or other government-issued identification.

If the tenant has a cosigner (see "About Cosigners," below), you'll need to add a line for the cosigner's signature.

If you alter our form by writing or typing in changes, you and all tenants must initial the changes when you sign the document, so as to forestall any possibility that a tenant will claim you unilaterally inserted changes after the tenant signed.

CAUTION

Don't sign a lease until all terms are final. All of your expectations should be written into the lease or rental agreement (or any attachments, such as tenant rules and regulations) before you and the tenant sign the document. Never sign an incomplete document assuming last-minute changes can be made later.

Give one copy of the signed lease or rental agreement to the tenant(s), and keep the other one for your files. (If you are renting to more than one tenant, you don't need to prepare a separate agreement for each cotenant. After all of you have signed the agreement, cotenants can make their own copies.)

Signing the Lease or Rental Agreement Electronically

It's often more convenient to sign a lease or rental agreement electronically than to ask everyone to sign in person. Fortunately, in most situations electronic signatures (e-signatures) are just as valid and enforceable as in-person signatures.

Perhaps the simplest way for landlords to avoid e-signature problems is to use a commercial e-signature program such as PandaDoc, HelloSign, DocuSign, or SignNow. These programs handle the formalities of making e-signatures valid for you. For example, they obtain the users' consent before allowing them to sign, authenticate the signatures, distribute copies of the signed documents to all the parties, and keep detailed records of the e-signing process. The cost of using these programs is fairly low—some even allow users to e-sign a few documents per month free of charge.

If you don't use a commercial e-signature program, but want to use e-signatures on your leases, rental agreements, and other rental documents, follow these steps to make the e-signatures valid and enforceable:

1. Get consent from your tenants to discuss the rental and exchange documents electronically. The best practice—and one that's required in some places—is for the parties to agree to electronic communications in a written document (or email) that's separate from the lease or rental agreement.

2. Make sure your tenants know that they are agreeing to be bound to the terms of a document when they e-sign—they're not signing to indicate they merely received it or reviewed it. You can tell them in your email with the attached document, or require them to click a box that alerts them to the binding nature of their signature, which they must do before they sign.

3. Give your tenants other options. Let them know they can sign documents in person if they prefer.

4. Follow up with hard copies. Provide all tenants and anyone else who signs (like a cosigner) with a paper copy of the signed document.

5. Retain copies (electronic or paper) of the fully executed documents.

Many landlords obtain e-signatures by emailing documents to the tenants and having them return scans of the signed documents. Most of the time, this is a valid and enforceable way of executing documents. If you're going to do this, send the document to be signed in a format that can't be altered (such as a read-only PDF). And, email the document to each person separately (not in a cc'd email) to make sure that it's received and signed by the intended signer.

About Cosigners

Some landlords require cosigners on rental agreements and leases, especially when renting to students who are financially dependent on someone else. The cosigner signs a separate agreement on the rental agreement or lease, under which the cosigner agrees to cover any rent or damage-repair costs the tenant fails to pay.

In practice, a cosigner's promise to guarantee the tenant's rent obligation might have less legal value than you might think. This is because the threat of eviction is the primary factor that motivates a tenant to pay the rent, and, obviously, you cannot evict a cosigner. Also, because you'll have to sue the cosigner separately from the renter if there's a problem, actually doing so might be more trouble than it's worth. This is especially true if the cosigner lives in another state, because the amount of money you're owed will rarely justify hiring a lawyer and collecting a judgment.

In sum, the benefits of having a lease or rental agreement cosigned by someone who won't be living on the property are largely psychological. But these benefits could still be worth something: A tenant who thinks you can (and will) notify and sue a cosigning relative or friend might be less likely to default on the rent. Similarly, a cosigner asked to pay the tenant's debts might persuade the tenant to pay.

Because of the practical difficulties associated with cosigners, many landlords refuse to consider them. Refusing to accept a cosigner is legal in every situation but one: If a tenant with a disability who has insufficient income (but is otherwise suitable) asks you to accept a cosigner who will cover the rent if needed, you must relax your blanket rule at least to the extent of investigating the suitability of the proposed cosigner. If that person is solvent and stable, federal law requires you to accommodate the applicant by accepting the cosigner, in spite of your general policy. (*Giebeler v. M & B Associates*, 343 F.3d 1143 (9th Cir. 2003).)

If you decide to accept a cosigner, you should have that person fill out a separate rental application and agree to a credit check—after all, a cosigner who has no resources or connection to the tenant will be completely useless. Should the tenant and the prospective cosigner object to these inquiries and the costs of a credit check, you might wonder how serious they are about the guarantor's willingness to stand behind the tenant. Once you're satisfied that the cosigner can back up the tenant, add a line at the end of the lease or rental agreement for the dated signature, phone, and address of the cosigner.

CAUTION

If you later amend the rental agreement or change the lease, have the cosigner sign the new version. Generally speaking, cosigners are bound only to the terms of the exact lease or rental agreement they cosign.

TIP

Help tenants understand the lease or rental agreement before they sign it. Too many landlords thrust a lease or rental agreement at tenants and expect them to sign it unread. Instead, encourage tenants to ask questions about anything that's unclear, or actually review each clause with them. It will save you lots of hassles later on.

Some states require landlords who discuss the lease or rental agreement with tenants in a language other than English to provide a written translation. For example, California requires landlords who negotiate primarily in Spanish, Chinese, Tagalog, Vietnamese, or Korean to give the applicant an unsigned, translated version of the lease before asking the applicant to sign. This rule doesn't apply (that is, you may supply your English version only) if tenants supply their own translator who isn't a minor and can fluently speak and read both languages.

Even if a translation is not legally required, you want your tenants to know and follow the rules. If most or all of your communications with the tenant about the lease or rental agreement are in a language other than English, you should give the tenant a written translation. (We include Spanish versions of our lease and rental agreement forms on Nolo's website. See Appendix B for the link to forms in this book.)

Lease-Option Contracts (Rent-to-Buy)

Occasionally, landlords of single-family houses will agree to rent to tenants who would like to eventually own the house. In periods of economic downturn, these arrangements are especially attractive to tenants who might not have the down payment money to purchase the property outright (or the good credit required for a loan), but expect their finances to improve over a period of one or more years. These tenants would like the option to buy their rented home, and would also like the opportunity to have some of their rent money applied toward the house purchase price.

Rent-to-buy can also be attractive for the landlord, who might intend to sell in the near future and would like to avoid the hassle and expense of putting the house on the market (selling to a resident tenant avoids staging costs and brokers' fees). In addition, a tenant who hopes to someday own the property will be motivated to take good care of it, and to honor other aspects of the lease.

When a landlord and tenant agree to a rent-to-buy (also called "rent-to-own") arrangement, they sign an agreement (typically called a "lease-option contract") that gives the tenant the right (the "option") of buying the house in the future, providing certain conditions are met. The option agreement should be separate from the lease, but refer to it. The agreement covers issues like:

- the amount of the option fee and how it will be paid
- the date by which or the window of time in which the tenant has to exercise (or lose) the option
- how much (if any) of the monthly rent will be applied to the house purchase price, and
- the sale price of the home.

Many landlords are wary of rent-to-buy arrangements, for good reasons. The major drawback is that giving a tenant the option to buy the rental house ties the landlord down; you can't easily sell it to someone else, and you might find it difficult to use the property as collateral for a loan.

A second major disadvantage is that in some states, purchase options trigger disclosures regarding any defects and the condition of the property—the same disclosures that sellers must make when engaging in a normal sale. Depending on the laws of your state, this might involve inspections and considerable work and expense.

When thinking about offering an option to buy, keep the following additional issues in mind.

Paying for the Option

An option curtails the ability of the owner to use the house for collateral. For example, if you want to finance your child's college education by getting a second mortgage on the property, you might have difficulty doing so. Because you're giving up a valuable right when granting the option, you can expect to be compensated. You'll need to negotiate how much the option right should cost; ideally, your tenant will pay you up front, though you could also agree to monthly payments, in addition to the rent.

Sale Price of the House

When you give a tenant an option to buy, you'll need to either name the price in your option contract or supply an objective method for determining the price later. Naming the price now risks misreading the market, and you could end up with a sale price that turns out to be less than the actual market value at the time of sale.

You can avoid this risk by waiting to decide the price, but you must set up a fail-safe method for arriving at it. For example, your contract might say, "Market value as determined by licensed brokers, one each chosen by landlord and tenant; and if the brokers cannot agree, the price to be determined by a third who will be chosen by the two brokers." If you simply say, "Fair market value at the time the option is exercised," or "Price to be negotiated at the time," and you and the tenant cannot agree on a price, you won't be able to go to court and get a judge to settle it for you. In other words, the option will fall apart.

When the Tenant Must Exercise the Option, and Under What Circumstances

You'll want to give tenants a specific window of time, or a deadline, by which they must tell you that they're exercising the option. You can specify that the option be exercised within several months of the end of the underlying lease—this gives you time to begin planning for a sale or a successor tenant. Or, you could set a deadline (like the end of the first year of a multiyear lease), specifying that exercising the option will terminate the lease.

You'll also need to decide whether the tenant must have been "squeaky clean" in order to take advantage of the option—whether any prior lease defaults will bar the exercise (current lease violations should give you grounds to refuse to honor the option, as explained below). For instance, you might not want a tenant who has a history of late rent to exercise the option, because a tenant who has trouble making timely rent payments will probably have a hard time making mortgage payments, too. You might also want to insist on certain financial criteria, such as a minimum credit score.

Spell out the manner in which you will accept the tenant's decision. Written notification is preferable, and personal delivery is the best method (certified mail is a good second choice).

Tenant Improvements and Rent

Many tenants will want the ability to begin improving "their" home, with the value of the improvements credited against the selling price. If you agree, be sure to consider what will happen if the tenant decides not to buy the home—will you reimburse the tenant?

Similarly, tenants might ask you to apply a portion of the rent toward a down payment. As with improvements, you'll need to address what will happen if the tenant doesn't exercise the option, or if the sale doesn't go through.

What Happens If You Need to Evict?

If drafted properly, your option contract won't curtail your ability to terminate the underlying lease if the tenant fails to pay the rent, causes damage, or otherwise gives you solid legal grounds for ending the tenancy. Option contracts should specify that the tenants may exercise the option only if they are in "good standing" with respect to the lease. A tenant whose lease you've terminated is obviously not in good standing. Be sure you don't become obligated to return any option fees already paid.

"Right of Refusal" and "Right of Offer"

Instead of entering into a full-blown option contract, some landlords agree to give their tenants preferential treatment when and if the property goes on the market. Although offering special treatment might help the landlord avoid some of the tricky issues mentioned above, it still poses some drawbacks.

A "right of refusal" allows the tenant to match or improve on any deal the landlord hammers out with a third-party buyer. Once the landlord has secured a buyer, the landlord must give the tenant an opportunity to buy the property on the same or better terms. These arrangements are nothing but a headache for a seller, because it means that any potential buyer runs the risk of having the tenant trump the deal that the buyer has painstakingly hammered out. Knowing this, buyers won't bother negotiating with these sellers, and seasoned brokers (on both sides) avoid these situations like the plague.

A "right of first refusal" is much milder. With this right, the landlord promises to give the tenant the first opportunity to buy the home at the price named by the landlord. If the tenant declines, the home goes on the market. The landlord cannot artificially inflate the offering price, in order to get rid of the tenant—the asking price must be commercially reasonable. But as many happy sellers find out, sometimes you don't really know what the house will go for, and selling at your named price might deprive you of a lucrative bidding war (which the tenant could always join, too).

Landlords don't give away rights of first refusal or offer—like options, these rights come at a price.

Get Legal Advice

Think long and hard about whether your interests would be served by giving tenants an option to buy, or even rights of first refusal or offer. If you decide to proceed, consult an attorney who specializes in real estate law and a tax specialist before signing a lease-option contract. Remember, you're dealing with a very expensive investment—once the tenant exercises the option, it's the same as a sales contract. Structuring the option contract (or offer rights) in ways that don't protect your interests could be financially disastrous. You'll also need professional help in preparing a house sales contract.

Month-to-Month Residential Rental Agreement

Clause 1. Identification of Landlord and Tenant

This Agreement is between _____Marty Nelson_____ ("Tenant") and

___Alex Stevens_____ ("Landlord").

Each Tenant is jointly and severally liable for the payment of rent and performance of all other terms of this

Agreement.

Clause 2. Identification of Premises

Subject to the terms and conditions in this Agreement, Landlord rents to Tenant, and Tenant rents from

Landlord, for residential purposes only, the premises located at ___137 Howell St., Philadelphia, Pennsylvania____

_____ ("Premises").

Rental of the Premises also includes: _____

_____ .

Rental of the Premises excludes: _____

_____ .

Clause 3. Limits on Use and Occupancy

The Premises are to be used only as a private residence for Tenant(s) listed in Clause 1 of this Agreement, and

their minor children: ____N/A_____ . Occupancy by guests

for more than ___ten days every six months_____ is prohibited without Landlord's written consent and will

be considered a breach of this Agreement.

Clause 4. Term of the Tenancy

The rental will begin on ___September 15, 20xx_____ , and continue on a month-to-month

basis. Landlord may terminate the tenancy or modify the terms of this Agreement by giving the Tenant

_____30_____ days' written notice. Tenant may terminate the tenancy by giving the Landlord

_____30_____ days' written notice.

Clause 5. Payment of Rent

Regular monthly rent

Tenant will pay to Landlord a monthly rent of $___1,800_____ , payable in advance on the first day of

each month, except when that day falls on a weekend or legal holiday, in which case rent is due on the next

business day. Rent will be paid as follows, or in another manner as Landlord designates from time to time:

Delivery of payment

Rent will be paid:

☑ by mail, to ___Alex Stevens, 28 Franklin Street, Philadelphia, Pennsylvania 19120___

☐ in person, at _____

☐ electronically, to _____

Form of payment

Landlord will accept payment in the form of:

☐ cash

☑ personal check made payable to ___Alex Stevens_____

☑ certified funds or money order payable to ___Alex Stevens_____

☐ credit or debit card

☐ other electronic funds transfer: _____

Prorated first month's rent

☑ On signing this Agreement, Tenant will pay to Landlord for the period of ___September 15, 20xx___

through ___September 30, 20xx___ the sum of $___900___ as rent, payable in advance of the start

of the tenancy.

☐ Upon move-in, Tenant will owe as rent the prorated rent specified above, plus one full month's rent in the

amount designated above, for a total of $_____.

Clause 6. Late Charges

Because Landlord and Tenant agree that actual damages for late rent payments are very difficult or impossible

to determine, Landlord and Tenant agree to the following:

- Tenant will pay Landlord a late charge if Tenant fails to pay the rent in full within ___3___ days after

  the date it is due.

- The late charge will be $___10___ plus $___5___ for each individual day that the rent continues

  to be unpaid. The total late charge for any one month will not exceed $___45___ .

Landlord does not waive the right to insist on payment of the rent in full on the date it is due.

Clause 7. Returned Check and Other Bank Charges

If any check offered by Tenant to Landlord in payment of rent or any other amount due under this Agreement

is returned for lack of sufficient funds, a "stop payment," or any other reason, Landlord will make a demand for

payment and otherwise pursue remedies as allowed by law.

Clause 8. Security Deposit

On signing this Agreement, Tenant will pay to Landlord the sum of $ __1,800__ as a security deposit. Tenant may not, without Landlord's prior written consent, apply this security deposit to the last month's rent or to any other sum due under this Agreement. Within __30 days__ after Tenant has vacated the Premises, returned keys, and provided Landlord with a forwarding address, Landlord will return the deposit in full or give Tenant an itemized written statement of the reasons for, and the dollar amount of, any of the security deposit retained by Landlord, along with a check for any deposit balance.

The security deposit of $1,800 will be held at: __Federal Bank, 1 Federal Street, Philadelphia, Pennsylvania 19120__

Clause 9. Utilities

Tenant will pay all utility charges, except for the following, which will be paid by Landlord:

__garbage and water__ .

Clause 10. Prohibition of Assignment and Subletting

Tenant will not sublet any part of the Premises or assign this Agreement without the prior written consent of Landlord. Violating this clause is grounds for terminating the tenancy.

- ☑ a. Tenant will not sublet or rent any part of the Premises for short-term stays of any duration, including but not limited to vacation rentals.
- ☐ b. Short-stay rentals are prohibited except as authorized by law. Any short-stay rental is expressly conditioned upon the Tenant's following all regulations, laws, and other requirements as a condition to offering a short-stay rental. Failure to follow all laws, ordinances, regulations, and other requirements, including any registration requirement, will be deemed a material, noncurable breach of this Agreement and will furnish cause for termination.

Clause 11. Tenant's Maintenance Responsibilities

Tenant agrees to: (1) keep the Premises clean, sanitary, and in good condition and, upon termination of the tenancy, return the Premises to Landlord in a condition identical to that which existed when Tenant took occupancy, except for ordinary wear and tear; (2) immediately notify Landlord of any defects or dangerous conditions in and about the Premises of which Tenant becomes aware; and (3) reimburse Landlord, on demand by Landlord, for the cost of any repairs to the Premises, including Landlord's personal property therein, damaged by Tenant or Tenant's guests or business invitees through misuse or neglect.

Tenant has examined the Premises, including appliances, fixtures, carpets, drapes, and paint, and has found them to be in good, safe, and clean condition and repair, except as noted in the Landlord-Tenant Checklist.

Clause 12. Repairs and Alterations by Tenant

    a. Except as provided by law, or as authorized by the prior written consent of Landlord, Tenant will not make any repairs or alterations to the Premises, including nailing holes in the walls or painting the rental unit.

    b. Tenant will not, without Landlord's prior written consent, alter, rekey, or install any locks to the Premises or install or alter any security alarm system. Tenant will provide Landlord with a key or keys capable of unlocking all such rekeyed or new locks as well as instructions on how to disarm any altered or new security alarm system.

Clause 13. Violating Laws and Causing Disturbances

Tenant is entitled to quiet enjoyment of the Premises. Tenant and guests or invitees will not use the Premises or adjacent areas in such a way as to: (1) violate any law or ordinance, including laws prohibiting the use, possession, or sale of illegal drugs; (2) commit waste (severe property damage) or cause or tolerate a nuisance; or (3) annoy, disturb, inconvenience, or interfere with the quiet enjoyment and peace and quiet of any other tenant or nearby resident.

Clause 14. Damage to the Premises

In the event the Premises are partially or totally damaged or destroyed by fire or other cause, the following will apply:

☐ a. Premises totally damaged and destroyed. Landlord will have the option to: (1) repair such damage and restore the Premises, with this Agreement continuing in full force and effect, except that Tenant's rent will be abated while repairs are being made; or (2) give written notice to Tenant terminating this Agreement at any time within thirty (30) days after such damage, and specifying the termination date; in the event that Landlord gives such notice, this Agreement will expire and all of Tenant's rights pursuant to this Agreement will cease.

☐ b. Premises partially damaged by fire or other cause. Landlord will attempt to repair such damage and restore the Premises within thirty (30) days after such damage. If only part of the Premises cannot be used, Tenant must pay rent only for the usable part, to be determined by Landlord. If Landlord is unable to complete repairs within thirty (30) days, this Agreement will expire and all of Tenant's rights pursuant to this Agreement will terminate at the option of either party. Whether the Premises are totally or partially destroyed will be decided by Landlord, in the exercise of its sole discretion.

☐ c. In the event that Tenant, or Tenant's guests or invitees, in any way caused or contributed to the damage of the Premises, Landlord will have the right to terminate this Agreement at any time, and Tenant will be responsible for all losses, including, but not limited to, damage and repair costs as well as loss of rental income.

☐ d. Landlord will not be required to repair or replace any property brought onto the Premises by Tenant.

Clause 15. Renters' Insurance

Tenant acknowledges that Landlord's property insurance policy will not cover damage to or loss of Tenant's personal property. Tenant will obtain a renters' insurance policy that will:

- reimburse Landlord for cost of fire or water damage caused by Tenant or Tenant's guests, and vandalism to the Premises

- indemnify Landlord against liability to third parties for any negligence on the part of Tenant, Tenant's guests, or invitees; and

- cover damage to Tenant's personal possessions to a minimum of $100,000.

Tenant will provide Landlord with proof of such policy by giving Landlord a certificate of insurance issued by the insurance company within fifteen (15) days of _September 15, 20xx_. The policy will include Landlord as an "additional insured." Tenant will provide Landlord with a certificate of insurance upon every renewal. Tenant will not allow such policy to expire during the rental term. Failure to obtain and maintain a renters' insurance policy will be treated as a material breach of this Agreement.

Clause 16. Pets

No animal may be kept on the Premises without Landlord's prior written consent, except animals needed by tenants who have a disability, as that term is understood by law, and _one dog weighing less than 20 pounds_, under the following conditions: _Tenant complies with rules set out in "Attachment A, Addition to Clause 16, Pets,"_ attached to this Agreement.

Clause 17. Landlord's Right to Access

Landlord or Landlord's agents may enter the Premises in the event of an emergency, to make repairs or improvements, or to show the Premises to prospective buyers or tenants. Landlord may also enter the Premises to conduct an annual inspection to check for safety or maintenance problems. Except in cases of emergency, Tenant's abandonment of the Premises, court order, or where it is impractical to do so, Landlord will give Tenant _24 hours'_ notice before entering.

Clause 18. Extended Absences by Tenant

Tenant will notify Landlord in advance if Tenant will be away from the Premises for _seven_ or more consecutive days. During such absence, Landlord may enter the Premises at times reasonably necessary to maintain the property and inspect for damage and needed repairs.

Clause 19. Possession of the Premises

a. *Tenant's failure to take possession.*

If, after signing this Agreement, Tenant fails to take possession of the Premises, Tenant will still be responsible for paying rent and complying with all other terms of this Agreement.

b. *Landlord's failure to deliver possession.*

If Landlord is unable to deliver possession of the Premises to Tenant for any reason not within Landlord's control, including, but not limited to, failure of prior occupants to vacate or partial or complete destruction of the Premises, Tenant will have the right to terminate this Agreement upon proper notice as required by law. In such event, Landlord's liability to Tenant will be limited to the return of all sums previously paid by Tenant to Landlord.

Clause 20. Tenant Rules and Regulations

☑ Tenant acknowledges receipt of, and has read a copy of, the Tenant Rules and Regulations, which are labeled Attachment ___B___ and attached to and incorporated into this Agreement by this reference. Tenant understands that serious or repeated violations of the rules may be grounds for termination.

Clause 21. Payment of Court Costs and Attorneys' Fees in a Lawsuit

In any action or legal proceeding to enforce any part of this Agreement, the prevailing party (*choose one:* ~~will not~~/will) recover reasonable attorneys' fees and court costs.

Clause 22. Disclosures

Tenant acknowledges that Landlord has made the following disclosures regarding the Premises:

☑ *Disclosure of Information on Lead-Based Paint and/or Lead-Based Paint Hazards* and the pamphlet *Protect Your Family From Lead in Your Home*

☐ Other disclosures: _____

Clause 23. Authority to Receive Legal Papers

The Landlord, any person managing the Premises, and anyone designated by the Landlord are authorized to accept service of process and receive other notices and demands, which may be delivered to:

☑ The Landlord, at the following address: _28 Franklin Street, Philadelphia, Pennsylvania 19120_

☐ The manager, at the following address: _____

☐ The following person, at the following address: _____

Clause 24. Additional Provisions

Additional provisions are as follows: _____N/A_____

_____

_____

_____

_____ .

Clause 25. Validity of Each Part

If a court holds any portion of this Agreement to be invalid, its invalidity will not affect the validity or enforceability of any other provision of this Agreement.

Clause 26. Grounds for Termination of Tenancy

The failure of Tenant or Tenant's guests or invitees to comply with any term of this Agreement, or the misrepresentation of any material fact on Tenant's Rental Application, is grounds for termination of the tenancy, with appropriate notice to Tenant and procedures as required by law.

Clause 27. Entire Agreement

This document constitutes the entire Agreement between the parties, and no promises or representations, other than those contained here and those implied by law, have been made by Landlord or Tenant. Any modifications to this Agreement must be in writing, signed by Landlord and Tenant.

Sept. 1, 20xx	*Alex Stevens*	Landlord
Date	Landlord or Landlord's Agent	Title

28 Franklin Street
Street Address

Philadelphia	Pennsylvania	19120	215-555-1578
City	State	Zip	Phone

alex@alex.com
Email

Sept. 1, 20xx	*Marty Nelson*	marty@marty.com	215-555-8751
Date	Tenant	email	Phone

Date	Tenant	email	Phone

2

Choosing Tenants: Your Most Important Decision

Choosing tenants is the most important decision any landlord makes. To do it well and stay out of legal trouble, you need a good system. Follow the steps in this chapter to maximize your chances of selecting tenants who will pay their rent on time, keep their units in good condition, and not cause legal or practical problems.

How to Advertise Rental Property

You can advertise rental property in many ways:
- posting a notice online
- using a "For Rent" sign
- taking out an ad in a local newspaper
- posting flyers on neighborhood bulletin boards
- posting a notice with university, alumni, or corporate housing offices
- listing with a local real estate broker
- buying ads in apartment rental guides or magazines, or
- hiring a property management company that will advertise your rentals as part of the management fee.

What will work best depends on a number of factors, including the characteristics of the rental property (such as rent, size, and amenities), its location, your budget, and how soon you need to find a tenant.

While large-scale landlords have great success with paid, nationally oriented advertising, many smaller landlords find marketing their rentals on a more personal level to be a better strategy. If you're renting only a few properties, you usually won't need to spend a lot of money on advertising—sometimes free is best. For example, you can spread the word about your rental through local social media and by word of mouth. Friends, colleagues, neighbors, and even current tenants can be great sources for finding tenants.

No matter how you let people know about the availability of your rental units, follow these simple rules to stay out of legal hot water:

Describe the rental unit enthusiastically but accurately. For practical reasons, avoid abbreviations and real estate jargon in your ad. Include basic details, such as:
- rent and deposit
- room size—particularly number of bedrooms and baths
- location—either the general neighborhood or street address
- move-in date and term—fixed-term lease or month-to-month rental agreement
- special features
- pets (whether you allow them, and any restrictions, such as dog breeds that your insurance prohibits)
- phone number, email, or website for more details (unless you're going to show the unit only at an open house and don't want to take calls), and
- date and time of any open house.

If you have any important rules (legal and nondiscriminatory, of course), such as no smoking, put them in your ad. Letting prospective tenants know about important policies can save you from talking to a lot of unsuitable people.

Be sure your ad can't be construed as discriminatory. The best way to do this is to focus on only the rental property—not on any particular type of tenant. Specifically, ads should never mention sex, race, religion, disability, or age (unless yours is legally recognized senior citizens housing). And ads should never imply through words, photographs, or illustrations that you prefer to rent to people because of their age, sex, or race. (See "Avoiding Illegal Discrimination," below, for more on the subject.)

State a market-rate price in your ad. Or, put another way, if an applicant who is otherwise acceptable (has a good credit history and impeccable references and meets all the criteria

Online Services

Countless online services exist to help you reach potential tenants. Do a bit of research to learn which sites are used most by people looking to rent in your area, as site usage varies by region. Here are some of the more established places renters look for listings:

Online community posting boards allow you to list your rentals at no or low charge and are a good place to start.

- **Craigslist.** Craigslist (Craigslist.org) has separate sites for every major metropolitan area. Visit the "Housing" section on your community's site to find the best place to post your listing.
- **Facebook.** Many communities form locally oriented "Groups" on Facebook where you can post rental listings. To find these local groups, search for your zip code, area code, or city's name in Facebook.
- **Online community groups**. Neighborhood groups, such as NextDoor, can be a good place to list your vacancy.

National apartment listing services are also available, with the largest ones representing millions of apartment units in the United States. Some of the most established are:

- Rentals.com
- Doorsteps.com
- Apartments.com
- Zillow.com
- ForRent.com
- Zumper.com
- Rent.com, and
- ApartmentGuide.com.

These national sites offer a wide range of services, from simple text-only ads that provide basic information on your rental to full-scale virtual tours and floor plans of the rental property. Services typically include mobile apps, too. Prices vary widely depending on the type of ad, how long you want it to run, and any services you purchase (some websites provide tenant-screening services).

Before you use any online apartment rental service, make sure it's reputable. Find out how long the company has been in business and how they handle problems with apartment listings.

explained below) shows up promptly and agrees to all the terms set out in your ad, that person should be able to rent your property for the price you have advertised. By contrast, if you suddenly find a reason why it will cost significantly more, you are likely to be in violation of your state's false advertising laws. This doesn't mean you're always legally required to rent at your advertised price, however. If a tenant asks for more services or significantly different lease terms that you feel justify more rent, it's fine to bargain and raise your price, as long as your proposed increase doesn't violate any rent control laws.

Don't advertise something you don't have. Some large landlords, management companies, and rental services have advertised units that weren't really available in order to produce a large number of prospective tenants who could then be directed to higher-priced or inferior units. Such bait-and-switch advertising is illegal under consumer fraud laws, and many property owners have been prosecuted for such practices.

Don't overhype security measures. Don't exaggerate—in writing or orally—the safety of your property or the security measures you provide. Not only will you have begun the landlord-tenant relationship on a note of insincerity, but you might be legally obligated to actually provide what you described. Or, if you fail to do so, or fail to conscientiously maintain promised security measures in working order (such as outdoor lighting or an electronic gate on the parking garage), a court or jury could find your failure to be a material factor that allowed a crime to occur on the premises. And, if this happens, chances are good you will be held liable for at least a portion of a tenant's losses or injuries.

Renting Property That's Still Occupied

It's always easier to wait until the old tenant moves out before showing a rental unit to prospective tenants. This gives you the chance to refurbish the unit and avoids problems such as promising the place to a new tenant, only to have the existing tenant not move out on time or leave the place a mess.

To eliminate any gap in rent, however, you might want to show a rental unit while current tenants are still there. This can create a conflict; in most states, you have a right to show the still-occupied property to prospective tenants, but your current tenants are still entitled to a reasonable level of privacy. (For details, see Clause 15 of the lease and rental agreement in Chapter 1.)

To minimize disturbing your current tenant, follow these guidelines:

- Before implementing your plans to find a new tenant, discuss them with outgoing tenants so you can be as accommodating as possible.
- Give current tenants as much notice as possible before entering and showing a rental unit to prospective tenants.
- Limit the number of times you show the unit in a given week, and make sure your current tenants agree to any evening and weekend visits.
- Consider reducing the rent slightly for the existing tenant if showing the unit is an imposition.
- If possible, avoid putting a sign on the rental property itself, because this almost guarantees that your existing tenants will be bothered by strangers. Or, if you must put up a sign, make sure it warns against disturbing the occupant and includes contact information. "For Rent: Shown by Appointment Only. Call 555-1700. Do Not Disturb Occupants" should work fine.

If, despite your best efforts to protect their privacy, the current tenants are uncooperative or hostile, it really is best to wait until they leave before showing the unit. Also, if the current tenant is a complete slob or has damaged the place, you'll be far better off to apply paint and elbow grease after they leave before trying to rerent it.

Accepting Rental Applications

Ask all prospective tenants to fill out a written rental application that includes information on the applicant's employment, income, credit, and rental housing history, including up-to-date references. It's legal (and a good idea) to ask for the applicant's Social Security and driver's license numbers or, if the applicant doesn't have one of these, some other form of identifying information. For example, instead of a Social Security number, you could accept an ITIN (Individual Taxpayer Identification Number), which is issued by the IRS to persons who are required to file income taxes but who can't obtain a Social Security number (SSN). ITINs are issued to nonimmigrants (people who are in the United States legally but don't have the right to live here permanently). Almost anyone planning on staying in the United States long enough to rent an apartment (like someone with a student visa) will have an ITIN. If you refuse to rent to someone who has an ITIN but not an SSN, you might be courting a fair housing claim. You can also ask if the applicant has declared bankruptcy or been evicted. (You'll also get much of this information from a credit report, as discussed below.)

FORM

Rental Application form. You'll find a downloadable Rental Application on the Nolo website; the link is included in Appendix B of this book. A filled-in sample rental application is shown below.

Before giving prospective tenants a rental application, complete the box at the top, filling in the property address, the first month's rent, the rental term, and any deposit or credit check fee that tenants must pay before moving in. (Credit check fees are discussed later in this chapter.) If you're charging any other fee, such as a nonrefundable cleaning deposit, note this as well—if you're sure that the nonrefundable fee is legal in your state. (See "Don't Charge Nonrefundable Fees" in Chapter 1 for details.)

Here are some basic guidelines for accepting rental applications:

- Each prospective tenant—everyone age 18 or older—should completely fill out and sign a separate written application.

This is true whether you're renting to a married couple or to unrelated roommates, a complete stranger, or the cousin of your current tenant.

- Always make sure that prospective tenants complete the entire rental application, including Social Security number, driver's license or other identifying information (such as a passport number or ITIN), current employment, bank, and emergency contacts. You might need this information later to track down a tenant who skips town leaving unpaid rent or abandoned property. Also, you might need the Social Security number or other identifying information, such as a passport, to request an applicant's credit report.

- Request proof of identity and immigration status. Many landlords ask prospective tenants to show their driver's license or other photo identification as a way to verify that applicants are using their real names. Except in California (Cal. Civ. Code § 1940.3), Colorado (Colo. Rev. Stat. § 38-12-1203), and New York City (NYC Admin. Code § 8-107(5)(a)), you may also ask applicants for proof of identity and eligibility to work under U.S. immigration laws (be aware that additional states and localities are considering and possibly passing similar measures). Proof includes documents like a work permit, a passport, or a naturalization certificate, using Form I-9 (*Employment Eligibility Verification*) from the U.S. Citizenship and Immigration Services, or USCIS, a bureau of the U.S. Department of Homeland Security. This form (and instructions for completing it) are available from the USCIS website at www.uscis.gov/i-9, or by phone at 800-375-5283. Under federal fair housing laws, you may not selectively ask for such immigration information—that is, you must ask all

Rental Application

A separate application is required from each applicant age 18 or older.

Date and time received by Landlord _____

THIS SECTION TO BE COMPLETED BY LANDLORD

Address of property to be rented: ___178 West 81st Street, Apt. 4F, NYC___

Rental term: ☐ month-to-month ☑ lease from ___March 1, 20xx___ to ___February 28, 20xx___

Amounts Due Prior to Occupancy

First month's rent: .... $____3,000____

Security deposit: .... $____3,000____

Credit check fee: .... $_____38_____

Other (specify): _____ $_____

TOTAL $____6,038____

Applicant

Full Name—include all names you use or have used in the past: ___Hannah Silver___

Home Phone: ___609-555-3789___   Work Phone: ___609-555-4567___

Cell Phone: ___609-555-3790___   Email: ___hannah@coldmail.com___

Social Security Number: ___123-00-4567___   Driver's License Number/State: ___D123456/New Jersey___

Other Identifying Information: _____

Vehicle Make: ___Toyota___ Model: ___Corolla___ Color: ___White___ Year: ___2015___

License Plate Number/State: ___NJ1234567/New Jersey___

Additional Occupants

List everyone, including minor children, who will live with you:

Full Name	Relationship to Applicant
Dennis Olson	Husband

Rental History

FIRST-TIME RENTERS: INSTEAD ATTACH A DESCRIPTION OF YOUR HOUSING FOR THE PAST FIVE YEARS.

Current Address: ___39 Maple Street, Princeton, New Jersey 08540___

Dates Lived at Address: ___May 2011–date___ Rent $ ___2,000___ Security Deposit $ ___4,000___

Landlord/Manager: ___Jane Tucker___ Landlord/Manager's Phone: ___609-555-7523___

Reason for Leaving: ___New job in NYC___

Previous Address: ___1215 Middlebrook Lane, Princeton, New Jersey 08540___

Dates Lived at Address: ___June 2008–May 2011___ Rent $ _1,800_ Security Deposit $ _1,000_

Landlord/Manager: ___Ed Palermo___ Landlord/Manager's Phone: _609-555-3711_

Reason for Leaving: ___Better apartment___

Previous Address: ___1527 Highland Drive, New Brunswick, New Jersey 08444___

Dates Lived at Address: ___Jan. 2007–June 2008___ Rent $ _800_ Security Deposit $ _800_

Landlord/Manager: ___Millie & Joe Lewis___ Landlord/Manager's Phone: _609-555-9999_

Reason for Leaving: ___Wanted to live closer to work___

Employment History

EMPLOYEES: ATTACH TAX RETURNS FROM THE MOST RECENT TWO YEARS, PLUS PAY STUBS FROM THE PAST SIX MONTHS.
SELF-EMPLOYED APPLICANTS: INSTEAD ATTACH TAX RETURNS FROM THE MOST RECENT TWO YEARS.

Name and Address of Current Employer: ___Argonworks, 54 Nassau Street, Princeton, New Jersey___

_____ Phone: (609) _555-2333_

Name of Supervisor: ___Tom Schmidt___ Supervisor's Phone: (609) _555-2333_

Dates Employed at This Job: ___2008–date___ Position or Title: _Marketing Director_

Name and Address of Previous Employer: ___Princeton Times___

___13 Junction Rd., Princeton, NJ___ Phone: (609) _555-1111_

Name of Supervisor: ___Dory Krossber___ Supervisor's Phone: (609) _555-2366_

Dates Employed at This Job: ___Jan. 2007–June 2008___ Position or Title: _Marketing Associate_

Income

1. Your gross monthly employment income (before deductions): $ _8,000_

2. Average monthly amounts of other income (specify sources): $ ___

___Note: This does not include my husband's income. See his application.___ $ ___

___ $ ___

TOTAL: $ _8,000_

Bank/Financial Accounts

	Account Number	Bank/Institution	Branch
Savings Account:	1222345	N.J. Federal	Trenton, NJ
Checking Account:	789101	Princeton S&L	Princeton, NJ
Money Market or Similar Account:	234789	City Bank	Princeton, NJ

Credit Card Accounts

Major Credit Card: ☑VISA ☐MC ☐Discover Card ☐Am Ex ☐Other: _____

Issuer: _____City Bank_____ Account No. _____1234 5555 6666 7777_____

Balance $ _____1,000_____ Average Monthly Payment $ _____1,000_____

Major Credit Card: ☐VISA ☐MC ☐Discover Card ☐Am Ex ☑Other: _____Dept. Store_____

Issuer: _____City Bank_____ Account No. _____2345 0000 9999 8888_____

Balance $ _____1,000_____ Average Monthly Payment $ _____1,000_____

Loans

Type of Loan (mortgage, car, student loan, etc.)	Name of Creditor	Account Number	Amount Owed	Monthly Payment

Other Major Obligations (such as child support, alimony, tax liens, etc.)

Type	Payee		Amount Owed	Monthly Payment

Pets

Type	Breed	Sex	Age	Neutered/spayed	Weight	Years owned
None now, but we might want to get a cat some time						
				None		

Miscellaneous

Describe water-filled furniture you want to have in the rental property: _____

_____ .

Do you smoke?   ☐ yes ☑ no

Have you ever: Filed for bankruptcy?   ☐ yes ☑ no   How many times _____

Been sued?   ☐ yes ☑ no   How many times _____

Sued someone else?   ☐ yes ☑ no   How many times _____

Been evicted?   ☐ yes ☑ no   How many times _____

Explain (include dates) any "yes" listed above: _____

_____

_____

References and Emergency Contact

Personal Reference: _Joan Stanley_   Relationship: _Friend, coworker_

Address: _785 Spruce Street, Princeton, New Jersey 08540_

Email: _____   Phone: (609) _555-4578_

Personal Reference: _Marnie Swatt_   Relationship: _Friend_

Address: _82 East 59th Street, #12B, NYC_

Email: _____   Phone: (212) _555-8765_

Contact in Emergency: _Connie & Martin Silver_   Relationship: _Parents_

Address: _7852 Pierce Street, Somerset, New Jersey 08321_

Email: _____   Phone: (609) _555-7878_

Source

Where did you learn of this vacancy? _Ryan Cowell, Broker_

I certify that all the information given above is true and correct and understand that my lease or rental agreement may be terminated if I have made any material false or incomplete statements in this application. I authorize verification of the information provided in this application from my credit sources, credit bureaus, current and previous landlords and employers, and personal references. This permission will survive the expiration of my tenancy.

Hannah Silver   February 15, 20xx
Applicant   Date

Notes (Landlord/Manager): _____

_____

_____

_____

_____

_____

_____

_____

_____

prospective tenants, not just those you suspect might be in the country illegally. It's illegal to discriminate on the basis of race, color, or national origin, although you may reject someone on the basis of immigration status.

- Be sure all potential tenants sign the rental application, authorizing you to verify the information and references and to run a credit report. (Some employers and banks require written authorization before they will talk to you.) You might also want to prepare a separate authorization, signed and dated by the applicant, so that you don't need to copy the entire application and send it off every time a bank or employer wants proof that the tenant authorized you to verify the information.

Finally, note that this application doesn't ask applicants for their dates of birth (DOB). Many fair housing experts believe that doing so is risky, should a disappointed applicant attempt to challenge your rejection as an instance of age discrimination—having the date on the application at least establishes that you knew of the applicant's age. Some landlords still ask for the DOB, in case a credit reporting company requests it. You should be able to order a credit report and a screening report using the applicant's Social Security number or ITIN; if vendors balk, you might want to ask for the DOB.

 FORM

Reference and Credit Check Consent form. You'll find a downloadable copy of the Consent to Contact References and Perform Credit Check on the Nolo website; the link is included in Appendix B of this book. A filled-in sample consent form is shown below.

Consent to Contact References and Perform Credit Check

I authorize _____ Jan Gold _____

to obtain information about me from my credit sources, current and previous landlords, employers, and personal

references, to enable _____ Jan Gold _____ to

evaluate my rental application.

I give permission for the landlord or its agent to obtain a consumer report about me for the purpose of this

application, to ensure that I continue to meet the terms of the tenancy, for the collection and recovery of any

financial obligations relating to my tenancy, or for any other permissible purpose.

_____ *Michael Clark* _____
Applicant Signature

_____ Michael Clark _____
Printed Name

_____ 123 State Street, Chicago, Illinois _____
Address

_____ 312-555-9876 _____
Phone Number

_____ February 2, 20xx _____
Date

Checking References, Credit History, and More

If an application looks good, your next step is to dig deeper. The time and money you spend are some of the most cost-effective expenditures you'll ever make.

> ⊘ **CAUTION**
>
> **Be consistent in your screening.** You risk a charge of illegal discrimination if you screen certain categories of applicants more stringently than others—for example, requiring credit reports only from minorities. (See "Avoiding Illegal Discrimination," below, for more on the subject.)

Here are six elements of a very thorough screening process. You should always go through at least the first three to check out the applicant's previous landlords and income and employment, and run a credit check.

Check With Current and Previous Landlords and Other References

Always call current and previous landlords or managers for references—even if you already have a written letter of reference from them. It's worth the time if it helps you weed out a tenant who might have presented you with a fake letter. Also call employers and personal references listed on the application.

To organize the information you gather from these calls, use the Tenant References form, which lists key questions to ask landlords, employers, and other references.

> ⊙ **TIP**
>
> **Check out pets, too.** If the prospective tenant has a dog or cat, ask previous landlords whether the pet caused damage or problems for other tenants

or neighbors. It's also a good idea to meet the dog or cat, so you can make sure that it's well-groomed and well-behaved. You must, however, accommodate an applicant with a mental or physical disability whose dog serves as a support animal. (See the discussion of pet rules in Chapter 1, Clause 14.)

Take notes of all your conversations. You can indicate your reasons for refusing an individual on the Tenant References form—for example, negative credit information, bad references from a previous landlord, or your inability to verify information. You'll want a record of this information so that you can survive a fair housing challenge if a disappointed applicant files a discrimination complaint against you.

> 📄 **FORM**
>
> **Tenant References form.** You'll find a downloadable copy of the Tenant References screening form on the Nolo website; the link is included in Appendix B of this book. A filled-in sample Tenant References form is shown below.

Verify Income and Employment

Make sure that all tenants have the income to pay the rent each month. Call the prospective tenant's employer to verify income and length of employment.

Some employers won't release information without require written authorization from the employee. You'll need to send the employer a signed copy of the release included at the bottom of the rental application form or the separate Consent to Contact References and Perform Credit Check form. If for any reason you question the income information you get from the employer, you may also ask applicants for copies of recent paycheck stubs.

Tenant References

Name of Applicant: _____ Michael Clark _____

Address of Rental Unit: _____ 123 State Street, Chicago, Illinois _____

Previous Landlord or Manager

Contact (name, property owner or manager, address of rental unit): __ Kate Steiner, 345 Mercer Street, Chicago, Illinois;

____ (312) 555-5432 _____

Date: _____ February 4, 20xx _____

Questions

When did tenant rent from you (move-in and move-out dates)? ____ December 2012 to date _____

What was the monthly rent? ___ $1,250 _____   Did tenant pay rent on time?   ☐ Yes ☑ No

If rent was not paid on time, did you have to give tenant a legal notice demanding the rent?   ☐ Yes ☑ No

If rent was not paid on time, provide details _____ He paid rent a week late a few times _____

_____

Did you give tenant notice of any lease violation for other than nonpayment of rent?   ☐ Yes ☑ No

If you gave a lease violation notice, what was the outcome? _____

Was tenant considerate of neighbors—that is, no loud parties and fair, careful use of common areas?

_____ Yes, considerate _____

_____

Did tenant have any pets? ☑ Yes ☐ No   If so, were there any problems? _____ He had a cat, contrary to

_____ rental agreement _____

Did tenant make any unreasonable demands or complaints?   ☐ Yes ☑ No   If so, explain: _____

_____

Why did tenant leave? _____ He wants to live someplace that allows pets _____

_____

Did tenant give the proper amount of notice before leaving?   ☑ Yes ☐ No

Did tenant leave the place in good condition? Did you need to use the security deposit to cover damage?

_____ No problems _____

Any particular problems you'd like to mention? _____ No _____

_____

Would you rent to this person again? _____ Yes, but without pets _____

_____

Other comments: _____

_____

Employment Verification

Contact (name, company, position): ___Brett Field, Manager, Chicago Car Company___

Date: ___February 5, 20xx___   Salary $ ___80,000 + bonus___

Dates of Employment: ___March 2011 to date___

Comments: ___No problems. Fine employee. Michael is responsible and hard working.___

Personal Reference

Contact (name and relationship to applicant): ___Sandy Cameron, friend___

Date: ___February 5, 20xx___   How long have you known the applicant? ___Five years___

Would you recommend this person as a prospective tenant? ___Yes___

Comments: ___Michael is very neat and responsible. He's reliable and will be a great tenant.___

Credit and Financial Information

Mostly fine—see attached credit report.

Notes, Including Reasons for Rejecting Applicant

Applicant had a history of late rent payments and kept a cat, contrary to the rental agreement.

It's also reasonable to require documentation of other sources of income, such as Social Security, disability payments, workers' compensation, welfare, child support, or alimony.

How much income is enough? Think twice before renting to someone if the rent will take more than one-third of their gross income, especially if they have a lot of debts.

Obtain a Credit Report

Private credit reporting agencies collect and sell credit files and other information about consumers. Landlords commonly check a prospective tenant's credit history with at least one credit reporting agency, to see how responsible the person is about managing money. Jot your findings down on the Tenant References form, discussed above.

How to Get a Credit Report

A credit report contains a gold mine of information. You can find out, for example, whether a prospective tenant has a history of paying rent or bills late, has gone through bankruptcy, or has been evicted. (Your legal right to get information on evictions, however, might vary from state to state.) Credit reports usually cover the past 7 to 10 years.

Depending on the type of report you order, you might also get an applicant's credit score (the most popular being the "FICO"), a number that purports to indicate the risk that an individual will default on payments.

To run a credit check, you'll normally need a prospective tenant's name, address, and Social Security number, or ITIN (Individual Taxpayer Identification Number). Three credit bureaus have cornered the market on credit reports:

- Equifax (Equifax.com)
- Experian (Experian.com), and
- TransUnion (TransUnion.com).

Although you generally cannot order a credit report directly from the big three bureaus, the bureaus have other options you might find helpful. For example, Experian has an option called "Experian Connect" (https://connect.experian.com) that allows prospective tenants to buy their credit report and credit score online, and give you access. This service provides you with a VantageScore, another type of credit score that's similar to FICO.

TransUnion also allows you to get credit information about potential tenants by creating a "SmartMove" account (MySmartMove.com). You send applicants an online invitation through the account. Once applicants receive the invite, they supply their personal information, and you can then view their credit report, a criminal report (subject to federal, state, and local laws that limit or restrict access to some records), an eviction report, a leasing recommendation, and a "ResidentScore." A ResidentScore is similar to a credit score, but TransUnion created it specifically for tenant screening purposes. ResidentScores range from 350 to 850, the same range that FICO and newer VantageScore models use. The higher the score, the better.

CAUTION

Take tenant scores with a grain of salt. If you use a screening service that provides you with a recommendation about a tenant—whether it be a "thumbs up" or a score—beware. The recommendation generated by the service might be based on erroneous information, such as mistakes in a credit report, or misleading data, such as an arrest that didn't actually lead to a conviction. Whenever possible, look at the data behind the recommendation—you might spot obvious errors that the program didn't, or you might not want to give as much weight to a single factor as the program did. There's also mounting evidence that these screening recommendations are often racially biased and lead to people of color being wrongfully denied housing.

All three of the credit bureaus also offer tenant screening services (as do many property management websites, such as Avail (Avail.co), and TurboTenant (TurboTenant.com)). Using these screening services has pros and cons.

On the plus side, the information they provide is geared to the rental housing context (whereas a credit score was designed to predict whether the applicant would repay a loan). The method also protects applicants' credit scores, in that the report counts only as a "soft inquiry" to the applicant's file (multiple requests for credit reports can significantly lower a credit score). Importantly, SSNs are not revealed to the landlord. Either the landlord or the applicant can pay for the service.

Applicants initiate the screening process by filling out an application to generate a report. The report contains a recommendation on whether to rent to this applicant, based on credit, criminal, and eviction history. (Note that some states and cities limit how and when landlords can consider applicants' criminal histories. For a bit more money, landlords can ask for a credit score, too.

On the negative side, some states do not post criminal data, so landlords who are evaluating applicants who have lived in those states will be paying for a service that isn't available (not to mention that someone doesn't have to live in a particular state to commit a crime there).

In addition, the service requires some work on the part of the applicants (they must complete an authentication form, to deter identity theft). This step will deter some applicants (but an applicant who isn't serious enough to complete the process arguably is not the one for you, either).

Your state or local apartment association might also offer credit reporting services.

Tenants who are applying for more than one rental might obtain their own reports, make copies, and ask you to accept their copies. Federal law doesn't require you to accept an applicant's copy—you can require applicants to pay a credit check fee for you to run a new report. However, certain states—Wisconsin and Washington, for example—are exceptions: State law in Wisconsin forbids landlords from charging for a credit report if, before the landlord asks for a report, the applicant offers one from a consumer reporting agency and the report is less than 30 days old. (Wis. Adm. Code ATCP § 134.05(4)(b).) In Washington, landlords must advise tenants whether they will accept a screening report done by a consumer reporting agency (in which case the landlord may not charge the tenant a fee for a screening report). Landlords who maintain a website that advertises residential rentals must include this information on the home page. (Wash. Rev. Code § 59.18.257.)

Credit Check Fees

It's legal in most states to charge prospective tenants a fee for the cost of the credit report itself and for your time and trouble. Any credit check fee should be reasonably related to the cost of the credit check—$20 to $30 is common.

Some landlords don't charge credit check fees, preferring to absorb the cost as they would any other cost of business. For low-end units, charging an extra fee can be a barrier to attracting tenants, and a tenant who pays a fee, but is later rejected, is likely to be annoyed and possibly more apt to claim that your rejection was based on a discriminatory reason.

Our rental application informs prospective tenants whether you charge a credit check fee. Make it clear to prospective tenants that paying a credit check fee does not guarantee the tenant will get the rental unit.

TIP

It's a mistake to collect a credit check fee from lots of people. If you expect a large number of applicants, you'd be wise not to accept fees from everyone. Instead, read over the applications first and do a credit check only on applicants you're seriously considering. That way, you won't waste your time (and prospective tenants' money) collecting fees from unqualified applicants.

CAUTION

It is illegal to charge a credit check fee if you don't use it for the stated purpose and pocket it instead. Return any credit check fees you don't use for that purpose.

What You're Looking for in a Credit Report

Be leery of applicants with lots of debts—especially people whose monthly payments plus the rent obligation exceed 40% of their gross income. Also, look at the person's bill-paying habits, and, of course, pay attention to lawsuits and evictions.

Sometimes, your only choice is to rent to someone with poor or fair credit—or even no credit (for example, a student or recent graduate). If that's your situation, you could condition acceptance on:

- positive references from previous landlords and employers
- a creditworthy cosigner for the lease (see the discussion on cosigners at the end of Chapter 1)
- a good-sized deposit—as much as you can collect under state law and the market will bear (see Clause 8 of the form agreements in Chapter 1), and
- proof of specific steps taken to improve bad credit—for example, enrollment in a debt counseling group.

CAUTION

Take special care to store credit reports in a safe place, where only you and those who "need to know" have access to them. When you no longer need the reports, according to the "Disposal Rule" of the Fair and Accurate Credit Transactions Act, you must destroy them. Use a shredder or burn the credit reports, and delete any reports kept on your computer or phone using a commercial electronic "shredding" product.

Verify Bank Account Information

If an individual's credit history raises questions about financial stability, you might want to double-check the bank accounts listed on the rental application. If so, you'll probably need an authorization form such as the one included at the bottom of the rental application, or the separate Consent to Contact References and Perform Credit Check form (discussed above). Banks differ as to the type of information they will provide over the phone. Generally, without a written authorization, banks will confirm only that an individual has an account there and that it is in good standing.

CAUTION

Be wary of an applicant who doesn't have a checking or savings account. Tenants who offer to pay cash or with a money order should be viewed with extreme caution. Perhaps the individual bounced so many checks that the bank dropped the account or the income comes from a shady or illegitimate source —for example, from drug dealing.

Review Court Records

When prospective tenants have previously lived in your area, you might want to review local court records to see whether collection or eviction lawsuits have been filed against them. Checking court records might seem redundant—some of this information might be available on credit reports—but now and then it's a valuable tool. You won't violate antidiscrimination laws as long as you check the records of every applicant who reaches this stage of your screening process. Because court records are kept for many years, this kind of information can supplement references from recent landlords. Talk to the court clerk at the local court that handles eviction cases for information on how to check court records.

Use Megan's Law to Check State Databases of Sex Offenders

Not surprisingly, most landlords don't want tenants with criminal records, particularly convictions for violent crimes or crimes against children. Checking a prospective tenant's credit report, as recommended above, might be one way to find out about a person's criminal history.

"Megan's Law" can also be a useful source of information. This federal crime prevention law charges the FBI with keeping a nationwide database of persons convicted of sexual offenses against minors and violent sexual offenses against anyone. (42 U.S.C. §§ 14071 and following.) Every state has its own version of Megan's Law that requires certain convicted sexual offenders to register with local law enforcement officials and supply their addresses.

For information on your access to this type of database, and restrictions on your use of information derived from a Megan's Law database, contact your local law enforcement agency. California landlords may not access their state's database unless they are doing so to protect a person "at risk." This means that routine checking is not legal. (Cal. Penal Code § 290.46(j)(1).) Massachusetts, Nevada, and New Jersey have some restrictions, too. To find out how to access your state's sex offender registry,

you can also contact the Parents for Megan's Law (PFML) Hotline at 888-ASK-PFML, or check this organization's website at www. parentsformeganslaw.org (you can search for your state's sex offender registry under the "Services" menu—click on "Sex Offender Information").

Protect Personally Identifiable Information

When screening applicants, you'll collect a lot of personal and potentially sensitive information, including names, Social Security numbers, and more. Because the misuse of this personally identifiable information (known as "PII") can be so harmful to victims, many states require those who handle PII—including landlords—to follow security protocols and to report the unintended leaking of PII. Even if your state hasn't imposed specific requirements on use and handling, you should to take steps to protect the PII you obtain.

What Is PII?

PII is any information that someone could use to identify a particular person. For example, knowing a name and birthdate, someone might be able to tie that information to an actual person. Driver's license numbers, Social Security numbers, and email addresses are just a few examples of PII landlords often collect.

As a general rule, ask only for what's necessary to determine who will be a good tenant. The information we've suggested that you obtain during your screening process is the minimum amount you'll need to confidently evaluate your applicants.

Storing PII

Most landlords' records contain PII. (For information about what items should be in your records and how to maintain records, see "Organize Your Tenant Records" in Chapter 3.)

State PII laws often require PII holders to take "reasonable steps" to protect PII. What's reasonable for your business depends on factors such as how you collect PII, how you store it, and how many people have access to it. At the very least, give others access to PII only when necessary, and consider developing a set of written rules for how to store PII. Whenever possible, password-protect PII, encrypt messages containing PII, and keep physical documents containing PII in one secured place with limited access.

Destroying PII

Deciding when to destroy PII can be a tough call—you need to maintain thorough records, but you also don't want to hold on to PII longer than necessary. For most landlords, it's safe to destroy rental records four years after the tenancy ends. You'll also need to consider how long you should keep records for tax purposes. Beyond these basic recommendations, consider scheduling regular audits of your files to check for unneeded PII.

No matter how long you keep rental records, you should have written procedures on how to destroy PII. Some examples of PII destruction practices are:

- Destroy PII as soon as it's no longer needed.
- Black out and shred documents containing PII before throwing them away or recycling.
- Delete or overwrite unneeded electronic files. Hitting "delete" will not be enough to prevent someone from reconstructing these files, so consider using a software application that prevents reconstruction.

What to Do If PII Is Stolen

Even when you take reasonable security measures, the PII of your applicants (and tenants) might become exposed. If this happens, check your state law—some states require you to report PII security breaches to affected consumers and even to the state itself, depending on the number of people affected by the breach. In any situation,

determine what PII was exposed, who was affected, and whether it's likely the PII will be misused. If you have any reason to believe the PII will be misused, contact the people whose information was taken as soon as possible. You should also evaluate how the PII was accessed, and take measures such as changing passwords or moving files to make sure it doesn't happen again.

RESOURCE

Stay current on the status of PII law in your state by going to The National Conference of State Legislatures' website (www.ncsl.org) and searching for "data security laws." For information on electronic record destruction, check out the Massachusetts Institute of Technology site (web.mit. edu) and search for "removing sensitive data." The FTC has a clear and thorough explanation of the Disposal Rule on its website (www.ftc.gov) as well as tips and advice on how to dispose of consumer reports. (On the FTC home page, search for the article's name: Disposing of Consumer Report Information? Rule Tells How.) Consider visiting this site on a regular basis to stay informed about any changes to or tips on complying with the Disposal Rule.

Consumer Reports: A Special Form of PII

Consumer reports—any report you obtain from a consumer reporting company for purposes of screening potential tenants—require special handling. The consumer report used most often by landlords is a credit report. Under the "Disposal Rule" of the Fair and Accurate Credit Transactions Act, when you no longer need a consumer report, you must destroy it in a manner that is reasonable for your business and that prevents anyone from using or accessing the report without permission. The Federal Trade Commission (FTC)—the organization which enforces the Disposal Rule— suggests shredding paper with PII and permanently erasing electronic files with PII.

Avoiding Illegal Discrimination

Federal and state antidiscrimination laws limit what you can say and do in the tenant selection process. Basically, you need to keep in mind three important points:

1. You are legally free to choose among prospective tenants as long as your decisions are based on legitimate business criteria. You are entitled to reject people for the following reasons:

   • poor credit history

   • income that you reasonably regard as insufficient to pay the rent

   • negative references from previous or current landlords indicating problems—such as property damage or consistently late rent payments—that make someone a bad risk

   • convictions for relevant criminal offenses

   • inability to meet the legal terms of a lease or rental agreement, such as someone who can't come up with the security deposit or who wants to keep a pet when your policy is no pets, or

   • more people than you want to live in the unit—assuming that your limit on the number of tenants is clearly tied to health and safety or legitimate business needs. (See Clause 3 discussion of occupancy limits in Chapter 1.)

2. Antidiscrimination laws identify the illegal reasons to refuse to rent to a tenant. The federal Fair Housing Act and Fair Housing Amendments Act (42 U.S.C. §§ 3601–3619, 3631) prohibit discrimination on the basis of race or color, religion, national origin, gender, age, familial status (pregnancy or children), and physical or mental disability (including recovering alcoholics and people with a past drug addiction). Many states and cities also prohibit discrimination based on marital status, source of income, military status, sexual orientation, or gender identity.

RESOURCE

More on housing discrimination rules. For more information on the rules and regulations of the Fair Housing Act, contact HUD's Housing Discrimination Hotline at 800-669-9777 or check the HUD website at www.HUD.gov. You can also contact a local HUD office.

For information on state and local housing discrimination laws, contact your state fair housing agency. HUD's website also contains a list of state agencies and contact information.

3. Consistency is crucial when dealing with prospective tenants. If you don't treat all tenants more or less equally—for example, if you arbitrarily set tougher standards for renting to a member of an ethnic minority (such as requiring a higher income level or proof of legal residence status), you are violating federal laws and opening yourself up to expensive lawsuits and the possibility of being hit with large judgments. On the other hand, if you require all prospective tenants to meet the same income standard and to supply satisfactory proof of their legal eligibility to work (as well as meet your other criteria), you will get the needed information, but in a nondiscriminatory way.

CAUTION

Accept applications from everyone who's interested. Even if, after talking to someone on the phone, you doubt that a particular tenant can qualify, it's best to politely take all applications. Unless you can point to something in writing that clearly disqualifies a tenant, you are on shaky legal ground: Refusing to take an application might anger prospective tenants and make them likely to look into the possibility of filing a discrimination complaint. Make decisions later about who will rent the property. Be sure to keep copies of all applications. (See discussion of record keeping in Chapter 3.)

The Rights of Tenants With Disabilities

The Fair Housing Acts require that landlords *accommodate* the needs of tenants with disabilities, at the landlord's own expense. (42 U.S.C. § 3604(f)(3)(B).) You are expected to adjust your rules, procedures, or services in order to give a person with a disability an equal opportunity to use and enjoy a dwelling unit or a common space. Accommodations include such things as providing a close-in, spacious parking space for a tenant who uses a wheelchair (assuming you provide parking). Your duty to accommodate tenants with disabilities does not mean that you must bend every rule and change every procedure at the tenant's request. You are expected to accommodate "reasonable" requests, but need not undertake changes that would seriously impair your ability to run your business.

The Fair Housing Acts also require landlords to allow tenants with disabilities to make reasonable *modifications* of their living unit at their expense if that is what is needed for the person to comfortably and safely live in the unit. (42 U.S.C. § 3604(f)(3)(A).) For example, a person with a disability has the right to modify the living space to the extent necessary to make the space safe and comfortable, as long as the modifications won't make the unit unacceptable to the next tenant, or the tenant with a disability agrees to undo the modification when they leave. An example of a modification undertaken by a tenant with a disability is lowering countertops for a tenant who uses a wheelchair.

You are not obliged to allow a tenant with a disability to modify a unit at will, without your prior approval. You are entitled to ask for a reasonable description of the proposed modifications, proof that they will be done in a workmanlike manner, and evidence that the tenant is obtaining any necessary building permits. Moreover, if a tenant proposes to modify the unit in such a manner that will require restoration when the tenant leaves (such as the repositioning of lowered kitchen counters), you may require that the tenant pay into an interest-bearing escrow account the amount estimated for the restoration. (The interest belongs to the tenant.)

Choosing—and Rejecting— an Applicant

After you've collected applications and done some screening, you can start evaluating applicants, using the basic criteria discussed above. Start by eliminating the worst risks: people with negative references from previous landlords, a history of nonpayment of rent, or poor credit or recent and numerous evictions. Then make your selection.

Assuming you choose the best-qualified candidate (based on income, credit history, and references), you have no legal problem. But what if you have a number of more or less equally qualified applicants? Can you safely choose an older white man over a young black woman?

The answer is a qualified "yes." If two people rate equally, you can legally choose either one without legal risk in any particular situation. But be extra careful not to take the further step of always selecting a person of the same sex, age, or ethnicity. For example, if you are a large landlord who is frequently faced with tough choices and who always avoids an equally qualified minority or disabled applicant, you are exposing yourself to charges of discrimination.

Information You Should Keep on Rejected Applicants

It's crucial that your tenant-screening system documents how and why you chose a particular tenant.

Note your reasons for rejection— such as poor credit history, pets (if you don't accept pets), or a negative reference from a previous landlord—on the tenant references form or other document, so that you have a paper trail if a tenant accuses you of illegal discrimination. You want to be able to back up your reason for rejecting the person. Keep organized files of applications and other materials and notes on prospective tenants for at least three years after you rent a particular unit. (See "Organize Your Tenant Records" in Chapter 3.) Keep in mind that if a rejected applicant files a complaint with a fair housing agency or files a lawsuit, your file will be made available to the applicant's lawyers. Knowing that, choose your words carefully, avoiding the obvious (slurs and exaggerations) and being scrupulously truthful.

Information You Must Provide Rejected Applicants

If you don't rent to someone because of an insufficient credit report or negative information in the report, you must give the applicant the name and address of the agency that reported the negative information or furnished the insufficient report. This is a requirement of the federal Fair Credit Reporting Act (FCRA). (15 U.S.C. §§ 1681 and following.) The notices are known as "adverse action reports."

In these cases, you must tell applicants that they have a right to obtain a copy of the file from the agency that reported the negative information, by requesting it within the next 60 days, or by asking within one year of having asked for their last free report. You must also tell rejected applicants that the credit reporting agency didn't make the decision to reject them and cannot explain the reason for the rejection. Finally, you must tell applicants that they can dispute the accuracy of their credit report and add their own

consumer statement to their report. The law doesn't require you to communicate an applicant's right to disclosure in writing, but it's a good idea to do so (and to keep a copy of the rejection letter in your files). That way, you'll have irrefutable proof that you complied with the law if you're challenged in court. Use the Notice of Denial Based on Credit Report or Other Information form, shown below, to comply with the federal Fair Credit Reporting Act when you reject an applicant because of an insufficient credit report or negative information in the report.

FORM
Rejection letter form. You'll find a downloadable copy of the Notice of Denial Based on Credit Report or Other Information on the Nolo website; the link is included in Appendix B of this book. A filled-in sample notice of denial form is shown below.

Exceptions: The federal requirements do not apply if you reject someone based on information that the applicant furnished or that you or your employee learned on your or their own.

Conditional Acceptances

You might want to make an offer to an applicant but condition that offer on the applicant paying more rent or a higher security deposit (one that's within any legal limits, of course), supplying a cosigner, or agreeing to a different rental term than you originally advertised. If your decision to impose the condition resulted from information you gained from a credit report or a report from a tenant screening service, you have to accompany the offer with an adverse action report (described in the section immediately above). Use the Notice of Conditional Acceptance Based on Credit Report or Other Information, shown below.

Notice of Denial Based on Credit Report or Other Information

To: _Ryan Paige_
Applicant

1 Mariner Square
Street Address

Seattle, Washington 98101
City, State, and Zip Code

Your rights under the Fair Credit Reporting Act and Fair and Accurate Credit Transactions (FACT) Act of 2003. (15 U.S.C. §§ 1681 and following.)

THIS NOTICE is to inform you that your application to rent the property at _75 Starbucks Lane, Seattle, WA 98108_

been denied because of [*check all that apply*]:

☑ Insufficient information in the credit report provided by:

Credit reporting agency: _ABC Credit Bureau_

Address, phone number, URL: _310 Griffey Way, Seattle, Washington 98140; Phone: 206-555-1212; www.abccredit.com_

☐ Negative information in the credit report provided by:

Credit reporting agency: _____

Address, phone number, URL: _____

☑ The credit score supplied on the credit report, _511_ , was used in whole or in part when making the selection.

☑ The consumer credit reporting agency noted above did not make the decision not to offer you this rental. It only provided information about your credit history. You have the right to obtain a free copy of your credit report from the consumer credit reporting agency named above, if your request is made within 60 days of this notice or if you have not requested a free copy within the past year. You also have the right to dispute the accuracy or completeness of your credit report. The agency must reinvestigate within a reasonable time, free of charge, and remove or modify inaccurate information. If the reinvestigation does not resolve the dispute to your satisfaction, you may add your own "consumer statement" (up to 100 words) to the report, which must be included (or a clear summary) in future reports.

☐ Information supplied by a third party other than a credit reporting agency or you and gathered by someone other than myself or any employee. You have the right to learn of the nature of the information if you ask me in writing within 60 days of the date of this notice.

Jason McGuire   _10-01-20xx_
Landlord/Manager   Date

Notice of Conditional Acceptance Based on Credit Report or Other Information

To: __William McGee__
Applicant

__1257 Bay Avenue__
Street Address

__Anytown, Florida 12345__
City, State, and Zip Code

Your application to rent the property at _____37 Ocean View Drive, #10-H, Anytown, Florida 12345_____

_____ [rental property address] has been accepted, conditioned on your

willingness and ability to: ____Supply a cosigner that is acceptable to the landlord____

_____

Your rights under the Fair Credit Reporting Act and Fair and Accurate Credit Transactions (FACT) Act of 2003. (15 U.S.C. §§ 1681 and following.)

Source of information prompting conditional acceptance

My decision to conditionally accept your application was prompted in whole or in part by:

☑ Insufficient information in the credit report provided by

    Credit reporting agency: _____Mountain Credit Bureau_____

    Address, phone number, URL: ____75 Baywood Drive, Anytown, Florida 12345; 800-123-4567;____
      __www.mountaincredit.com__

☐ Negative information in the credit report provided by:

    Credit reporting agency: _____

    Address, phone number, URL: _____

_____

☑ The consumer credit reporting agency noted above did not make the decision to offer you this conditional acceptance. It only provided information about your credit history. You have the right to obtain a free copy of your credit report from the consumer credit reporting agency named above, if your request is made within 60 days of this notice or if you have not requested a free copy within the past year. You also have the right to dispute the accuracy or completeness of your credit report. The agency must reinvestigate within a reasonable time, free of charge, and remove or modify inaccurate information. If the reinvestigation does not resolve the dispute to your satisfaction, you may add your own "consumer statement" (up to 100 words) to the report, which must be included (or a clear summary) in future reports.

☐ Information supplied by a third party other than a credit reporting agency or you and gathered by someone other than myself or any employee. You have the right to learn of the nature of the information if you ask me in writing within 60 days of the date of this notice.

Jane Thomas _____   _May 15, 20xx_ _____
Landlord/Manager   Date

FORM

Conditional acceptance form. You'll find a downloadable copy of the Notice of Conditional Acceptance Based on Credit Report or Other Information on the Nolo website; the link is included in Appendix B of this book. A filled-in sample notice of conditional acceptance form is shown above.

Choosing a Tenant-Manager

Many landlords hire a manager to handle all the day-to-day details of running a rental property, including fielding tenants' routine repair requests and collecting the rent. If you hire a resident manager, get a completed rental application and check references and other information carefully. If you use a property management company, it will do this work for you. (See below.)

The person you hire as a manager will occupy a critical position in your business. Your manager will interact with every tenant and will often have access to their personal files and their homes. Legally, you have a duty to protect your tenants from injuries caused by employees you know (or should know) pose a risk of harm to others. If someone gets hurt or has property stolen or damaged by a manager whose dubious background you didn't check carefully, you could be sued, so it's crucial that you be especially vigilant when hiring a manager.

When you hire a manager, you should sign two separate agreements:

- an employment agreement that covers manager responsibilities, hours, and pay, and that can be terminated at any time for any reason by either party, and
- a month-to-month rental agreement that can be terminated by either of you with the amount of written notice (typically 30 days) required under state law.

Whether or not you compensate a manager with reduced rent or regular salary, be sure you comply with your legal obligations as an employer, such as following laws governing minimum wage and overtime.

RESOURCE

A comprehensive legal resource for landlords. *Every Landlord's Legal Guide,* by Marcia Stewart, Janet Portman, and Ann O'Connell (Nolo), provides detailed advice on hiring a manager, including how to prepare a property manager agreement, and your legal obligations as an employer, such as following laws governing minimum wage and overtime.

Property Management Companies

Owners of large apartment complexes often use property management companies, as do absentee owners. Some absentee owners hire property managers simply because they live too far away to be involved in everyday details; others hire property managers out of necessity—some states require owners who live out of state to hire local, licensed property managers. If you're considering renting out property you own in another state, research whether that state requires properties to have an in-state manager.

Property management companies generally take care of renting units, collecting rent, taking tenant complaints, arranging repairs and maintenance, and evicting troublesome tenants (not every management company will handle evictions, however). Of course, some of these responsibilities can be shared with or delegated to resident managers who, in some instances, might work for the management company.

A variety of relationships between owners and management companies is possible, depending on your wishes and how the particular management company chooses to do business. For example, if you own one or more big buildings, the management company will probably recommend hiring a resident manager. But if your rental property has only a few units, or you own a number of small buildings spread over a good-sized geographical area, the management company will probably suggest simply responding to tenant requests and complaints from its central office.

One advantage of working with a management company is that you avoid all the legal hassles of being an employer: paying payroll taxes, buying workers' compensation insurance, and withholding income tax. The management company is an independent contractor, not an employee. It hires and pays the people who do the work. Typically, you sign a contract spelling out the management company's duties and fees. Most companies charge a fixed percentage—about 6% to 12%—of the total rent collected. (The salary of any resident manager is additional.) This gives the company a good incentive to keep the building filled with rent-paying tenants.

Another advantage is that good management companies are usually well informed about the law, keep thorough records, and are adept at staying out of legal hot water in such areas as discrimination, invasion of privacy, and returning deposits.

The primary disadvantage of hiring a management company is the expense. For example, if you pay a management company 10% of the $14,000 you collect in rent each month from tenants in a 12-unit building, this amounts to $1,400 a month and $16,800 per year. While many companies charge less than 10%, it's still quite an expense—even if you adjust for the fact that the property manager's fee is tax deductible. Also, if the management company works from a central office with no one on-site, tenants might feel that management is too distant and unconcerned with their day-to-day needs.

Management companies have their own contracts, which you should read thoroughly and understand before signing. Be sure you understand how you'll pay the company and its exact responsibilities.

Shop around for a management company—not all are created equal. A management company with a reputation for treating tenants poorly or ignoring service requests can hurt your chances of finding high-quality tenants. And, even though a management company is an independent entity, under certain circumstances a court could find you partially responsible for its misdeeds. Interview people at the company and ask them about past lawsuits or complaints. Ask other landlords in the area about their experiences with the company. In particular, try to learn the eviction rate in buildings they manage. Unusually large numbers of evictions might spell sloppiness in tenant screening or, worse, deliberate indifference. Keep in mind that many management companies get paid apart from their monthly fee every time they advertise and screen applicants, giving them an incentive to perform that task as often as possible.

And, finally, be sure to check online reviews. Online reviews will give you insight into what tenants think about the management company. Give the reviews whatever weight you think is appropriate, keeping in mind that most reviews are written either by people who the company asked for reviews or who had terrible experiences.

Getting the Tenant Moved In

Legal disputes between landlords and tenants can be almost as emotional as divorce court battles. While some might be inevitable, many disputes could be defused at the start if tenants were better educated as to their legal rights and responsibilities. A clearly written and easy-to-understand lease or rental agreement that's signed by all adult occupants of your rental unit is the best way to start a tenancy. (See Chapter 1.) But there's more that can be done to help establish a positive relationship when new tenants move in. Most important, you should:

- inspect the property, fill out a landlord-tenant checklist with the tenant, and photograph or video the rental unit, and
- prepare a move-in letter highlighting important terms of the tenancy and your expectations, such as how to report repair problems.

Inspect and Photograph the Unit

Using a landlord-tenant checklist that reflects the condition of the rental property at the beginning and end of the tenancy, along with taking photos and video, is an excellent way to protect both you and your tenant when the tenant moves out and wants the security deposit returned. Without a record of the condition of the unit, disputes over who caused any damage are hard to settle.

The checklist will provide good evidence as to why you withheld all or part of a security deposit. Coupled with a system to regularly keep track of the rental property's condition, the checklist will also be extremely useful to you if a tenant withholds rent, breaks the lease and moves out, or sues you outright, claiming the unit needs substantial repairs.

FORM

Landlord-Tenant Checklist form.
You'll find a downloadable copy of the Landlord-Tenant Checklist on the Nolo website; the link is included in Appendix B of this book. A filled-in sample Landlord-Tenant Checklist is shown below.

States That Require a Landlord-Tenant Checklist

A number of states require landlords to give new tenants a written statement on the condition of the rental premises at move-in time, including a comprehensive list of existing damages. Check "Required Landlord Disclosures" in Appendix A for the exact requirements in your state, including the type of inspection required at the end of the tenancy. In some states (including California) you will need to do a "pre-move out inspection," which will give the tenant notice of (and a chance to avoid) intended deductions for cleaning and damage.

How to Fill Out the Checklist

You and the tenants should fill out the checklist together. If that's impossible, complete the form, make a copy, and give it to the tenants to review. Ask the tenants to note any disagreement promptly and return the checklist to you within a few days.

The checklist is in two parts: the General Condition of Rental Unit and Premises, and Checklist for Furnished Property. If your rental isn't furnished, you can delete the second part.

You will fill out the first column—*Move-In Condition*—on or before the tenant's move-in date. You'll fill out the second column—*Move-Out Condition*—when the tenant moves out and you inspect the unit again.

Landlord-Tenant Checklist

Property Address: 572 Fourth Street Apt. 11 Washington, D.C.

General Condition of Rental Unit and Premises

	Move-In Condition Date of Walk-Through: May 1, 20xx	Move-Out Condition Date of Walk-Through:
Living Room		
Flooring	OK, slight wearing from normal use	
Walls & Ceiling	OK	
Light Fixtures	OK	
Window Treatments	Miniblinds on both windows discolored	
Windows & screens	West window rattles, others OK	
Doors & handles/locks	OK	
Fireplace	OK	
Smoke detector & CO detector	Both present and OK	
Other	N/A	
Kitchen		
Flooring	Cigarette burn hole near island	
Walls & Ceiling	OK	
Light Fixtures	OK	
Window treatments	OK	
Windows & screens	OK	
Doors & handles/locks	N/A	
Cabinets	OK, a few knobs are loose	
Counters	Stained near stove	
Stove/oven/range	OK	
Refrigerator	OK	
Dishwasher	OK	
Garbage disposal	N/A	
Microwave	OK	
Stove hood	Burners filthy (grease)	
Sink & plumbing	OK	
Other appliances	N/A	
Smoke detector & CO detector	Smoke detector OK, no CO in kitchen	
Other	N/A	

	Move-In Condition Date of Walk-Through: May 1, 20xx	Move-Out Condition Date of Walk-Through:
Dining Room		
Flooring	OK	
Walls & Ceiling	Cracks in ceiling	
Light Fixtures	Dirty but works OK	
Window treatments	OK	
Windows & screens	OK	
Doors & handles/locks	OK	
Smoke detector & CO detector	N/A	
Other	N/A	
Bathroom		
Flooring	OK	
Walls & ceiling	Wallpaper peeling near ceiling, small patch of mildew. Landlord will clean mildew by 5/15	
Light fixtures	OK	
Window treatments	OK	
Windows & screens	OK	
Doors & handles/locks	OK	
Bathtub/shower (incl. attached door)	Tub chipped	
Sink, counters, & plumbing	OK, tenant notes discoloration of plastic faucet handle	
Cabinets & storage	OK	
Mirror(s)	Some blackening	
Toilet	Base of toilet dirty	
Ceiling fan/ventilation	OK	
Other	N/A	
Bedroom #1		
Flooring	OK	
Walls & ceiling	OK	
Light fixtures	OK	
Window treatments	Horizontal blinds don't go up all the way	
Windows & screens	OK	
Doors & handles/locks	Lock on door not working	
Closet	Water stain on closet floor	
Smoke detector & CO detector	Both OK	
Other	N/A	

	Move-In Condition Date of Walk-Through: May 1, 20xx	Move-Out Condition Date of Walk-Through:
Bedroom #2		
Flooring	OK	
Walls & ceiling	OK	
Light fixtures	Dented	
Window treatments	Horizontal blinds don't go up all the way	
Windows & screens	OK	
Doors & handles/locks	OK	
Closet	Piece of built-in shelf missing	
Smoke detector & CO detector	Both OK	
Other	N/A	
Other Areas		
Heating, A/C (mechanical room)	OK	
Lawn/garden	N/A	
Stairs and landings	N/A	
Patio, terrace, deck, etc.	Needs staining, otherwise OK	
Basement	N/A	
Garage	N/A	
Attic	N/A	
Entryway	N/A	
Laundry room	N/A	
Other	N/A	

☑ Tenants acknowledge that all smoke detectors were tested in their presence and found to be in working order, and that the testing procedure was explained to them. Tenants agree to promptly notify Landlord in writing should any smoke detector appear to be malfunctioning or inoperable. Tenants will not refuse Landlord access for the purpose of inspecting, maintaining, repairing, or installing legally-required smoke detectors.

☑ Tenants acknowledge that all carbon monoxide detectors were tested in their presence and found to be in working order, and that the testing procedure was explained to them. Tenants agree to promptly notify Landlord in writing should any carbon monoxide detector appear to be malfunctioning or inoperable. Tenants will not refuse Landlord access for the purpose of inspecting, maintaining, repairing, or installing legally-required carbon monoxide detectors.

Checklist for Furnished Property

	Move-In Condition Date of Walk-Through: May 1, 20xx	Move-Out Condition Date of Walk-Through:
Living Room		
Coffee table	Two scratches on top	
End tables	OK	
Lamps	OK	
Chairs	OK	
Sofa	OK, a bit worn but no stains	
Decorative items (unattached mirrors, rugs, pictures, vases, etc.)	Rug has small tear	
Electronics	Modem and router in living room; both functioning well	
Other	N/A	
Kitchen		
No furnishings in kitchen		
Dining Room		
Chairs	4 dining room chairs, one wobbles	
Stools	N/A	
Table	OK	
Lamps	N/A	
Decorative items (unattached mirrors, rugs, pictures, vases, etc.)	1 framed painting, OK condition	
Electronics	N/A	
Other	One wooden buffet, scuffed and worn condition	
Bathroom		
Shelves & storage (unattached)	N/A	
Shower curtain & rod	Rod slightly rusted, no curtain	
Hamper	N/A	
Linens	N/A	
Decorative items (unattached mirrors, rugs, pictures, vases, etc.)	Two magnifying mirrors, good condition	
Other	Scale, working condition	

	Move-In Condition Date of Walk-Through: May 1, 20xx	Move-Out Condition Date of Walk-Through:
Bedroom #1		
Bed(s)	1 queen size frame, box spring, mattress. All brand new.	
Chairs	N/A	
Bureau	N/A	
Chests	N/A	
Dressing table	N/A	
Bedside tables	2 small wooden, good condition	
Lamps	2 bedside lamps, good condition	
Linens	N/A	
Decorative items (unattached mirrors, rugs, pictures, vases, etc.)	Woven wall hanging, good condition	
Electronics	Flat screen TV, new	
Other	N/A	
Bedroom #2		
Bedroom #2 has no furnishings		
Other Areas		
Desks	N/A	
Shelves	Shoe shelf in entry	
Books, games, media	N/A	
Decorative items (unattached mirrors, rugs, pictures, vases, etc.)	N/A	
Electronics	Video doorbell, newly installed, located outside entry door	
Tools (yard and workshop)	N/A	
Trash & recycling bins	N/A	
Outdoor furniture	Metal café set on deck-small table and 2 chairs. Brand new.	
Recreational equipment	N/A	
Other	N/A	

Use this space to provide any additional explanation:

_____

Landlord-Tenant Checklist completed on moving in on _____ May 1, 20xx _____

and approved by:

_____ *Bennie Cohen* _____ and _____ **Maria Crouse** _____
Landlord/Manager   Tenant

_____ *Sandra Martino* _____
                                             Tenant

_____
                                             Tenant

Landlord-Tenant Checklist completed on moving out on _____

and approved by:

_____ and _____
Landlord/Manager   Tenant

_____
                                             Tenant

_____
                                             Tenant

Each room has its own section in the Checklist. You can change the entries by adding or deleting rows and columns. For example, the downloadable form has only one bedroom section, but if your rental has more than one bedroom, simply copy the Bedroom section, paste it into the table, and label it Bedroom #2. You can also delete sections and items that don't apply to your property.

General Condition of Rental Unit and Premises

In the *Move-In Condition* column, make detailed notes about items that aren't working or are dirty, scratched, or in poor condition. For example, don't simply note that the refrigerator "needs fixing" if the ice maker doesn't work—it's just as easy to write "ice maker broken, should not be used, expect to accomplish repair within a month of tenants' move-in." If the tenants use the ice maker anyway and cause water damage, they cannot claim that they weren't aware it wasn't working properly.

You should remedy any mold, pest, or other habitability issues before new tenants move in. However, if you didn't notice the problem until the move-in inspection, describe it in the Checklist and note that you will be repairing it within a certain timeframe. (And don't forget to follow through on your promise to repair!)

Mark "OK" next to items that are in satisfactory condition—basically, clean, safe, sanitary, and in good working order.

Checklist for Furnished Property

If your rental is furnished, use this section. You can delete items that aren't present in your rental, or you can place "N/A" in the applicable box. You can also add as many items or rooms to the Checklist as you need.

CAUTION

As part of your move-in procedures, make sure you test all smoke detectors, carbon monoxide (CO) detectors, and fire extinguishers in the tenant's presence and confirm they are in good working order (the readiness arrow on the fire extinguisher should be in the green, not near the red). Explain to the tenant how to test the smoke and CO detectors, and explain the signs of a failing detector (for example, a beeping noise). Alert tenants to their responsibility to regularly test smoke and CO detectors, and explain how to replace the battery when necessary. Be sure the tenants check the boxes at the end of the Checklist acknowledging that the smoke and CO detectors were tested in their presence and shown to be in working order. By doing this, you'll limit your liability if a detector fails and results in fire damage or injury. Testing and demonstrating the use of smoke and CO detectors at move-in is required in many cities and states.

Sign the Checklist

After you and the tenants agree on the matters covered in the Checklist, each of you should sign and date every page, as well as any attachments (such as a separate list of furnishings). Keep the original checklist for yourself and attach a copy to the tenants' lease or rental agreement. (This Checklist is referred to in Clause 11 of the form agreements in Chapter 1.)

Keep the Checklist up to date if you repair, replace, add, or remove items or furnishings after the tenants move in. Both you and the tenants should initial and date any changes on the original, signed Checklist.

Photograph the Rental Unit

Taking photos or videos of the unit before new tenants move in is another excellent way to record the initial condition of the rental. You'll be able to compare your "after" pictures at the end of the tenancy with the "before" pictures, as well as refer to the written record you created via the Checklist. And, if tenants claim that damage was present when they moved in, you can show them the records to refresh their memory.

If you end up in mediation or court for not returning the full security deposit, having a visual record of the unit's condition will be invaluable. Photos and videos can also help if you have to sue a former tenant for cleaning and repair costs that end up being more than the deposit amount.

Whether you take photos with your phone or use a separate camera, be sure that the photos are date- and time-stamped. If you make a video, clearly state the time and date when the video was made. Provide copies of the photos and videos to the tenants. Don't trust your phone or even your computer's hard drive to keep this evidence safe—upload the files to a secure place on the cloud (several companies offer cloud storage at very low monthly prices).

You should repeat this process when the tenants leave, as part of your standard move-out procedure. (Chapter 4 discusses how to prepare a move-out letter.)

Send New Tenants a Move-In Letter

A move-in letter supplements the lease or rental agreement and provides basic information, such as the manager's phone number and office hours.

You can also use a move-in letter to explain any procedures and rules that are too detailed or numerous to include in your lease or rental agreement. (Alternatively, large landlords might want to use a set of tenant rules and regulations to cover some of these issues. See Clause 18 of the form agreements in Chapter 1.)

Here are some items you might want to cover in a move-in letter:

- how and where to report maintenance and repair problems
- any lock-out or rekey fees
- use of grounds and garage
- your policy regarding rent increases for additional roommates
- location of garbage cans, available recycling programs, and trash pickup days
- maintenance dos and don'ts, such as how to avoid overloading circuits and use the garbage disposal properly, and
- any other issues, such as pool hours, elevator operation, laundry room usage, and storage space.

Do not add important terms or conditions to the move-in letter that should have been part of the lease or rental agreement. It's too late! For example, if you don't want to heat the pool during the winter, your lease should explain that the rental comes with the use of a heated pool during specified months. If you announce in a move-in letter that the pool will be unusable for six months of the year, you're inviting trouble from tenants who might reasonably claim that your reduction in services is a breach of the lease.

Because every rental situation is unique, we can't supply you with a generic move-in letter that works for everyone. However, you can use the sample shown here as a model in preparing your own.

We recommend asking tenants to sign the last page of your move-in letter to indicate that they have read it. As an extra precaution, you can ask tenants to initial each page. After everyone has signed, keep a copy for your records and give one to the tenants.

Review your move-in letter before you provide it to a new tenant, and update it as needed.

Move-In Letter

Date ___September 1, 20xx___

Tenant ___Frank O'Hara___

Street Address ___139 Porter Street___

City and State ___Madison, Wisconsin 53704___

Dear ___Frank___ ,
                           Tenant

Welcome to ___Apartment 45 B at Happy Hill Apartments___

_____ (address of rental unit). We hope you will enjoy living here. This letter is to explain what you can expect from the management and what we'll be looking for from you.

1. Rent: ___Rent is due on the first day of the month. There is no grace period for the payment of rent. (See Clauses 5 and 6 of your rental agreement for details, including late charges.) Also, we don't accept postdated checks.___

2. New Roommates: ___If you want someone to move in as a roommate, please contact us first. If your rental unit is big enough to accommodate another person, we will arrange for the new person to fill out a rental application. If it's approved, all of you will need to sign a new rental agreement. Depending on the situation, there might be a rent increase to add a roommate. Note that under our written agreement, you may not sublet without our prior approval. This includes short-term vacation rentals through Airbnb or similar services.___

3. Notice to End Tenancy: ___To terminate your month-to-month tenancy, you must give at least 28 days' written notice. We have a written form available for this purpose. We may also terminate the tenancy, or change its terms, on 28 days' written notice. If you give less than 28 days' notice, you will still be financially responsible for rent for the balance of the 28-day period.___

4. Deposits: ___Your security deposit will be applied to costs of cleaning, damages, or unpaid rent after you move out. You may not apply any part of the deposit toward any part of your rent in the last month of your tenancy. (See Clause 8 of your rental agreement.)___

5. Manager: ___Sophie Beauchamp (Apartment #15, phone 555-1234, email Sophie@sophie.com) is your resident manager. You should pay your rent to her at that address and promptly let her know of any maintenance or repair problems (see #7, below) and any other questions or problems. She's in her office every day from 8 a.m. to 10 a.m. and from 4 p.m. to 6 p.m. and can be reached by phone at other times.___

6. Landlord-Tenant Checklist: ___By now, Sophie Beauchamp should have taken you on a walk-through of your apartment to check the condition of all walls, drapes, carpets, and appliances and to test the smoke alarms and fire extinguisher. These are all listed on the Landlord-Tenant Checklist, which you should have reviewed carefully and signed. When you move out, we will ask you to check each item against its original condition as described on the Checklist.___

7. Maintenance/Repair Problems: __We are determined to maintain a clean, safe building in which all systems are in__ __good repair. To help us make repairs promptly, we will give you Maintenance/Repair Request forms to report to the__ __manager any problems in your apartment. (Extra copies are available from the manager.) In an emergency, or when__ __it's not convenient to use this form, please call the manager at 555-1234.__

8. Semiannual Safety and Maintenance Update: __To help us keep your unit and the common areas in excellent__ __condition, we'll ask you to fill out a form every six months updating any problems on the premises or in your__ __rental unit. This will allow you to report any potential safety hazards or other problems that otherwise might be__ __overlooked.__

9. Annual Safety Inspection: __Once a year, we will ask to inspect the condition and furnishings of your rental unit__ __and update the Landlord-Tenant Checklist. In keeping with state law, we will give you reasonable notice before the__ __inspection, and you are encouraged to be present for it.__

10. Insurance: __Under the terms of your rental agreement, you are required to purchase renters' insurance. The__ __building property insurance policy will not cover the replacement of your personal belongings if they are lost due__ __to fire, theft, or accident. In addition, you could be found liable if someone is injured on the premises you rent as__ __a result of your negligence. If you damage the building itself—for example, if you start a fire in the kitchen and it__ __spreads—you could be responsible for large repair bills.__

11. Moving Out: __It's a little early to bring up moving out, but please be aware that we have a list of items that should__ __be cleaned before we conduct a move-out inspection. If you decide to move, please ask the manager for a copy of__ __our Move-Out Letter, explaining our procedures for inspection and returning your deposit.__

12. Changes to Your Contact Information: __Please notify us if your phone numbers change, so we can reach you__ __promptly in an emergency.__

Please let us know if you have any questions.

Sincerely,

Tom Guiliano
Landlord/Manager

September 1, 20xx
Date

I have read and received a copy of this statement.

Frank O'Hara
Tenant

September 1, 20xx
Date

FORM

Move-In Letter form. You'll find a down-loadable copy of the Move-In Letter on the Nolo website; the link is included in Appendix B. A filled-in sample move-in letter is shown above.

Cash Rent and Security Deposit Checks

Every landlord's nightmare is a new tenant whose deposit or first rent check bounces.

To avoid this, never sign a lease or rental agreement, or let a tenant move furniture into your property or give the tenant a key, until you have the tenant's cash, certified check, or money order for the first month's rent and security deposit. Alternatively, deposit the tenant's check at the bank and make sure it clears before the move-in date. (While you have the tenant's first check, photocopy it for your records. The information on it can be helpful if you need to sue to collect a judgment from the tenant.) Be sure to give the tenant a signed receipt for the deposit.

Clause 5 of the form lease and rental agreements in Chapter 1 requires tenants to pay rent on the first day of each month. If the move-in date is other than the first day of the month, rent is prorated between that day and the end of that month.

Organize Your Tenant Records

Develop a system for recording all significant tenant complaints and repair requests, as well as your responses. This will provide a valuable paper trail should disputes develop later. Without good records, the outcome of a dispute could come down to your word against your tenant's—always a precarious situation. If you're not using one of the many available online tenant management programs, here's some advice on how to DIY your records.

Set up a file folder on each property, with individual files for each tenant. Include the following documents in each tenant's file:

- tenant's rental application, credit report, and references, including information about any cosigners
- the signed lease or rental agreement, plus any changes or addenda
- the Landlord-Tenant Checklist, plus photos or video made at move-in (or a note as to where to find these online), and
- a signed move-in letter.

After a tenant moves in, add these documents to the individual's file:

- copies of your written requests for entry
- copies of rent increase notices
- records of repair requests and details of how and when they were handled (if you keep repair records on the computer, you should regularly back up files from past months; if you have a master system to record all requests and complaints in one log, you would save that log separately, not necessarily put it in every tenant's file)
- safety and maintenance updates and inspection reports, and
- correspondence (including copies of important emails and texts).

Your computer can also be a valuable tool to keep track of tenants. Set up a simple spreadsheet for each tenant with spaces for the following information:

- address or unit number
- move-in date
- phone number (cell, home, work)
- email
- name, address, and phone number of employer
- credit information and up-to-date banking information
- monthly rent amount and rent due date

- amount and purpose of deposits plus any information your state requires on location of deposit and interest payments
- details about the tenant's pet or service animal, if applicable
- vehicle make, model, color, year, and license plate number
- emergency contacts, and
- whatever else is important to you.

Once you enter the information into your spreadsheet, you'll be able to sort the list by address or other variables and easily print labels for rent increases or other notices.

If you own many rental properties, keeping your own records might become more cumbersome the longer you're in business (and accumulate more tenant records). Consider using a property management software program that allows you to keep track of every aspect of your business, from the tracking of rents to the follow-up on repair requests.

Organize Income and Expenses for Schedule E

If you are a sole proprietor, partnership, or LLC, you will report your rental income on Schedule E of your personal tax return, Form 1040. The Schedule is relatively simple. For each address (which could include multiple rental units), you report the year's rent and list enumerated expenses (the first page of Schedule E is reproduced below). You can download a fillable version of Schedule E from www.IRS.gov.

Many landlords find it easiest to use *QuickBooks* or another accounting software package to track their income and expenses. You can also use programs designed specifically for completing Schedule E, notably *Quicken Home & Business* (it comes with a built-in rent center for managing rentals). Programs such as these allow you to track income, expenses, and tax deductions, and convert the information into a Schedule E at tax time. You can also design your own spreadsheet using Excel or a similar program to keep track of rental income and expenses. Finally, there's always the old-fashioned way of making your own paper ledger of income and expenses.

Of course, the system you use to track income and expenses is only as good as the information you enter. To maximize tax deductions, keep receipts and records of all rental-property–related expenses, such as interest payments on mortgage loans, property taxes, professional fees (your accountant, attorney, property manager), insurance, repairs, mileage related to trips to and on behalf of the property, advertising and tenant screening, and membership fees. Note all income from rent, late fees, and the like.

RESOURCE
For detailed information on completing Schedule E and valuable tax advice for landlords, see *Every Landlord's Tax Deduction Guide*, by Stephen Fishman (Nolo). For personalized advice, consult an accountant or tax professional (buying this book and consulting with a tax pro are both tax-deductible expenses).

SCHEDULE E (Form 1040)	Supplemental Income and Loss	OMB No. 1545-0074
Department of the Treasury Internal Revenue Service	(From rental real estate, royalties, partnerships, S corporations, estates, trusts, REMICs, etc.) Attach to Form 1040, 1040-SR, 1040-NR, or 1041. Go to *www.irs.gov/ScheduleE* for instructions and the latest information.	2022 Attachment Sequence No. **13**

Name(s) shown on return | Your social security number

Part I Income or Loss From Rental Real Estate and Royalties

Note: If you are in the business of renting personal property, use **Schedule C**. See instructions. If you are an individual, report farm rental income or loss from **Form 4835** on page 2, line 40.

A Did you make any payments in 2022 that would require you to file Form(s) 1099? See instructions . . . . . ☐ Yes ☐ No
B If "Yes," did you or will you file required Form(s) 1099? . . . . ☐ Yes ☐ No

1a Physical address of each property (street, city, state, ZIP code)

A
B
C

1b Type of Property (from list below)	2 For each rental real estate property listed above, report the number of fair rental and personal use days. Check the QJV box only if you meet the requirements to file as a qualified joint venture. See instructions.		Fair Rental Days	Personal Use Days	QJV
A		A			☐
B		B			☐
C		C			☐

Type of Property:
1 Single Family Residence   3 Vacation/Short-Term Rental   5 Land   7 Self-Rental
2 Multi-Family Residence   4 Commercial   6 Royalties   8 Other (describe) _____

			Properties:		
			A	B	C
Income:					
3	Rents received	3			
4	Royalties received	4			
Expenses:					
5	Advertising	5			
6	Auto and travel (see instructions)	6			
7	Cleaning and maintenance	7			
8	Commissions	8			
9	Insurance	9			
10	Legal and other professional fees	10			
11	Management fees	11			
12	Mortgage interest paid to banks, etc. (see instructions)	12			
13	Other interest	13			
14	Repairs	14			
15	Supplies	15			
16	Taxes	16			
17	Utilities	17			
18	Depreciation expense or depletion	18			
19	Other (list) _____	19			
20	Total expenses. Add lines 5 through 19 . . .	20			
21	Subtract line 20 from line 3 (rents) and/or 4 (royalties). If result is a (loss), see instructions to find out if you must file **Form 6198**	21			
22	Deductible rental real estate loss after limitation, if any, on **Form 8582** (see instructions)	22	( )	( )	( )

23a	Total of all amounts reported on line 3 for all rental properties	23a	
b	Total of all amounts reported on line 4 for all royalty properties	23b	
c	Total of all amounts reported on line 12 for all properties	23c	
d	Total of all amounts reported on line 18 for all properties	23d	
e	Total of all amounts reported on line 20 for all properties	23e	
24	**Income.** Add positive amounts shown on line 21. **Do not** include any losses	24	
25	**Losses.** Add royalty losses from line 21 and rental real estate losses from line 22. Enter total losses here	25	( )
26	**Total rental real estate and royalty income or (loss).** Combine lines 24 and 25. Enter the result here. If Parts II, III, IV, and line 40 on page 2 do not apply to you, also enter this amount on Schedule 1 (Form 1040), line 5. Otherwise, include this amount in the total on line 41 on page 2 .	26	

For Paperwork Reduction Act Notice, see the separate instructions.   Cat. No. 11344L   **Schedule E (Form 1040) 2022**

Changing or Ending a Tenancy

At some point after you've signed a lease or rental agreement, you might want to make changes—perhaps to increase the rent, or to let the tenant bring in a roommate or keep a pet. This chapter shows how to modify a signed lease or rental agreement. It also discusses how you—or your tenant—can end a tenancy, and offers tips on how to head off problems such as a tenant giving inadequate notice or breaking the lease. This chapter also summarizes the basic rules for returning security deposits.

How to Modify Signed Rental Agreements and Leases

All amendments to your lease or rental agreement should be in writing and signed by everyone who signed the original lease, including you, the tenants, and any cosigners.

Amending a Fixed-Term Lease

If you use a fixed-term lease, you cannot unilaterally alter the terms of the tenancy. You can't raise the rent or change the terms of the lease until the end of the lease period unless the lease allows it or the tenant agrees. If the tenant agrees to changes, however, follow the directions below for amending the rental agreement.

Amending a Month-to-Month Rental Agreement

If you want to change one or more clauses in a month-to-month rental agreement, no law requires that you get the tenant's consent. Legally, you simply send the tenant a notice of the change.

Most states require 30 days' advance notice (subject to any rent control laws) to change a month-to-month tenancy. (See the "State Rules on Notice Required to Change or Terminate a Month-to-Month Tenancy" chart in Appendix A for a list of each state's notice requirements, and Clause 4 of the rental agreement in Chapter 1.) You'll need to consult your state statutes for the specific information on how you must deliver a notice to the tenant. (Most allow you to use first-class mail.)

TIP

Contact the tenant and explain the changes. It makes good personal and business sense for you or your manager to contact the tenant personally and explain a rent increase or other changes before you deliver a written notice. If the tenant is opposed to your proposal, your personal efforts will allow you to explain your reasons.

Most of the time, you don't need to redo the entire rental agreement in order to make a change or two. Just keep a copy of the amendment with the original rental agreement. If the change is small and simply alters part of an existing clause—such as increasing the rent or making the rent payable every 14 days instead of every 30 days—you can cross out the old language, write in the new (don't forget to indicate when the new rent kicks in), and sign in the margin next to the new words. Make sure the tenant also signs next to the change. Add the date that the two of you signed, in case a dispute later arises as to when everyone agreed to the new rent.

Preparing a New Lease or Rental Agreement

In some cases, however, you might want the tenant to sign a new rental agreement. For example, if you're adding a clause or making several changes, you'll probably find it easier to substitute a whole new agreement for the old one. If you prepare an entire new agreement, be sure that you and the tenant write "Canceled by mutual consent, effective (date)" on the old one, and sign it. To avoid the possibility of two inconsistent agreements operating at the same time, be sure that there is no time overlap between the old and new agreements. Similarly, so that the tenant is always subject to a written agreement, don't allow any gap between the cancellation date of the old agreement and the effective date of the new one.

 TIP

Adding a new tenant should result in a new agreement. Even when a new tenant is filling out the rest of a former tenant's lease term under the same conditions, it's never wise to allow the new resident to operate under the same lease or rental agreement. Start over and prepare a new agreement in the new tenant's name. (See Clause 10 of the form agreements in Chapter 2.)

Ending a Month-to-Month Tenancy

This section discusses a landlord's and a tenant's responsibilities when ending a month-to-month tenancy.

Landlords: Giving Notice to the Tenant

You can end a month-to-month tenancy simply by giving the proper amount of notice. You don't usually have to state a reason, unless state or local law requires it. In most places, all you need to do is give the tenant a simple written notice that complies with your state's minimum notice requirement and states the date on which the tenancy will end. After that date, the tenant no longer has the legal right to occupy the premises.

In most states, and for most rentals, landlords who want to terminate a month-to-month tenancy must provide the same amount of notice as tenants—typically 30 days (discussed below). But this isn't the rule everywhere. (See the "State Rules on Notice Required to Change or Terminate a Month-to-Month Tenancy" chart in Appendix A.) State and local rent control laws can also impose notice requirements on landlords. Different rules apply when you want a tenant to move because the tenant has violated a material term of the rental agreement—for example, by failing to pay rent. If so, the required notice periods are usually much shorter.

Restrictions to Ending a Tenancy

The general rules for terminating a tenancy often don't apply in the following situations:

- **Rent control laws.** Many rent control cities and some states require "just cause" (a good reason) to end a tenancy, which typically includes moving in a close relative and refurbishing the unit. You will likely have to state your legal reason in the termination notice you give the tenant.

- **Discrimination.** It is illegal to end a tenancy because of a tenant's race, religion, or sex; because they have children; or for any other reason constituting illegal discrimination.

- **Retaliation.** You cannot legally terminate a tenancy to retaliate against a tenant for exercising any tenant-related right under the law, such as the tenant's right to complain to governmental authorities about defective housing conditions or, in many states, to withhold rent because of a health or safety problem the landlord has failed to correct. Chapter 16 of Nolo's *Every Landlord's Legal Guide* covers how to avoid tenant retaliation claims.

Each state (and even some cities) has its own detailed rules and procedures for preparing and serving termination notices, making it impossible to provide state-specific forms and instructions in this book. Consult a landlords' association or a local landlord-tenant organization, along with your state statutes, for information and sample forms. Once you find out how much notice you must give, how the notice must be delivered, and any other requirements, you'll be in good shape to handle this work yourself—usually with no lawyer needed.

Tenants: Giving Notice to the Landlord

In most states, a tenant who decides to move out must give you at least 30 days' notice. Some states allow less than 30 days' notice in certain situations —for example, when a tenant must leave early due to military orders or health problems. And, in some states, tenants who pay rent more frequently than once a month can give notice to terminate that matches their rent payment interval—for example, tenants who pay rent every two weeks would have to give 14 days' notice. Special rules apply to tenants in active military service. (See "Special Rules for Active Military Tenants," below.)

To educate your tenants, your rental agreement should include your state's notice requirements for ending a tenancy. (See Clause 4 of the form agreements in Chapter 1.) It's also wise to list termination notice requirements in the move-in letter you send to new tenants (discussed in Chapter 3).

For details about your state's requirements, see the "State Rules on Notice Required to Change or Terminate a Month-to-Month Tenancy" table in Appendix A.

Insist on a Tenant's Written Notice of Intent to Move

In many states, a tenant's notice must be in writing and give the exact date the tenant plans to move out. Even if it's not required by law, it's a good idea to insist that the tenant give you notice in writing (as does Clause 4 of the form agreements in Chapter 1).

Insisting on written notice will prove essential should your old tenants not move as planned after you've signed a lease or rental agreement with a new tenant. Not only will a written notice support your position if, at the last minute, the tenants try to claim that they didn't really set a firm move-out date, but it will also be invaluable if a new tenant sues you to recover the costs of temporary housing or storage fees because you could not deliver possession of the unit. In turn, you can sue the old (holdover) tenants for causing the problem by failing to move out. You will have a much stronger case against the holdover tenants if you can produce a written promise to move on a specific date, instead of your version of a conversation (which the tenants will undoubtedly dispute).

A sample tenant's notice of intent to move out form is shown below. Give a copy of this form to any tenant who announces a plan to move.

FORM

Tenant's Intent to Move Out form. You'll find a downloadable copy of the Tenant's Notice of Intent to Move Out on the Nolo website; the link is included in Appendix B of this book. A filled-in sample Tenant's Notice of Intent to Move Out form is shown below.

Tenant's Notice of Intent to Move Out

Date _____April 3, 20xx_____

Landlord __Anne Sakamoto_____

Street Address ___888 Mill Avenue_____

City and State___Nashville, Tennessee 37126_____

Dear _____Ms. Sakamoto_____ ,
                              Landlord

This is to notify you that the undersigned Tenant(s), ___Patti and Joe Ellis_____

_____ , will be moving from

___999 Brook Lane, Apartment Number 11_____ ,

on ___May 3, 20xx_____ , ___30 days_____ from today. This

provides at least _____30 days'_____ written notice as required in the rental

agreement.

Sincerely,

_Patti Ellis_____
Tenant
_Joe Ellis_____
Tenant

_____
Tenant

Special Rules for Active Military Tenants

Tenants who are in the active military or other specified federal agencies, or who enter military service after signing a lease or rental agreement, may terminate when they receive permanent change of station orders or are deployed to a new location for 90 days or more. (Servicemembers Civil Relief Act, 50 App. U.S.C. §§ 3901 and following.) Tenants must mail written notice of their intent to terminate their tenancy for military reasons to the landlord or manager.

Rental agreements. Once the tenant mails or delivers the notice, the tenancy will terminate 30 days after the day that rent is next due. For example, if rent is due on the first of June and the tenant mails a notice on May 28, the tenancy will terminate on July 1. This rule takes precedence over any longer notice periods that might be specified in your rental agreement or by state law. If state law or your agreement provides for shorter notice periods, however, the shorter notice will control. Recently, many states have passed laws that offer the same or greater protections to members of the state defense force or National Guard.

Leases. A tenant who enters military service after signing a lease may terminate the lease by following the procedure for rental agreements, above. For example, suppose a tenant signs a one-year lease in April, agreeing to pay rent on the first of the month. The tenant enlists October 10 and mails you a termination notice on October 11. In this case, you must terminate the tenancy on December 1, 30 days after the first time that rent is next due (November 1) following the mailing of the notice. This tenant will have no continuing obligation for rent past December 1, even though this is several months before the lease expires.

Preparing a Move-Out Letter

Chapter 3 explains how a move-in letter can help get a tenancy off to a good start. Similarly, a move-out letter can also help reduce the possibility of disputes, especially over the return of security deposits. Send the letter as soon as you receive notice of the tenant's intent to leave. Your move-out letter should explain the following:

- how you expect the rental unit to be left, including specific cleaning requirements
- details on your final inspection procedures and how you'll determine the level of cleaning and damage repair that you require
- the kinds of deposit deductions that you can legally make, and
- when and how you will send any refund.

See below for more detail on returning security deposits and on final inspection procedures.

 FORM

Tenant's Move-Out Letter form. You'll find a downloadable copy of the Move-Out Letter on the Nolo website; the link is included in Appendix B of this book. A filled-in sample move-out letter form is shown below.

Accepting Rent After a Tenant Gives a 30-Day Notice

If you accept rent for any period beyond the date the tenants told you they are moving out, you will likely cancel the termination notice. Accepting (and documenting in writing) past-due rent from a tenant who has given notice will not cancel a termination notice, however.

Move-Out Letter

Date ___July 5, 20xx_____

Tenant ___Jane Wasserman_____

Street Address ___123 North Street, Apartment #23_____

City and State ___Atlanta, Georgia 30360_____

Dear ___Jane_____,
Tenant

We hope you have enjoyed living here. In order that we can mutually end our relationship on a positive note, this move-out letter describes how we expect your unit to be left and what our procedures are for returning your security deposit.

Basically, we expect you to leave your rental unit in the same condition it was when you moved in, except for normal wear and tear. To refresh your memory on the condition of the unit when you moved in, I've attached a copy of the Landlord-Tenant Checklist you signed at the beginning of your tenancy. I'll be using this same form to inspect your unit when you leave.

Specifically, here's a list of items you should thoroughly clean before vacating:

- ☑ Floors
    - ☑ sweep wood floors
    - ☑ vacuum carpets and rugs (shampoo if necessary)
    - ☑ mop kitchen and bathroom floors
- ☑ Walls, baseboards, ceilings, and built-in shelves
- ☑ Kitchen cabinets, countertops and sink, stove and oven—inside and out
- ☑ Refrigerator—clean inside and out, empty it of food, and turn it off, with the door left open
- ☑ Bathtubs, showers, toilets, and plumbing fixtures
- ☑ Doors, windows, and window coverings
- ☑ Other _____

  Microwave oven—clean inside and out

If you have any questions as to the type of cleaning we expect, please let me know.

Please don't leave anything behind—that includes bags of garbage, clothes, food, newspapers, furniture, appliances, dishes, plants, cleaning supplies, or other items that belong to you.

Please be sure you have disconnected phone and utility services, changed your address for regular deliveries and subscriptions, and sent the post office a change of address form.

Once you have cleaned your unit and removed all your belongings, please call me at ___555-1234___ to arrange for a walk-through inspection and to return all keys. Please be prepared to give me your forwarding address where we may mail your security deposit.

It's our policy to return all deposits either in person or at an address you provide within ___one month___ _____ after you move out. If any deductions are made—for past-due rent or because the unit is damaged or not sufficiently clean—they will be explained in writing.

If you have any questions, please contact me at ___555-1234___.

Sincerely,

Denise Parsons

Landlord/Manager

Suppose, after giving notice, the tenant asks for a little more time in which to move out. Assuming no new tenant is moving in and you're willing to accommodate the request, prepare a written agreement setting out what you have agreed to in detail, and have the tenant sign it. See the sample letter, below, extending the tenant's move-out date.

> CAUTION
> **If you collected the "last month's rent" when the tenant moved in, don't accept rent for the last month of the tenancy.** You are legally obligated to use this money for the last month's rent. Accepting an additional month's rent might extend the tenant's tenancy.

When the Tenant Doesn't Give the Required Notice

All too often, tenants will provide a "too short" notice of intent to move. And it's not unheard of for tenants to move out with no notice or with a wave as they toss the keys on your desk.

Tenants who leave without giving enough notice have lost the right to occupy the premises but are still obligated to pay rent through the end of the required notice period. For example, when the notice period is 30 days, but the tenants move out 20 days after telling you of their plan to move, they still owe you rent for the remaining 10 days.

In most states, you have a legal duty to try to rerent the property before you can charge tenants for giving you too little notice, but few courts

expect a landlord to accomplish this in less than a month. (This rule, called the landlord's duty to mitigate damages, is discussed below.) You can also use the security deposit to cover unpaid rent (also discussed below).

When You or Your Tenant Violate the Rental Agreement

The discussion below concerned terminations that are not tied to serious misbehavior by the landlord or tenant. The notice period for such terminations is typically generous, at least 30 days. But under certain conditions, landlord or tenant may terminate on much shorter notice.

Terminations by Tenants

If you seriously violate the rental agreement and fail to fulfill your legal responsibilities—for example, by not correcting serious health or safety problems—a tenant might legally be able to move out with no written notice or by giving less notice than is otherwise required. Called "constructive eviction," this doctrine typically applies only when living conditions are intolerable—for example, when a tenant hasn't had heat for an extended period in the winter, or when a tenant's use and enjoyment of the property has been substantially impaired because of drug dealing in the building.

The laws regarding constructive eviction vary slightly from state to state.

Generally, when a landlord is on notice that a rental unit has serious habitability problems and those conditions continue for an extended period of time, the tenant is entitled to move out on short notice or, in extreme cases, without giving notice.

Terminations by Landlords

Along the same lines, landlords can evict tenants who violate a lease or rental agreement, or an important law, using short notice periods. For example, you may give a "notice to quit" to a tenant who fails to pay rent or damages the premises, using less notice than is required to end a tenancy when misbehavior is not involved (typically 3 to 5 days, rather than 30 days). When tenants don't leave as demanded, the next step is an eviction lawsuit. Because state eviction rules and procedures vary greatly, the details of how to evict a tenant are beyond the scope of this book.

How Fixed-Term Leases End

A lease lasts for a fixed term, typically one year. As a general rule, neither you nor the tenant may unilaterally terminate the tenancy or change a material condition during the period of the lease, unless the other party has violated the terms of the lease. (There's an exception for tenants who join the military and want to terminate a lease, as explained in "Special Rules for Active Military Tenants," above.)

Most of the time, the lease simply ends of its own accord at the end of the lease term, and the tenant moves out. Alternatively, you could sign a new lease, with the same or different terms. As every landlord knows, however, life is not always so simple. Sooner or later, a tenant will stay beyond the end of the term without signing a new lease, or leave before the lease term ends without any legal justification for doing so.

Giving Notice to the Tenant

Because a lease specifies when it will end, you might not think it's necessary to remind the tenants of the expiration date. But doing so is a very good

practice, and some states or cities (especially those with rent control) actually require it.

We suggest giving the tenant at least 60 days' written notice that the lease is going to expire. This reminder has several advantages. It can:

- **Get the tenants out on time.** Two months' notice allows plenty of time for the tenants to look for another place if they don't—or you don't—want to renew the lease.

- **Give you time to renegotiate the lease.** If you'd like to continue renting to your present tenant but also want to change some lease terms or increase the rent, your notice serves to remind the tenant that the terms of the old lease won't automatically continue. Encourage the tenant to stay, but mention that you need to make some changes to the lease.

- **Allow you to find a new tenant quickly.** If you know a tenant is going to move, you can show the unit to prospective tenants ahead of time and minimize the time the space is vacant. You must still respect the current tenant's privacy. (Chapter 2 discusses showing the unit to prospective tenants.)

RENT CONTROL

Your options might be limited in a rent control area. When your property is subject to rent or eviction controls, your ability to end your relationship with a current tenant might be limited. Many laws require "just cause" for refusing to renew a lease, which generally means that only certain reasons (such as the tenant's failure to pay rent, or your desire to move in a close relative) justify nonrenewal. If your law requires "just cause," and if your decision not to renew doesn't meet the law's "just clause" test, you might end up with a perpetual month-to-month tenant. Check your rent control laws carefully.

Sample Letter Extending Tenant's Move-Out Date

June 20, 20xx

Kalinda Blake
777 Broadway Terrace, Apartment #3
Richmond, Virginia 23233

Dear Kalinda:

On June 1, you gave me a 30-day notice of your intent to move out on July 1. You have since requested to extend your move-out to July 18 because of last-minute problems with closing escrow on your new house. This letter is to verify our understanding that you will move out on July 18, instead of July 1, and that you will pay prorated rent for 18 days (July 1 through July 18). Prorated rent for 18 days, based on your monthly rent of $1,200 or $40 per day, is $720.

Please sign below to indicate your agreement to these terms.

Sincerely,

Fran Moore, Landlord

Agreed to by Kalinda Blake, Tenant:

Signature ___*Kalinda Blake*_____

Date ___June 20, 20xx_____

When the Tenant Remains After the Lease Expires

It's fairly common for a tenant to remain in a unit even though the lease has ended. If this happens, you have a choice: You can continue renting to the tenant, or you can take legal steps to get the tenant out.

When a tenant stays beyond the end of the lease, and you accept rent money without signing a new lease, in most states you will have created a new, month-to-month tenancy on the same terms that were in the old lease. In a few states, accepting rent might even have created a new lease for the same term—such as one year. In other words, you'll be stuck with the terms and rent in the old lease, for at least the first 30 days. If you want to change the terms in a new lease, you must abide by the law regarding giving notice for a month-to-month tenancy (discussed above). It will usually take you at least a month while you go about giving notice to your now month-to-month tenant.

To avoid the problem of tenants staying longer than you want, notify tenants that you expect them to leave no later than the lease expiration date, and don't accept rent after this date. If a tenant wants to stay a few days after a lease expires and you agree, put your agreement in a letter. (See the sample letter extending the tenant's move-out date, above.)

When the Tenant Leaves Early

Tenants who leave before a fixed-term lease expires (with or without notifying you), and who refuse to pay rent for the remainder of the lease, have "broken the lease." Once the tenants leave for good, you have the legal right to take possession of the premises and rerent to another tenant.

A key question that arises is, how much do tenants with a lease owe when they break the lease? Let's start with the general legal rule.

Tenants who sign a lease agree at the outset to pay a fixed amount of rent: the monthly rent multiplied by the number of months of the lease. The tenants are obligated to pay this amount in monthly installments over the term of the lease. The fact that payments are made monthly doesn't change the tenants' responsibility to pay rent for the entire lease term. And even when tenants give you notice of their intention to leave early, you are still owed the money for the rest of the term. As discussed below, depending on the situation, you can use the tenants' security deposit to cover part of the shortfall, or sue the tenants for rent owed.

TIP

Require tenants to notify you of extended absences. Clause 18 of the form lease and rental agreements (Chapter 2) requires tenants to inform you when they will be gone for an extended time, such as two or more weeks.

By requiring tenants to notify you of long absences, you'll know whether the rental has been abandoned or the tenant is simply on an extended trip. In addition, if you have such a clause and, under its authority, enter an apparently abandoned unit only to be confronted later by an indignant tenant, you can defend yourself by pointing out that the tenant violated the lease.

Your Duty to Mitigate Your Loss When the Tenant Leaves Early

When tenants break the lease without legal justification, in most states you can't just sit back and wait until the lease ends, and then sue the departed tenant for the total amount of your lost rent. Instead, you must try to rerent the property reasonably quickly and subtract the rent you receive from rent due on the remaining months of the lease (plus any past-due rent).

When Leaving Early Is Justified

The blanket rule that a tenant who breaks a lease owes you the rent for the entire lease term is subject to important exceptions. A tenant who leaves early might be off the hook for the remaining rent when:

- **The rental is unsafe or otherwise uninhabitable.** When you don't live up to your obligations to provide habitable housing, a court will conclude that you have "constructively evicted" the tenant. That releases the tenant from further obligations under the lease.

- **You have rented—or could rent—the unit to someone else.** Most courts require landlords to try to soften ("mitigate") the ex-tenant's liability for the remaining rent, by attempting to find a new rent-paying tenant as soon as reasonably possible. The new tenant's rent is credited against what the former tenant owed. (This "mitigation of damages" rule is discussed below.)

- **The law allows the tenant to leave early.** A few states have laws that list allowable reasons to break a lease. For example, in Delaware, tenants need only give 30 days' notice to end a long-term lease if they need to move because their present employer relocated or because health problems (of the tenant or a family member) require a permanent move. (Del. Code tit. 25 § 5314.) In many states, victims of domestic violence, sexual assault, or stalking may terminate a lease (with proper notice) early without penalty. In all states, tenants who enter active military duty after signing a lease must be released after delivering proper notice. (See "Special Rules for Active Military Tenants," above.) If your tenant has a good reason for a sudden move, you might want to research your state's law to see whether the tenant will still be on the hook for rent.

- **The rental is damaged or destroyed.** If a tenant's home is significantly damaged—by natural disaster or any other reason beyond the tenant's control—the tenant has the right to move out. State laws vary on the extent of the landlord's responsibility, depending on the cause of the damage. When a fire, flood, tornado, earthquake, or other natural disaster makes the dwelling unlivable; or when a third party is the cause of the destruction (for instance, a fire due to an arsonist), your best bet is to look to your insurance policy for help in repairing or rebuilding the unit and to assist your tenants in resettlement.

Even if this isn't the legal rule in your state, trying to rerent is a sound business strategy. It's much better to have rent coming in every month than to leave a rental unit vacant for months and hope that in the future you can sue and collect from a tenant who's probably long gone.

If you sue the tenant for the whole rent instead of making best efforts to rerent, you will collect only what the judge thinks is the difference between the fair rental value of the property and the original tenant's promised rent. How much you can recover will be affected by the rental market in your area; judges will usually account for the relative ease of finding new renters as well as any declines in rental rates. Even in areas where renters are easy to find, most judges will give you some time (probably at least 30 days) to find a new tenant.

How to Mitigate Your Damages

When you're sure that a tenant has moved out, you can turn your attention to rerenting the unit.

You don't need to relax your standards for acceptable tenants—for example, you are entitled to reject applicants with poor credit or rental histories. Also, you need not give the suddenly available property priority over other rental units that you'd normally attend to first.

You aren't required to rent the premises at a rate substantially below its fair market value. Keep in mind, however, that refusing to rent at less than the original rate might be foolish. If you're unable to ultimately collect from the former tenant, you will get *no* income from the property instead of less. You will have hurt no one but yourself.

The Tenant's Right to Find a Replacement Tenant

Tenants who wish to leave before the lease expires might offer to find a suitable new tenant, in an effort to be off the hook for future rent payments. Unless you have a new tenant waiting, you have nothing to lose by cooperating. And refusing to cooperate could hurt you: When you refuse to accept an excellent new tenant and then withhold the lease-breaking tenant's deposit or sue for unpaid rent, you could wind up losing in court because, after all, you turned down the chance to reduce your losses (mitigate your damages).

Of course, in a really tight rental market, you might be able to lease the unit easily at a higher rent, or you might already have an even better prospective tenant on your waiting list. In that case, a tenant who breaks the lease benefits you, and you might not be interested in any new tenant provided by the old one.

Be sure to sign a new lease with any new tenant you accept.

Keep Good Records

When you sue a former tenant, you need to be able to show the judge that you acted reasonably in your attempts to rerent the property. Don't rely on your memory and powers of persuasion to convince the judge. Keep detailed records, including:

- the original lease
- receipts for cleaning and painting, with photos of the unit showing the need for repairs, if any
- your expenses for storing or properly disposing of any belongings the tenant left
- receipts for advertising the property and bills from credit reporting agencies investigating potential renters
- a log of the time you spent showing the property, and the value of that time
- a log of any potential renters you rejected, along with your reasons for rejecting them, and
- a copy of the new lease as documentation that you had to accept less rent than what the original tenant paid, if applicable.

When You Can Sue

When a tenant leaves prematurely, you should first use the tenant's deposit to cover your rerental costs and any shortfall between the original and replacement rent amounts. However, if the deposit isn't enough to cover your losses, you might need to sue the former tenant.

Deciding *where* to sue is usually easy: For most landlord-tenant disputes, small claims court is the court of choice, because it's fast, affordable, and doesn't require a lawyer. The only exception is when your former tenant owes you more than your small claims court's dollar limits.

Knowing *when* to sue is trickier. You might be eager to start legal proceedings as soon as the original tenant leaves, but, if you do, you won't know the extent of your losses, because you might find another tenant who will make up part of the lost rent. Must you wait until the end of the original tenant's lease? Or can you bring suit when you rerent the property?

The standard approach, and one that all states allow, is to go to court after you rerent the property. At this point, your losses—your expenses and the rent differential, if any—are known and final. The disadvantage is that you haven't received rental income since the original tenant left, and the original tenant might be long gone and not, practically speaking, worth chasing down.

 RESOURCE

Nolo's book on small claims court. *Everybody's Guide to Small Claims Court*, by Cara O'Neill, provides detailed advice on bringing or defending a small claims court case, preparing evidence and witnesses for court, and collecting your court judgment when you win. *Everybody's Guide to Small Claims Court* will also be useful in defending yourself against a tenant who sues you in small claims court—for example, claiming that you failed to return a cleaning or security deposit.

Returning Security Deposits When a Tenancy Ends

Most states set very specific rules for the return of security deposits. A landlord's failure to return security deposits as legally required can result in substantial financial penalties.

Alerting Tenants to Final Inspection Procedures

Many landlords do a final inspection of the rental unit on their own and simply send the tenant an itemized statement with any remaining balance of the deposit. If at all possible, you should conduct the inspection with the tenant who's moving out, rather than by yourself (in fact, in some states the tenant must have notice and an opportunity to be present). Because state laws can be quite detailed as to rules and procedures for itemizing and returning security deposits, be sure to check your state statutes. (See "State Security Deposit Rules" in Appendix A.)

Inspecting the Unit When a Tenant Leaves

At the end of a tenancy, you'll need to inspect the unit to assess any necessary cleaning and damage repair (a few states require you to do a "pre-move out inspection," which gives tenants a heads-up on what needs to be cleaned or fixed in order to avoid deductions). At the final inspection, check the condition of each item on the Landlord-Tenant Checklist (described in Chapter 3) or a similar document that you and the tenant signed when the tenant moved in. If you didn't use the Landlord-Tenant Checklist or a similar form to inventory the condition of the rental property at move-in, you should still do a walk-through inspection when the tenant moves out. You won't have the benefit of the "before" documentation, but you can still review the condition of the unit together and identify items that need cleaning, repair, or replacement. As explained earlier, it's a good idea (and the law in some states) to involve the tenants in the final inspection. (See "Alerting Tenants to Final Inspection Procedures," above.)

Basic Rules for Returning Deposits

You can deduct from a tenant's security deposit the amount you need to fix damaged or dirty property (beyond ordinary wear and tear) or to make up unpaid rent. But you must make your deductions and return deposits correctly. The rules vary from state to state, but landlords usually have between 14 and 30 days after the tenant leaves to return the deposit. (See "State Security Deposit Rules" in Appendix A.)

State security deposit statutes typically require you to mail the following within the time limit to the tenant's last known address (or forwarding address if you have one):

- a written, itemized accounting of deductions, including back rent and costs of cleaning and damage repair, together with payment for any deposit balance, including any required interest
- the deposit that remains after any valid deductions, and
- any required interest.

Even if your state or law has no specific time limit for requiring itemization, promptly presenting the tenant with a written itemization of all deductions and a clear reason why each was made is an essential part of a savvy landlord's overall plan to avoid disputes with tenants. In general, we recommend 21 to 30 days as a reasonable time to return deposits.

Penalties for Violating Security Deposit Laws

If you don't follow state security deposit laws to the letter, you might pay a heavy price if a tenant sues you and wins. In addition to whatever amount you wrongfully withheld, you might have to pay the tenant punitive damages (penalties imposed when the judge feels that the defendant has acted especially outrageously) and court costs. In many states, if you "willfully" (deliberately and not through inadvertence) violate the security deposit statute, you could forfeit your right to retain any part of the deposit and could be liable for two or three times the amount wrongfully withheld, plus attorneys' fees and costs.

When the Deposit Doesn't Cover Damage and Unpaid Rent

If the security deposit doesn't cover what a tenant owes you for back rent, cleaning, or repairs, you can file a lawsuit against the former tenant.

RESOURCE

More information on deposits. *Every Landlord's Legal Guide*, by Marcia Stewart, Janet Portman, and Ann O'Connell (Nolo), provides complete details on state laws and sample forms for returning and itemizing security deposits.

State Landlord-Tenant Law Charts

How to Use the State Landlord-Tenant Law Charts

The State Landlord-Tenant Law Charts are comprehensive 50-state charts that give you two kinds of information:

- the state rules, such as notice periods and deposit limits (what the statutes and cases say), and
- specific citations for key statutes and cases, which you can use if you want to read the law yourself or look for more information.

When you're looking for information for your state, simply find your state along the left-hand list on the chart, and read to the right—you'll see the statute or case, and the rule.

RESOURCE

How to find your state's laws. If you would like to read the actual statute that we summarize in these charts, you can easily find it online. Many times, when you type the citation itself (the letters and numbers that identify the law, such as Cal. Civ. Code Sec. 1954) right into your browser, you'll get a results list with a link to the law. Or, search for your state's statutes (such as "Arizona statutes"). That will usually result in a link to the state's entire set of laws, and you can search for your citation within the table of contents on that site.

State Landlord-Tenant Statutes

Here are some of the key statutes pertaining to landlord-tenant law in each state. In some states, important legal principles are contained in court opinions, not codes or statutes. Court-made law and rent stabilization—rent control—laws and regulations are not reflected in this chart. Note that because some states exempt certain occupancies from their general landlord-tenant statutes, such as rentals of mobile homes and short-term rentals, it's a good idea to confirm that these statutes apply to your rental situation. You'll find the details about each state's exemption statutes, if any, in the chart titled "State Landlord-Tenant Exemption Statutes."

State	Statute	State	Statute
Alabama	Ala. Code §§ 35-9-1 to 35-9-100; 35-9A-101 to 35-9A-603	Maryland	Md. Code Real Prop. §§ 8-101 to 8-604; 8-901 to 8-911
Alaska	Alaska Stat. §§ 34.03.010 to 34.03.380	Massachusetts	Mass. Gen. Laws ch. 111, § 127L; ch. 186, §§ 1A to 31; ch. 186a, §§ 1 to 6; ch. 239, §§ 1 to 14
Arizona	Ariz. Rev. Stat. §§ 12-1171 to 12-1183; 33-301 to 33-381; 33-1301 to 33-1381; 36-1637	Michigan	Mich. Comp. Laws §§ 125.530; 554.131 to 554.201; 554.601 to 554.641; 600.2918
Arkansas	Ark. Code §§ 18-16-101 to 18-16-306; 18-16-501 to 18-16-509; 18-17-101 to 18-17-913	Minnesota	Minn. Stat. §§ 504B.001 to 504B.471
California	Cal. Civ. Code §§ 789.3; 790 to 793; 827; 1925 to 1934; 1940 to 1954.05; 1954.50 to 1954.605; 1961 to 1995.340; 2079.10a; Cal. Health & Safety Code §§ 25400.28; 26147 to 26148; Cal. Bus. & Prof. Code § 8538; Cal. Gov't. Code § 8589.45	Mississippi	Miss. Code §§ 89-7-1 through 89-7-125; 89-8-1 through 89-8-45
		Missouri	Mo. Rev. Stat. §§ 441.005 to 441.920; 442.055; 535.010 to 535.300
Colorado	Colo. Rev. Stat. §§ 13-40-101 to 13-40-123; 13-40.1-101 to 13-40.1-102; 38-12-101 to 38-12-105; 38-12-301 to 38-12-1007; 38-12-1201 to 38-12-1205	Montana	Mont. Code §§ 70-24-101 to 70-26-110; 70-27-101 to 70-27-212; 75-10-1305
		Nebraska	Neb. Rev. Stat. §§ 69-2302 to 69-2314; 76-1401 to 76-1449
Connecticut	Conn. Gen. Stat. §§ 19a-37, 47a-1 to 47a-75	Nevada	Nev. Rev. Stat. §§ 40.215 to 40.425; 118A.010 to 118A.530
Delaware	Del. Code tit. 25, §§ 5101 to 5907		
District of Columbia	D.C. Code §§ 42-3201 to 42-3651.08; D.C. Mun. Regs., tit. 14, §§ 300 to 399	New Hampshire	N.H. Rev. Stat. §§ 477:4-g; 540:1 to 540:30; 540-A:1 to 540-A:8; 540-B:1 to 540-B:10
Florida	Fla. Stat. §§ 83.40 to 83.683; 404.056; 715.10 to 715.111	New Jersey	N.J. Stat. §§ 2A:18-51 to 2A:18-61.67; 2A:18-72 to 2A:18-84; 2A:42-1 to 2A:42-96; 2A:42-144 to 2A:42-148; 46:8-1 to 46:8-64; 55:13A-7.14; 55:13A-7.18; 55:13A-7.19; N.J.A.C. §§ 5:10-5.1, 5:10-27.1
Georgia	Ga. Code §§ 44-1-16; 44-7-1 to 44-7-81		
Hawaii	Haw. Rev. Stat. §§ 368-1 to 368-4; 521-1 to 521-83		
Idaho	Idaho Code §§ 6-301 to 6-324; 55-208 to 55-308	New Mexico	N.M. Stat. §§ 47-8-1 to 47-8-51; N.M. Admin. Code § 20.4.5.13
Illinois	425 Ill. Comp. Stat. § 60/3; 430 Ill. Comp. Stat. § 135/10; 735 Ill. Comp. Stat. §§ 5/9-201 to 5/9-321; 765 Ill. Comp. Stat. §§ 705/0.01 to 742/30; 750/1 to 750/35; 755/1 to 755/999	New York	N.Y. Real Prop. Law §§ 220 to 238-a; Real Prop. Acts §§ 701 to 853; Mult. Dwell. Law (all); Mult. Res. Law (all); Gen. Oblig. Law §§ 7-101 to 7-109; N.Y. Envtl. Conserv. Law § 27-2405; N.Y. Exec. Law § 170-d; N.Y. Penal Law §§ 241.00 to 241.05; N.Y. Unconsol. Law §§ 8581 to 8597 (Emergency Housing Rent Control Law); 8601 to 8617 (Local Emergency Housing Rent Control Act); 8621 to 8634 (Emergency Tenant Protection Act); 9 NYCRR § 4665.15; N.Y. Pub. Serv. § 104
Indiana	Ind. Code §§ 8-1-2-1.2; 32-31-1-1 to 32-31-11-5; 36-1-24.2-1 to 36-1-24.2-4		
Iowa	Iowa Code §§ 562A.1 to 562A.37		
Kansas	Kan. Stat. §§ 58-2501 to 58-2573; 58-25,127; 58-25,137		
Kentucky	Ky. Rev. Stat. §§ 224.1-410; 383.010 to 383.715; 902 Ky. Admin. Regs. 47:200		
		North Carolina	N.C. Gen. Stat. §§ 42-1 to 42-14.2; 42-14.4 to 42-14.5; 42-25.6 to 42-76; 62-110
Louisiana	La. Rev. Stat. §§ 9:3251 to 9:3261.2; La. Civ. Code art. 2002; 2668 to 2729	North Dakota	N.D. Cent. Code §§ 23-13-15; 47-06-04; 47-16-01 to 47-16-41; 47-17-01 to 47-17-05
Maine	Me. Rev. Stat. tit. 14, §§ 6000 to 6046		

State Landlord-Tenant Statutes (continued)

Ohio	Ohio Rev. Code §§ 5321.01 to 5321.20	**Utah**	Utah Code §§ 57-17-1 to 57-17-5; 57-22-1 to 57-22-7; 57-27-201; 78B-6-801 to 78B-6-816
Oklahoma	Okla. Stat. tit. 41, §§ 101 to 136; 201; tit. 74, § 324.11a	**Vermont**	Vt. Stat. tit. 9, §§ 4451 to 4469a; 4471 to 4475
Oregon	Or. Rev. Stat. §§ 90.100 to 90.228; 90.243 to 90.265; 90.295 to 90.493; 105.005 to 105.168; 105.190; 479.270 to 479.280	**Virginia**	Va. Code §§ 54.1-2108.1; 55.1-1200 to 55.1-1262
Pennsylvania	68 Pa. Cons. Stat. §§ 250.101 to 399.19	**Washington**	Wash. Rev. Code §§ 43.31.605; 59.04.010 to 59.18.912; 59.24.010 to 59.24.060
Rhode Island	R.I. Gen. Laws §§ 34-18-1 to 34-18-57		
South Carolina	S.C. Code §§ 5-25-1330; 27-40-10 to 27-40-940	**West Virginia**	W.Va. Code §§ 37-6-1 to 37-6-30; 37-6A-1 to 37-6A-6; 37-7-1 to 37-7-5; W. Va. Code St. R. § 64-92-7
South Dakota	S.D. Codified Laws §§ 43-32-1 to 43-32-36		
Tennessee	Tenn. Code §§ 66-7-101 to 66-7-102; 66-7-104; 66-7-106 to 66-7-107; 66-7-109 to 66-7-112; 66-28-101 to 66-28-522	**Wisconsin**	Wis. Stat. §§ 704.01 to 704.95; Wis. Admin. Code ATCP §§ 134.01 to 134.10
		Wyoming	Wyo. Stat. §§ 1-21-1001 to 1-21-1017; 1-21-1201 to 1-21-1211; 1-21-1301 to 1-21-1304; 34-2-128 to 34-2-129
Texas	Tex. Prop. Code §§ 91.001 to 92.355		

State Laws on Attorneys' Fees and Court Costs Clauses

State	Statute	Rule
Alabama	Ala. Code § 35-9A-163(a)(3)	Leases and rental agreements cannot require the tenant to pay the landlord's attorneys' fees or costs of collection.
Alaska	Alaska Stat. Ann. § 34.03.040(a)(4)	Leases and rental agreements cannot require the tenant (or the landlord) to pay the landlord's attorneys' fees.
Arizona	Ariz. Rev. Stat. § 33-1315	Rental document may not provide that tenant pays landlord's attorneys' fees, except that it may provide that the prevailing party in a court action can be awarded attorneys' fees. Also, the prevailing party in an eviction action can be awarded attorneys' fees even if the rental document doesn't mention it.
Arkansas	No statute	
California	No statute	
Colorado	Colo. Rev. Stat. § 38-12-801	Leases and rental agreements cannot contain a clause that awards attorneys' fees and court costs to only one party. Any fees or costs clause must award attorneys' fees to the prevailing party in a court dispute concerning the rental agreement or the rental premises.
Connecticut	Conn. Gen. Stat. Ann. § 47a-4	A lease or rental agreement cannot require the tenant to pay attorneys' fees that amount to more than 15% of any judgment against the tenant in any action where money damages are awarded.
Delaware	Del. Code Ann. tit. 25, § 5111	Leases and rental agreements cannot contain a clause providing for the recovery of attorneys' fees in any action relating to the tenancy.
District of Columbia	D.C. Code Ann. § 42-3509.02	The Rent Administrator, Rental Housing Commission, or a court of competent jurisdiction may award reasonable attorneys' fees to the prevailing party, except in eviction actions authorized under D.C. Code Ann. § 42-3505.01.
Florida	Fla. Stat. Ann. § 83.48	No ban on attorneys' fees and costs clause. Both landlords and tenants are entitled to recover reasonable attorneys' fees and court costs from the nonprevailing party in a lawsuit brought to enforce the lease or rental agreement, and this right to attorneys' fees and costs cannot be waived in a lease or rental agreement.
Georgia	Ga. Code Ann. § 44-7-2	A clause that provides for the tenant to pay the landlord's attorneys' fees and costs will be void unless it also provides for the landlord to pay the winning tenant's attorneys' fees and costs.
Hawaii	Haw. Rev. Stat. Ann. § 521-35	Leases and rental agreements can require the tenant to pay the costs of a suit, unpaid rent, and reasonable attorneys' fees not exceeding 25% of the unpaid rent when a landlord sues for unpaid rent. Leases and rental agreements can also require that reasonable attorneys' fees and costs may be awarded to the prevailing party in any other landlord-tenant dispute.
Idaho	No statute	
Illinois	No statute	
Indiana	No statute	
Iowa	Iowa Code Ann. § 562A.11	Neither landlord nor tenant may agree to pay the other's attorneys' fees in a lease or rental agreement.
Kansas	Kan. Stat. Ann. § 58-2547	Neither landlord nor tenant may agree to pay the other's attorneys' fees in a lease or rental agreement.
Kentucky	Ky. Rev. Stat. Ann. § 383.570	Neither landlord nor tenant may agree to pay the other's attorneys' fees in a lease or rental agreement.
Louisiana	No statute	

State Laws on Attorneys' Fees and Court Costs Clauses (continued)

State	Statute	Rule
Maine	Me. Rev. Stat. Ann. tit. 14, § 6030	Leases and rental agreements cannot require tenant to pay landlord's legal fees in enforcing the lease or rental agreement. However, a lease or rental agreement can provide for the award of attorneys' fees to the prevailing party after a contested hearing to enforce the lease or rental agreement in cases of "wanton disregard" of the terms of the lease or rental agreement.
Maryland	No statute	
Massachusetts	Mass. Gen. Laws Ann. ch 186 § 20	Leases and rental agreements can require parties to pay attorneys' fees and court costs. If a lease or rental agreement provides that only the landlord can recover attorneys' fees and costs, the court will infer a provision that the tenant can also recover attorneys' fees and costs.
Michigan	Mich. Comp. Laws § 554.633(1)(g)	Leases and rental agreements cannot require a landlord or a tenant to pay the other's legal costs or attorneys' fees in a dispute arising under the lease or rental agreement.
Minnesota	Minn. Stat. Ann. § 504B.172	If a lease provides for recovery of attorneys' fees by the landlord, the tenant is also entitled to attorneys' fees if the tenant prevails in the same type of action. (Effective for leases entered into on or after August 1, 2011, and for leases renewed on or after August 1, 2012.)
Mississippi	No statute	
Missouri	No statute	
Montana	No statute	
Nebraska	Neb. Rev. Stat. § 76-1415	No lease or rental agreement can require the tenant to pay the landlord's or tenant's attorneys' fees.
Nevada	Nev. Rev. Stat. § 118A.220	A lease or rental agreement may not provide that the tenant agrees to pay the landlord's attorneys' fees, but it can provide that reasonable attorneys' fees may be awarded to the prevailing party in a court action.
New Hampshire	No statute	
New Jersey	N.J. Stat. § 2A:18-61.66	Leases and rental agreements can require parties to pay attorneys' fees and court costs. If a lease or rental agreement provides that only the landlord can recover attorneys' fees and costs, the court will infer a provision that the tenant can also recover attorneys' fees and costs.
New Mexico	No statute	
New York	N.Y. Real Prop. Law § 234	When a lease includes an attorneys' fees clause in case of a successful action based on tenant's failure to pay rent or perform covenants, the clause will also automatically apply to the landlord if the tenant is successful in the action.
North Carolina	N.C. Gen. Stat. § 42-46	Landlords can require tenants to pay attorneys' fees (in an amount no greater than 15% of the amount owed by the tenant or 15% of the monthly rent if it's for an eviction not related to nonpayment of rent) and court costs (filing fees and costs for service of process) if the amounts are disclosed in writing in the lease or rental agreement.
		Landlords can also file the following administrative fees (which must be written into the lease): Complaint-filing fee: Landlord can charge a complaint-filing fee of no more than the greater of $15 or 5% of the monthly rent. Court-appearance fee: Landlord can charge a court-appearance fee of 10% of the monthly rent, and only if the landlord's complaint is successful. Second-trial fee: Landlord can charge a fee for an appeal. The fee can't be more than 12% of the monthly rent, and landlord must prevail.
		Landlords can't waive these limits.

State Laws on Attorneys' Fees and Court Costs Clauses (continued)		
State	**Statute**	**Rule**
North Dakota	No statute	
Ohio	Oh. Rev. Code Ann. § 5321.13(C)	Leases and rental agreements cannot require either the landlord or tenant to pay attorneys' fees.
Oklahoma	Okla. Stat. tit. 41, § 113	Leases and rental agreements cannot require either party to pay the other's attorneys' fees.
Oregon	Or. Rev. Stat. §§ 20.096, 90.255	If a lease or rental agreement states that one party is entitled to attorneys' fees and costs if the party prevails in a claim based on the lease or rental agreement, the other party is also entitled to the same. The parties cannot waive this rule and agree that only one will get attorneys' fees and costs.
Pennsylvania	No statute	
Rhode Island	R.I. Gen. Laws § 34-18-17(a)(3)	Leases and rental agreements cannot require the tenant to pay the landlord's attorneys' fees under circumstances not allowed in the landlord-tenant act.
South Carolina	No statute	
South Dakota	No statute	
Tennessee	No statute	
Texas	Tex. Prop. Code § 24.006	If a written lease entitles the landlord to obtain attorneys' fees in an eviction lawsuit, or if the landlord's termination notice advises the tenant that the landlord will be entitled to fees if the tenant does not vacate before the eleventh day after the day of receipt, a prevailing tenant will also be entitled to obtain attorneys' fees.
Utah	No statute	
Vermont	No statute	
Virginia	Va. Code § 55.1-1208	A lease or rental agreement can't require the tenant to pay the landlord's attorneys' fees unless specifically allowed under the Virginia Residential Landlord and Tenant Act.
Washington	Wash. Rev. Code § 59.18.230	A lease or rental agreement may not provide that the tenant will pay the landlord's attorneys' fees.
West Virginia	No statute	
Wisconsin	Wis. Admin. Code § ATCP 134.08(4)	Lease or rental agreement cannot require tenant to pay landlord's attorneys' fees or costs incurred in any legal action or dispute arising under the agreement. This does not prevent the recovery of costs or attorneys' fees by a landlord or tenant pursuant to a court order in a small claims or other type of civil lawsuit.
Wyoming	No statute	

State Rules on Notice Required to Change or Terminate a Month-to-Month Tenancy

Except where noted, the amount of notice a landlord must give to increase rent or change another term of the rental agreement in month-to-month tenancy is the same as that required to end a month-to-month tenancy. Be sure to check state and local rent control laws, which might have different notice requirements.

State	Tenant	Landlord	Statute	Comments
Alabama	30 days	30 days	Ala. Code §§ 35-9A-302, 35-9A-441	A rule or regulation that substantially modifies the tenant's use of the rental isn't valid unless the tenant consents to it in writing.
Alaska	30 days	30 days	Alaska Stat. §§ 34.03.130, 34.03.290(b)	After giving reasonable notice, landlords may adopt new rules and regulations that don't substantially modify the rental agreement.
Arizona	30 days	30 days	Ariz. Rev. Stat. §§ 33-1342, 33-1375	After giving the tenant 30 days' notice, landlords may adopt new rules and regulations that don't substantially modify the rental agreement.
Arkansas	30 days	30 days	Ark. Code § 18-17-704	No state statute on the amount of notice required to change rent or other terms.
California	30 days	30 days to terminate if tenant has lived in property for under 12 months; if 12 months or longer, the landlord must have just cause to terminate. 30-90 days to change terms or increase rent, depending on size of increase.	Cal. Civ. Code §§ 827, 1946, 1946.2	At least 30 days' notice to change rental terms, but if the change is a proposed rent increase of more than 10% of the rental amount charged to that tenant at any time during the 12 months prior to the effective date of the increase, either in and of itself or when combined with any other rent increases for the 12 months prior to the effective date of the increase, then an additional 60 days' notice is required.
Colorado	21 days	21 days	Colo. Rev. Stat. §§ 13-40-107, 38-12-701, 38-12-702	No state statute on the amount of notice required to change rent or other terms, unless there is no written agreement, in which case the landlord must give 60 days' notice of a rent increase. For all tenancies, the landlord can increase the rent only once within any 12-month period of consecutive tenancy.
Connecticut		3 days	Conn. Gen. Stat. §§ 47a-9, 47a-23	Landlord must provide 3 days' notice to terminate tenancy. Landlord is not required to give a particular amount of notice of a proposed rent increase unless prior notice was previously agreed upon. If landlord makes a new rule or regulation resulting in a substantial modification of the rental agreement, it is not valid unless tenant agrees to it in writing.
Delaware	60 days	60 days	Del. Code tit. 25, §§ 5106, 5107	For termination, the 60-day notice period begins on the first day of the month following the day of actual notice. For change of terms, upon receiving notice of landlord's proposed change of terms tenant has 15 days to notify landlord of rejection of those terms and intent to terminate the lease. Otherwise, changes will take effect as announced.

State Rules on Notice Required to Change or Terminate a Month-to-Month Tenancy (continued)

State	Tenant	Landlord	Statute	Comments
District of Columbia	30 days	30–120 days, depending on reason for terminating the tenancy	D.C. Code §§ 42-3202, 42-3505.01, 42-3509.04(b)	No rent increases shall be effective until the first day on which rent is normally paid occurring more than 30 days after notice of the increase is given to the tenant. Landlords must have good reason (just cause) to terminate a month-to-month tenancy so long as the tenant is still paying rent.
Florida	15 days	15 days	Fla. Stat. § 83.57	No state statute on the amount of notice required to change rent or other terms.
Georgia	30 days	60 days	Ga. Code §§ 44-7-6, 44-7-7	No state statute on the amount of notice required to change rent or other terms.
Hawaii	28 days	45 days	Haw. Rev. Stat. §§ 521-21(d), 521-71	Landlord shall not increase rent without written notice given 45 consecutive days prior to the effective date of the increase. The landlord may terminate the rental agreement by notifying the tenant, in writing, at least 45 days in advance of the anticipated termination. The tenant may terminate the rental agreement by notifying the landlord, in writing, at least 28 days in advance of the anticipated termination.
Idaho	One month	One month to terminate; 15 or 30 days to change terms of tenancy.	Idaho Code §§ 55-208, 55-307	A "month" means a calendar month. For landlords: 30 days' notice to increase rent or end tenancy; 15 days' notice to change terms of lease other than rent.
Illinois	30 days	30 days	735 Ill. Comp. Stat. § 5/9-207	No state statute on the amount of notice required to change rent or other terms.
Indiana	One month	One month	Ind. Code §§ 32-31-5-4, 32-31-1-1	Unless agreement states otherwise, landlord must give 30 days' written notice to modify written rental agreement.
Iowa	30 days	30 days	Iowa Code §§ 562A.13(5), 562A.34	To end or change a month-to-month agreement, landlord must give written notice at least 30 days before the next time rent is due (not including any grace period). Each tenant shall be notified, in writing, of any rent increase at least 30 days before the effective date. Such effective date shall not be sooner than the expiration date of original rental agreement or any renewal or extension thereof.
Kansas	30 days	30 days	Kan. Stat. §§ 58-2556, 58-2570	After the tenant enters into the rental agreement, if a rule or regulation that effects a substantial modification of the rental agreement is adopted, such rule or regulation isn't enforceable against the tenant unless the tenant consents to it in writing.
Kentucky	30 days	30 days	Ky. Rev. Stat. §§ 383.610, 383.695	If a rule or regulation is adopted after the tenant enters into the rental agreement, which works a substantial modification of the bargain, it is not valid unless the tenant consents to it in writing.
Louisiana	10 days	10 days	La. Civ. Code Art. 2728	No state statute on the amount of notice required to change rent or other terms.

State Rules on Notice Required to Change or Terminate a Month-to-Month Tenancy (continued)

State	Tenant	Landlord	Statute	Comments
Maine	30 days	30 days	Me. Rev. Stat. tit. 14 §§ 6002, 6015	Landlord must provide 45 days' notice to increase rent.
Maryland	30 days	60 days	Md. Code Real Prop. § 8-402	These rules do not apply in Baltimore City.
Massachusetts	See comments	See comments	Mass. Gen. Laws ch. 186, § 12	Interval between days of payment or 30 days, whichever is longer.
Michigan	One month	One month	Mich. Comp. Laws § 554.134	No state statute on the amount of notice required to change rent or other terms.
Minnesota	See comments	See comments	Minn. Stat. §§ 504B.135, 504B.147	For terminations, notice period must be the interval between time rent is due or three months, whichever is less. If the lease provides a notice period for the landlord to end the tenancy that's different from the notice required by the tenant, the tenant can use either time period. The landlord can't give a notice to end the tenancy or raise the rent that is shorter than the time period for the tenant to give notice to end the tenancy.
Mississippi	30 days	30 days	Miss. Code §§ 89-8-11, 89-8-19	No state statute on the amount of notice required to change rent or other terms. A rule or regulation added or changed after the tenancy began is enforceable only if it does not substantially alter the terms of the tenancy and only when the landlord has given reasonable notice.
Missouri	One month	One month	Mo. Rev. Stat. § 441.060	No state statute on the amount of notice required to change rent or other terms.
Montana	30 days	30 days	Mont. Code §§ 70-24-441, 70-26-109	Landlord may change terms of tenancy with 15 days' notice.
Nebraska	30 days	30 days	Neb. Rev. Stat. §§ 76-1422, 76-1437	A rule or regulation adopted after the tenant enters into the rental agreement is enforceable if the landlord gives reasonable notice to tenant of its adoption and if it doesn't substantially modify the rental agreement.
Nevada	30 days	30 days	Nev. Rev. Stat. §§ 40.251, 118A.300	Landlords must provide 60 days' notice to increase rent. Tenants 60 years old or older, or physically or mentally disabled, may request an additional 30 days of possession, but only if they have complied with basic tenant obligations as set forth in Nev. Rev. Stat. Chapter 118A (termination notices must include this information).
New Hampshire	30 days	30 days	N.H. Rev. Stat. §§ 540:2, 540:3, 540:11	Landlord may terminate only for just cause. Tenant's termination: If the date of termination given in the notice does not coincide with the rent due date, tenant is responsible for the rent for the entire month in which the notice expires, up to the next rent due date, unless the terms of the rental agreement provide otherwise.

State Rules on Notice Required to Change or Terminate a Month-to-Month Tenancy (continued)

State	Tenant	Landlord	Statute	Comments
New Jersey	One month	One month	N.J. Stat. §§ 2A:18-56, 2A:18-61.1	Landlord may terminate only for just cause. The landlord may increase the rent only at the beginning of the term of the agreement. The landlord cannot increase the rent while an agreement exists. The landlord must offer the tenant the option of entering into a new agreement, at the increased rental rate, after the old agreement expires. If the tenant doesn't sign the new agreement and doesn't move at the expiration of the old agreement, and has been given a valid notice to quit and notice of rent increase, a new tenancy is automatically created at the increased rental rate. New Jersey landlords should check local ordinances, as they might have different rules regarding rent increase notice.
New Mexico	30 days	30 days	N.M. Stat. §§ 47-8-15(F), 47-8-23, 47-8-37	Landlord must deliver rent increase notice at least 30 days before rent due date. Landlord can change a rule or regulation in force when the tenancy began only after the landlord has given notice. Rules or regulations added after the tenancy began are enforceable only if they do not substantially alter the terms of the tenancy and only when the landlord has given notice.
New York	One month, within NYC and statewide	Within NYC and statewide, 30 to 90 days for terminations and rent increases of 5% or more	N.Y. Real Prop. Law §§ 226-c, 232-b	Terminations and rent increases of 5% over existing rent: Tenants occupying for a year or having a lease of at least one year: 30 days' notice. Tenants occupying from one to two years and lease holders of one- to two-year leases: 60 days' notice. Tenants occupying more than two years or having leases of two years or more: 90 days' notice.
North Carolina	7 days	7 days	N.C. Gen. Stat. § 42-14	No state statute on the amount of notice required to change rent or other terms.
North Dakota	One calendar month	One calendar month	N.D. Cent. Code §§ 47-16-07, 47-16-15	Landlord may change the terms of the lease to take effect at the expiration of the month upon giving notice in writing at least 30 days before the expiration of the month. Tenant may terminate with 25 days' notice if landlord has changed the terms of the agreement.
Ohio	30 days	30 days	Ohio Rev. Code § 5321.17	No state statute on the amount of notice required to change rent or other terms.
Oklahoma	30 days	30 days	Okla. Stat. tit. 41, §§ 111, 126	No state statute on the amount of notice required to change rent or other terms. Rules and regulations adopted after the start of the tenancy that substantially modify the terms of the rental are not valid or enforceable unless the tenant agrees in writing.

State Rules on Notice Required to Change or Terminate a Month-to-Month Tenancy (continued)

State	Tenant	Landlord	Statute	Comments
Oregon	30 days, or 72 hours (lack of bedroom exit only)	Termination: 30 days within the first year (except Portland and Milwaukie, which require a 90-day notice); 90 days after that, only for cause. A landlord with five or more residential dwelling units must also pay tenants the equivalent of one month's rent. Rent increase: See comments. Rules and regulations adopted after the start of the tenancy that substantially modify the terms of the rental are not valid or enforceable unless the tenant agrees in writing.	Or. Rev. Stat. §§ 90.262, 90.275, 90.323, 90.427, 90.460, 91.070	When the rental is in the same building or on the same property as the landlord's residence, and the property has no more than two dwelling units, unique termination periods and notice requirements apply. Temporary occupants are not entitled to notice. Rent cannot be increased during the first year of the tenancy. After that, the landlord must give at least 90 days' notice of an increase in rent, and the rent cannot be increased more than 7% plus the consumer price index (CPI) above the existing rent during any 12-month period. A landlord is exempt from the 7%+CPI increase limit if either: The unit's first certificate of occupancy was issued less than 15 years from the date of the rent increase notice, or the landlord accepts reduced rent as part of a federal, state, or local program or subsidy.
Pennsylvania		15 days	68 Pa. Stat. § 250.501	At the end of the term or due to a breach of the lease landlord must give 15 days' notice to terminate. If notice to terminate is due to tenant's failure to pay rent, notice required is 10 days.
Rhode Island	30 days	30 days	R.I. Gen. Laws §§ 34-18-16.1, 34-18-25, 34-18-37	Landlord must provide 30 days' notice to increase rent if tenant is age 62 or younger; if tenant is over 62 years old, landlord must provide 60 days' notice. Rules and regulations adopted after the start of the tenancy that substantially modify the terms of the rental are not valid or enforceable unless the tenant agrees in writing.
South Carolina	30 days	30 days	S.C. Code §§ 27-40-520, 27-40-770	Rules or regulations adopted after a tenant enters into a rental agreement do not apply to a tenant if the rules or regulations substantially modify the tenant's agreement with landlord and, after receiving notice upon adoption of the right to object, the tenant objects in writing to the landlord within 30 days after the rules are made.

State Rules on Notice Required to Change or Terminate a Month-to-Month Tenancy (continued)

State	Tenant	Landlord	Statute	Comments
South Dakota	One month	One month	S.D. Codified Laws §§ 43-8-8, 43-32-13	If tenant (or spouse or minor child) is in active duty in the military, landlord must give two months' notice (unless there is tenant misconduct, a sale of the property, or the property has passed into the landlord's estate). Landlord must give at least 30 days' notice to modify lease (including rent amount). Tenant may terminate lease within 15 days of receipt of the notice of modification.
Tennessee	30 days	30 days	Tenn. Code §§ 66-28-402, 66-28-512	A rule or regulation adopted after the tenant enters into the rental agreement is enforceable against the tenant if reasonable notice of its adoption is given and it does not work a substantial modification of the rental agreement.
Texas	One month	One month	Tex. Prop. Code §§ 91.001, 92.013	Landlord and tenant may agree in writing to different notice periods, or none at all. No state statute on the amount of notice required to change rent or other terms. A landlord shall give prior written notice to a tenant regarding a landlord rule or policy change that is not included in the lease agreement and that will affect any personal property owned by the tenant that is located outside the tenant's dwelling.
Utah		15 days	Utah Code § 78B-6-802	No state statute on the amount of notice required to change rent or other terms.
Vermont	One rental period, unless written lease says otherwise	30 days	Vt. Code tit. 9, §§ 4456(d), 4467	If there is no written rental agreement, for tenants who have continuously resided in the unit for two years or less, 60 days' notice to terminate; for those who have resided longer than two years, 90 days. If there is a written rental agreement, for tenants who have lived continuously in the unit for two years or less, 30 days; for those who have lived there longer than two years, 60 days.
Virginia	30 days	30 days	Va. Code §§ 55.1-1204, 55.1-1228, 55.1-1253	Rental agreement may provide for a different notice period. When a month-to-month tenant doesn't have a written lease, the law states that the lease is for 12 months by default, and its terms and conditions can be changed only by agreement of the parties. Rules and regulations changed or added after the start of the tenancy are valid only after landlord has given reasonable notice and they do not substantially modify the terms of the tenancy (substantial modifications are enforceable only after tenant has agreed in writing).

State Rules on Notice Required to Change or Terminate a Month-to-Month Tenancy (continued)

State	Tenant	Landlord	Statute	Comments
Washington	20 days before the end of the "rental period" (the rental period ends the day before rent is due); tenants who are members of the armed forces (as well as their spouses and dependents) may give less than 20 days' notice if they receive permanent change of station or deployment orders that don't allow a 20-day written notice.	Landlord must have a just cause, as enumerated in state law, to terminate a month-to-month tenancy, including one that has resulted from a lease-holding tenant remaining with the consent of the landlord (as a month-to-month tenant). Tenants whose leases are for 6 to 12 months may be terminated upon 60 days' notice in advance of the tenancy end date.	Wash. Rev. Code §§ 59.18.140, 59.18.200, 59.18.650	Landlord must give 60 days' notice to change rent, and any increase in rent may not become effective before the end of the term of the rental agreement, but if the rental is a subsidized tenancy, landlord can give 30 days' notice. If the landlord plans to change rental agreement to exclude children, the landlord shall give tenant at least 90 days' notice. All other changes require 30 days' written notice.
West Virginia	One month	One month	W.Va. Code § 37-6-5	No state statute on the amount of notice required to change rent or other terms.
Wisconsin	28 days	28 days	Wis. Stat. § 704.19	No state statute on the amount of notice required to change rent or other terms.
Wyoming			No statute	

State Rent Rules

Here are citations for statutes that set out rent rules in each state. When a state has no statute, the space is left blank. (See the "State Rules on Notice Required to Change or Terminate a Month-to-Month Tenancy" chart in this appendix for citations to raising rent.)

State	When Rent Is Due	Grace Period	Where Rent Is Due	Late Fees
Alabama	Ala. Code § 35-9A-161(c)		Ala. Code § 35-9A-161(c)	
Alaska	Alaska Stat. § 34.03.020(c)		Alaska Stat. § 34.03.020(c)	
Arizona	Ariz. Rev. Stat. §§ 33-1314(C), 33-1368(B)		Ariz. Rev. Stat. § 33-1314(C)	Ariz. Rev. Stat. § 33-1368(B) [1]
Arkansas	Ark. Code § 18-17-401	Ark. Code §§ 18-17-701 & 18-17-901	Ark. Code § 18-17-401	
California	Cal. Civ. Code § 1947		Cal. Civ. Code § 1962	*Orozco v. Casimiro*, 121 Cal. App.4th Supp. 7 (2004) [2]
Colorado		Colo. Rev. Stat. § 38-12-105(1)(a)		Colo. Rev. Stat. § 38-12-105(1)(b) [3]
Connecticut	Conn. Gen. Stat. § 47a-3a	Conn. Gen. Stat. § 47a-15a	Conn. Gen. Stat. § 47a-3a	Conn. Gen. Stat. §§ 47a-4(a)(8), 47a-15a [4]
Delaware	Del. Code tit. 25, § 5501(b)		Del. Code tit. 25, § 5501(b)	Del. Code tit. 25, § 5501(d) [5]
District of Columbia		D.C. Code § 42-3505.31		D.C. Code § 42-3505.31 [6]
Florida	Fla. Stat. § 83.46(1)			
Georgia	No statute [7]			
Hawaii	Haw. Rev. Stat. § 521-21(b)		Haw. Rev. Stat. § 521-21(b)	Haw. Rev. Stat. § 521-21(f) [8]
Idaho	No statute			
Illinois	735 Ill. Comp. Stat. § 5/9-218		735 Ill. Comp. Stat. § 5/9-218	
Indiana	*Watson v. Penn*, 8 N.E. 636 (Ind. 1886)			
Iowa	Iowa Code § 562A.9(3)		Iowa Code § 562A.9(3)	Iowa Code § 562A.9(3)(4) [9]

[1] Late fees must be set forth in a written rental agreement and be reasonable. (Arizona)

[2] Late fees must reflect landlord's actual damages; courts likely won't enforce a preset fee (liquidated damages clause). (California)

[3] Landlord can't charge tenant a late fee unless the rent payment is late by at least 7 calendar days. Late fee can't exceed the greater of $50 or 5% of the amount past due, and landlords must disclose late fees in lease or rental agreement. (Colorado)

[4] Landlords may not charge a late fee until 9 days after rent is due. (Connecticut)

[5] To charge a late fee, landlord must maintain an office in the county where the rental unit is located at which tenants can pay rent. If a landlord doesn't have a local office for this purpose, tenant has 3 extra days (beyond the due date) to pay rent before the landlord can charge a late fee. Late fee cannot exceed 5% of rent and cannot be imposed until the rent is more than 5 days late. (Delaware)

[6] Fee policy (including a statement of the maximum amount of late fees that may be charged) must be stated in the lease, and cannot exceed 5% of rent due or be imposed until rent is five days late (or later, if lease so provides). Landlord cannot evict for failure to pay late fee (may deduct unpaid fees from security deposit at end of tenancy). (District of Columbia)

[7] Although there is no specific statute regarding late fees, Georgia law states that all contracts for rent bear interest from the time rent is due. (Georgia)

[8] Late charge cannot exceed 8% of the amount of rent due. (Hawaii)

[9] When rent is $700 per month or less, late fees cannot exceed $12 per day, or a total amount of $60 per month; when rent is more than $700 per month, fees cannot exceed $20 per day or a total amount of $100 per month. (Iowa)

State	When Rent Is Due	Grace Period	Where Rent Is Due	Late Fees
		State Rent Rules (continued)		
Kansas	Kan. Stat. § 58-2545(c)		Kan. Stat. § 58-2545(c)	
Kentucky	Ky. Rev. Stat. § 383.565(2)		Ky. Rev. Stat. § 383.565(2)	
Louisiana	La. Civ. Code art. 2703		La. Civ. Code art. 2703	
Maine		Me. Rev. Stat. tit. 14, § 6028		Me. Rev. Stat. tit. 14, § 6028 [10]
Maryland				Md. Code Real Prop. § 8-208(d)(3) [11]
Massachusetts		Mass. Gen. Laws ch. 186, § 15B(1)(c); ch. 239, § 8A		Mass. Gen. Laws ch. 186, § 15B(1)(c) [12]
Michigan	*Hilsendegen v. Scheich*, 21 N.W. 894 (Mich. 1885)			
Minnesota				Minn. Stat. Ann. § 504B.177 [13]
Mississippi	No statute			
Missouri	Mo. Rev. Stat. § 535.060			
Montana	Mont. Code § 70-24-201(2)(c)		Mont. Code § 70-24-201(2)(b)	
Nebraska	Neb. Rev. Stat. § 76-1414(3)		Neb. Rev. Stat. § 76-1414(3)	
Nevada	Nev. Rev. Stat. § 118A.210		Nev. Rev. Stat. § 118A.200	Nev. Rev. Stat. §§ 118A.200, 118A.210(4) [14]
New Hampshire				N.H. Rev. Stat. § 540:8 [15]
New Jersey		N.J. Stat. § 2A:42-6.1	N.J. Stat. § 2A:42-6.1	N.J. Stat. § 2A:42-6.1 [16]
New Mexico	N.M. Stat. § 47-8-15(B)		N.M. Stat. § 47-8-15(B)	N.M. Stat. § 47-8-15(D) [17]

[10] Late fees cannot exceed 4% of the amount due for 30 days. Landlord must notify tenants, in writing, of any late fee at the start of the tenancy, and cannot impose it until rent is 15 days late. (Maine)

[11] Late fees cannot exceed 5% of the rent due. (Maryland)

[12] Late fees, including interest on late rent, may not be imposed until the rent is 30 days late.(Massachusetts)

[13] Late fee policy must be agreed to in writing, and may not exceed 8% of the overdue rent payment. The "due date" for late fee purposes does not include a date earlier than the usual rent due date, by which date a tenant earns a discount. (Minnesota)

[14] A court will presume that there's no late fee provision unless it's included in a written rental agreement, but the landlord can offer evidence to overcome that presumption. Landlord may charge a reasonable late fee as set forth in the rental agreement, but it cannot exceed 5% of the amount of the periodic rent, and the maximum amount of the late fee must not be increased based upon a late fee that was previously imposed. For tenancies that are longer than week-to-week, landlords can't charge a late fee until at least three calendar days after the rent due date. (Nevada)

[15] Landlord cannot demand an amount greater than the whole rent in arrears when rent is late. (New Hampshire)

[16] Landlord must wait 5 business days before charging a late fee, but only when the premises are rented or leased by senior citizens receiving Social Security Old Age Pensions, Railroad Retirement Pensions, or other governmental pensions in lieu of Social Security Old Age Pensions; or when rented by recipients of Social Security Disability Benefits, Supplemental Security Income, or benefits under Work First New Jersey. (New Jersey)

[17] Late fee policy must be in the lease or rental agreement and may not exceed 10% of the rent specified per rental period. Landlord must notify the tenant of the landlord's intent to impose the charge no later than the last day of the next rental period immediately following the period in which the default occurred. (New Mexico)

State	When Rent Is Due	Grace Period	Where Rent Is Due	Late Fees
New York		N.Y. Real Prop. Law § 238-a		N.Y. Real Prop. Law § 238-a [18]
North Carolina		N.C. Gen. Stat. § 42-46		N.C. Gen. Stat. § 42-46 [19]
North Dakota	N.D. Cent. Code § 47-16-20			
Ohio				*Campus Village Toledo Univ. Park, LLC v. Mowrer*, 68 N.E.3d 219 (Ohio App. 2016); Ohio Rev. Code § 5321.14 [20]
Oklahoma	Okla. Stat. tit. 41, § 109		Okla. Stat. tit. 41, § 109	*Sun Ridge Investors, Ltd. v. Parker*, 956 P.2d 876 (1998) [21]
Oregon	Or. Rev. Stat. § 90.220	Or. Rev. Stat. § 90.260	Or. Rev. Stat. § 90.220	Or. Rev. Stat. § 90.260 [22]
Pennsylvania	No statute			
Rhode Island	R.I. Gen. Laws § 34-18-15(c)	R.I. Gen. Laws § 34-18-35	R.I. Gen. Laws § 34-18-15(c)	
South Carolina	S.C. Code § 27-40-310(c)		S.C. Code § 27-40-310(c)	
South Dakota	S.D. Codified Laws § 43-32-12			
Tennessee	Tenn. Code § 66-28-201(c)	Tenn. Code § 66-28-201(d)	Tenn. Code § 66-28-201(c)	Tenn. Code § 66-28-201(d) [23]
Texas		Tex. Prop. Code § 92.019		Tex. Prop. Code §§ 92.019, 92.0191 [24]
Utah				Utah Code § 57-22-4(5) [25]
Vermont	Vt. Stat. tit. 9, § 4455			
Virginia	Va. Code § 55.1-1204	Va. Code § 55.1-1204	Va. Code § 55.1-1204	Va. Code § 55.1-1204 [26]

[18] Landlord must wait five days after the rent due date before imposing a late fee. A late fee may not be more than $50 or 5% of the rent, whichever is less. (New York)

[19] Late fee when rent is due monthly cannot be higher than $15 or 5% of the rental payment, whichever is greater (when rent is due weekly, may not be higher than $4.00 or 5% of the rent, whichever is greater); and may not be imposed until the rent is 5 days late. A late fee may be imposed only one time for each late rental payment. A late fee for a specific late rental payment may not be deducted from a subsequent rental payment so as to cause the subsequent rental payment to be in default. (North Carolina)

[20] Late fees won't be enforced if a court finds that they are an "unconscionable penalty." (Ohio)

[21] Reasonable late fees are allowed, but "per-day" or similar charges intended as penalties—rather than actual expenses—are invalid. (Oklahoma)

[22] Landlord must wait 4 days after the rent due date before imposing a late fee, and must disclose the late fee policy in the rental agreement. A flat fee must be "reasonable." A daily late fee may not be more than 6% of a reasonable flat fee, and cannot add up to more than 5% of the monthly rent. (Oregon)

[23] Landlord can't charge a late fee until the rent is 5 days late (the day rent is due is counted as the first day). If day five is a Sunday or legal holiday, landlord cannot impose a fee if the rent is paid on the next business day. Fee can't exceed 10% of the amount past due. (Tennessee)

[24] Late fee provision must be included in a written lease and cannot be imposed until the rent remains unpaid two full days after the date it is due. The fee must be reasonable: For properties that have four or fewer units, it cannot be more than 12% of the rent; for properties that have more than four units, it cannot be more than 10% of the rent; OR it must be related to the late payment of rent (such as expenses, costs, and overhead associated with the collection of late payment). Landlord may charge an initial fee and a daily fee for each day the rent is late--the combined fees are considered a single late fee. Tenants can ask landlords to provide a statement of whether they owe late fees. (Texas)

[25] Late fees can't exceed the greater of 10% of the rent agreed to in the lease or rental agreement, or $75. The fee must be disclosed in the lease or rental agreement unless the lease or rental agreement is month-to-month and the landlord provides the renter a 15-day notice of the charge. (Utah)

[26] Landlords cannot charge a tenant a late fee unless it is provided for in a written rental agreement or lease. No late charge shall exceed the lesser of 10% of the periodic rent or 10% of the remaining balance due and owed by the tenant. (Virginia)

		State Rent Rules (continued)		
State	**When Rent Is Due**	**Grace Period**	**Where Rent Is Due**	**Late Fees**
Washington		Wash. Rev. Code § 59.18.170		Wash. Rev. Code § 59.18.285 [27]
West Virginia	No statute			
Wisconsin				Wis. Adm. Code § ATCP 134.09(8) [28]
Wyoming	No statute			

[27] Nonrefundable fees must be described in lease or rental agreement; otherwise, they will be considered to be deposits. Landlords may not impose late fees until the rent is more than five days late. The fee may commence as of the first day the rent is overdue, and landlords may serve a notice to pay rent or quit as soon as the rent is overdue. If tenants can demonstrate in writing that their primary source of income is a regular, monthly source of governmental assistance that is not received until after the date rent is due in the rental agreement, landlords must adjust rental due date (to no more than five days after the date specified in the rental agreement). (Washington)

[28] Late fee policy must be in the rental agreement, landlord must first apply any prepaid rent (such as last month's rent) to the unpaid rent, and landlord may not charge a fee or impose a penalty for failure to pay the late rent fee. (Wisconsin)

State Security Deposit Rules

Here are the statutes and rules that govern a landlord's collection and retention of security deposits. Many states require landlords to disclose, at or near the time they collect the deposit, information about how deposits may be used, as noted in the Disclosure or Requirement section. Required disclosures of other issues, such as a property's history of flooding, are in the chart, "Required Landlord Disclosures."

Alabama

Ala. Code § 35-9A-201

Limit: One month's rent, except for pet deposits, deposits to cover undoing tenant's alterations, and deposits to cover tenant activities that pose increased liability risks.

Deadline for Landlord to Itemize and Return Deposit: 60 days after termination of tenancy and delivery of possession.

Alaska

Alaska Stat. § 34.03.070

Limit: Two months' rent, unless rent exceeds $2,000 per month. Landlord may ask for an additional month's rent as deposit for a pet that is not a service animal, but may use it only to remedy pet damage.

Disclosure or Requirement: Orally or in writing, landlord must disclose the conditions under which landlord may withhold all or part of the deposit.

Separate Account: Required (but may commingle prepaid rent with security deposits).

Advance Notice of Deduction: Not required.

Deadline for Landlord to Itemize and Return Deposit: 14 days if the tenant gives proper notice to terminate tenancy; 30 days if the tenant does not give proper notice or if landlord has deducted amounts needed to remedy damage caused by tenant's failure to maintain the property (Alaska Stat. § 34.03.120).

Arizona

Ariz. Rev. Stat. § 33-1321

Limit: One and one-half months' rent.

Disclosure or Requirement: If landlord collects a non- refundable fee, its purpose must be stated in writing. All fees not designated as nonrefundable are refundable.

Advance Notice of Deduction: Not required.

Deadline for Landlord to Itemize and Return Deposit: 14 days (excluding Saturdays, Sundays, and legal holidays); tenant has the right to be present at final inspection.

Arkansas

Ark. Code §§ 18-16-301 to 18-16-305

Exemption: Security deposit rules do not apply to landlords who own five or fewer units unless the management of the rental (including rent collection) is performed by a third party for a fee.

Limit: Two months' rent, but this limit does not apply to landlords who own 5 or fewer properties, unless the landlord has hired a third party to manage the property.

Advance Notice of Deduction: Not required.

Deadline for Landlord to Itemize and Return Deposit: 60 days.

California

Cal. Civ. Code §§ 1940.5(g), 1950.5

Limit: Two months' rent (unfurnished); three months' rent (furnished). If the tenant is an active service member, no more than one month's rent (unfurnished) or two months' rent (furnished). Add extra one-half month's rent for waterbed.

Advance Notice of Deduction: Required.

Deadline for Landlord to Itemize and Return Deposit: 21 days.

Colorado

Colo. Rev. Stat. §§ 38-12-102 to 38-12-104

Limit: No statutory limit.

Advance Notice of Deduction: Not required.

Deadline for Landlord to Itemize and Return Deposit: One month, unless lease agreement specifies longer period of time (which may be no more than 60 days); 72 hours (not counting weekends or holidays) if a hazardous condition involving gas equipment requires tenant to vacate.

State Security Deposit Rules (continued)

Connecticut

Conn. Gen. Stat. § 47a-21

Limit: Two months' rent (tenant younger than 62 years of age); one month's rent (tenant 62 years of age or older). Tenants who paid a deposit in excess of one month's rent, who then turn 62 years old, are entitled, upon request, to a refund of the amount that exceeds one month's rent.

Separate Account: Required.

Interest Payment: Interest payments must be made annually (or credited toward rent, at the landlord's option) and no later than 30 days after termination of tenancy. The interest rate must be equal to the average rate paid on savings deposits by insured commercial banks, rounded to the nearest 0.1%, as published by the Federal Reserve Board Bulletin.

Advance Notice of Deduction: Not required.

Deadline for Landlord to Itemize and Return Deposit: 30 days, or within 15 days of receiving tenant's forwarding address, whichever is later.

Delaware

Del. Code tit. 25, §§ 5311, 5514

Limit: One month's rent on leases for one year or more. For month-to-month tenancies, no limit for the first year, but after that, the limit is one month's rent (at the expiration of one year, landlord must give tenant a credit for any deposit held by the landlord that is in excess of one month's rent). No limit for furnished units. Tenant may offer to supply a surety bond in lieu of or in conjunction with a deposit, which landlord may elect to receive.

Separate Account: Required. Orally or in writing, the landlord must disclose to the tenant the location of the security deposit account.

Advance Notice of Deduction: Not required.

Deadline for Landlord to Itemize and Return Deposit: 20 days.

District of Columbia

D.C. Code § 42-3502.17; D.C. Mun. Regs. tit. 14, §§ 308 to 310

Exemption: Landlords cannot demand or receive a security deposit from a tenant in a rental unit occupied by the tenant as of July 17, 1985, when no security deposit had been required prior to that date.

Limit: One month's rent.

Disclosure or Requirement: In the lease, rental agreement, or receipt, landlord must state the terms and conditions under which the security deposit was collected (to secure tenant's obligations under the lease or rental agreement).

Separate Account: Required.

Interest Payment: Required. Interest payments at the prevailing statement savings rate must be made at termination of tenancy.

Advance Notice of Deduction: Not required.

Deadline for Landlord to Itemize and Return Deposit: 45 days.

Florida

Fla. Stat. §§ 83.43(12), 83.49

Limit: No statutory limit.

Disclosure or Requirement: Within 30 days of receiving the security deposit, the landlord must disclose in writing whether it will be held in an interest- or non-interest-bearing account; the name of the account depository; and the rate and time of interest payments. Landlord who collects a deposit must include in the lease the disclosure statement contained in Florida Statutes § 83.49.

Separate Account: Required. Landlord may post a security bond securing all tenants' deposits instead.

Interest Payment: Required. Interest payments, if any (account need not be interest bearing) must be made annually and at termination of tenancy. However, no interest is due a tenant who wrongfully terminates the tenancy before the end of the rental term.

State Security Deposit Rules (continued)

Advance Notice of Deduction: Required.

Deadline for Landlord to Itemize and Return Deposit: 15 to 60 days depending on whether tenant disputes deductions.

Georgia

Ga. Code §§ 44-7-30 to 44-7-37

Exemption: Landlord who owns ten or fewer rental units, unless these units are managed by an outside party, need not supply written list of preexisting damage, nor place deposit in an escrow account. Rules for returning the deposit still apply.

Limit: No statutory limit.

Disclosure or Requirement: Landlord must give tenant a written list of preexisting damage to the rental before collecting a security deposit.

Separate Account: Required. Landlord must place the deposit in an escrow account in a state- or federally regulated depository, and must inform the tenant of the location of this account. Landlord may post a security bond securing all tenants' deposits instead.

Advance Notice of Deduction: Required.

Deadline for Landlord to Itemize and Return Deposit: 30 days.

Hawaii

Haw. Rev. Stat. § 521-44

Limit: One month's rent. (Landlord may require an additional one month's rent as security deposit for tenants who keep a pet.)

Advance Notice of Deduction: Not required.

Deadline for Landlord to Itemize and Return Deposit: 14 days.

Idaho

Idaho Code § 6-321

Limit: No statutory limit.

Separate Account: Required. Security deposits for rentals that are managed by a third-party property manager must be held in a separate account at a federally insured financial institution. The account must be separate from the operating account. (These rules don't apply to managers who are owners, who have a real estate license, or who are nonprofit entities.)

Advance Notice of Deduction: Not required.

Deadline for Landlord to Itemize and Return Deposit: 21 days or up to 30 days if landlord and tenant agree.

Illinois

765 Ill. Comp. Stat. 710/1; 715/1 to 715/3

Limit: No statutory limit.

Disclosure or Requirement: If a lease specifies the cost for repair, cleaning, or replacement of any part of the leased premises; or the cleaning or repair of any component of the building or common area that will not be replaced, the landlord may withhold the dollar amount specified in the lease. Landlord's itemized statement must reference the specified dollar amount(s) and include a copy of the lease clause.

Interest Payment: Landlords who rent 25 or more units in either a single building or a complex located on contiguous properties must pay interest on deposits held for more than six months. The interest rate is the rate paid for minimum deposit savings accounts by the largest commercial bank in the state, as of December 31 of the calendar year immediately preceding the start of the tenancy. Within 30 days after the end of each 12-month rental period, landlord must pay any interest that has accumulated to an amount of $5 or more, by cash or credit applied to rent due, except when the tenant is in default under the terms of the lease. Landlord must pay all interest that has accumulated and remains unpaid, regardless of the amount, upon termination of the tenancy.

Advance Notice of Deduction: Not required.

Deadline for Landlord to Itemize and Return Deposit: For properties with 5 or more units, 30 to 45 days, depending on whether tenant disputes deductions or if statement and receipts are furnished.

State Security Deposit Rules (continued)

Indiana

Ind. Code §§ 32-31-3-1.1 to 32-31-3-19

Exemption: Does not apply to rental agreements entered into before July 1, 1989.

Limit: No statutory limit.

Advance Notice of Deduction: Not required.

Deadline for Landlord to Itemize and Return Deposit: 45 days.

Iowa

Iowa Code § 562A.12

Limit: Two months' rent.

Separate Account: Required.

Interest Payment: Interest payment, if any (account need not be interest bearing), must be made at termination of tenancy. Interest earned during first five years of tenancy belongs to landlord.

Advance Notice of Deduction: Not required.

Deadline for Landlord to Itemize and Return Deposit: 30 days.

Kansas

Kan. Stat. §§ 58-2548, 58-2550

Limit: One month's rent (unfurnished); one and one-half months' rent (furnished); for pets, add extra one-half month's rent.

Advance Notice of Deduction: Not required.

Deadline for Landlord to Itemize and Return Deposit: 14 days after the determination of the amount of any deductions, but in no event longer than 30 days after the end of the tenancy.

Kentucky

Ky. Rev. Stat. § 383.580

Limit: No statutory limit.

Disclosure or Requirement: Orally or in writing, landlord must disclose where the security deposit is being held and the account number.

Before accepting a security deposit, landlords must give tenants a list of preexisting damage that would justify a charge against the deposit, including the amount of the charge. Tenants have the right to inspect before taking possession. Both parties must sign the list, and if tenants disagree with its accuracy, they must state in writing the basis for their disagreement and sign the statement of dissent. A mutually signed listing is conclusive proof of the listed defects, but not as to latent (unobservable) defects.

Separate Account: Required.

Advance Notice of Deduction: Required.

Deadline for Landlord to Itemize and Return Deposit: 30 to 60 days depending on whether tenant disputes deductions.

Louisiana

La. Rev. Stat. § 9:3251

Limit: No statutory limit.

Advance Notice of Deduction: Not required.

Deadline for Landlord to Itemize and Return Deposit: One month.

Maine

Me. Rev. Stat. tit. 14, §§ 6031 to 6038

Exemption: Entire security deposit law does not apply to rental unit that is part of structure with five or fewer units, one of which is occupied by landlord.

Limit: Two months' rent.

Disclosure or Requirement: Upon request by the tenant, landlord must disclose orally or in writing the account number and the name of the institution where the security deposit is being held.

Separate Account: Required.

Advance Notice of Deduction: Not required.

Deadline for Landlord to Itemize and Return Deposit: 30 days (if written rental agreement) or 21 days (if tenancy at will).

Maryland

Md. Code Real Prop. §§ 8-203, 8-203.1, 8-208

Limit: Two months' rent.

Exemption: Security deposit statutes do not apply to a tenancy arising after the sale of owner-occupied residential property where the seller and purchaser agree that the seller may remain in possession of the property for not more than 60 days after the settlement.

State Security Deposit Rules (continued)

Separate Account: Required. Landlord may hold all tenants' deposits in secured certificates of deposit, or in securities issued by the federal government or the State of Maryland.

Interest Payment: For security deposits of $50 or more, when landlord has held the deposit for at least six months: Within 45 days of termination of tenancy, interest must be paid at the daily U.S. Treasury yield curve rate for 1 year, as of the first business day of each year, or 1.5% a year, whichever is greater, less any damages rightfully withheld. Interest accrues monthly but is not compounded, and no interest is due for any period less than one month. (See the Department of Housing and Community Development website for a calculator.) Deposit must be held in a Maryland banking institution.

Advance Notice of Deduction: Required.

Deadline for Landlord to Itemize and Return Deposit: 45 days.

Massachusetts

Mass. Gen. Laws ch. 186, § 15B

Limit: One month's rent.

Exemption: Security deposit rules do not apply to any lease, rental, occupancy, or tenancy of 100 days or less in duration, which lease or rental is for a vacation or recreational purpose.

Disclosure or Requirement: At the time of receiving a security deposit, landlord must furnish a receipt indicating the amount of the deposit; the name of the person receiving it and, if received by a property manager, the name of the lessor for whom the security deposit is received; the date on which it is received; and a description of the premises leased or rented. The receipt must be signed by the person receiving the security deposit.

Separate Account: Required. Within 30 days of receiving security deposit, landlord must disclose the name and location of the bank in which the security deposit has been deposited, and the amount and account number of the deposit.

Interest Payment: Landlord must pay tenant 5% interest per year or the amount received from the bank (which must be in Massachusetts) that holds the deposit. Interest should be paid yearly, and within 30 days of termination date. Interest will not accrue for the last month for which rent was paid in advance.

Advance Notice of Deduction: Not required.

Deadline for Landlord to Itemize and Return Deposit: 30 days.

Michigan

Mich. Comp. Laws §§ 554.602 to 554.616

Limit: One and one-half months' rent.

Disclosure or Requirement: Within 14 days of tenant's taking possession of the rental, landlord must furnish in writing the landlord's name and address for receipt of communications, the name and address of the financial institution or surety where the deposit will be held, and the tenant's obligation to provide in writing a forwarding mailing address to the landlord within 4 days after termination of occupancy. The notice shall include the following statement in 12-point boldface type that is at least 4 points larger than the body of the notice or lease agreement: "You must notify your landlord in writing within 4 days after you move of a forwarding address where you can be reached and where you will receive mail; otherwise your landlord shall be relieved of sending you an itemized list of damages and the penalties adherent to that failure."

Separate Account: Required. Landlord must place deposits in a regulated financial institution, and may use the deposits as long as the landlord deposits with the secretary of state a cash or surety bond.

Advance Notice of Deduction: Required. Tenants must dispute the landlord's stated deductions within 7 days of receiving the itemized list and balance, if any, or give up any right to dispute them.

Deadline for Landlord to Itemize and Return Deposit: 30 days.

State Security Deposit Rules (continued)

Minnesota

Minn. Stat. §§ 504B.151, 504B.175, 504B.178, 504B.195

Limit: No statutory limit. If landlord collects a "prelease deposit" and subsequently rents to tenant, landlord must apply the prelease deposit to the security deposit.

Disclosure or Requirement: Before collecting rent or a security deposit, landlord must provide a copy of all outstanding inspection orders for which a citation has been issued, pertaining to a rental unit or common area, specifying code violations that threaten the health or safety of the tenant, and all outstanding condemnation orders and declarations that the premises are unfit for human habitation. Citations for violations that do not involve threats to tenant health or safety must be summarized and posted in an obvious place. With some exceptions, landlord who has received notice of a contract for deed cancellation or notice of a mortgage foreclosure sale must so disclose before entering a lease, accepting rent, or accepting a security deposit; and must furnish the date on which the contract cancellation period or the mortgagor's redemption period ends.

Interest Payment: Landlord must pay 1% simple, noncompounded interest per year. (Deposits collected before 8/1/03 earn interest at 3%, up to 8/1/03, then begin earning at 1%.) Any interest amount less than $1 is excluded.

Advance Notice of Deduction: Not required.

Deadline for Landlord to Itemize and Return Deposit: Three weeks after tenant leaves and landlord receives forwarding address; five days if tenant must leave due to building condemnation.

Mississippi

Miss. Code § 89-8-21

Limit: No statutory limit.

Advance Notice of Deduction: Not required.

Deadline for Landlord to Itemize and Return Deposit: 45 days.

Missouri

Mo. Stat. § 535.300

Limit: Two months' rent.

Advance Notice of Deduction: Not required.

Deadline for Landlord to Itemize and Return Deposit: 30 days.

Montana

Mont. Code §§ 70-25-101 to 70-25-206

Limit: No statutory limit.

Disclosure or Requirement: Before signing a lease, landlords must give tenants a signed statement of the physical condition of the premises, including a statement (if applicable) that the premises have never been leased. Upon request, landlords must furnish a separate written statement of the damage and cleaning charges of the departing tenants. Landlords who fail to comply may not deduct any sums for damage or cleaning unless the landlord can establish by "clear and convincing evidence" that the tenant, tenant's family, licensees, or invitees were responsible.

Advance Notice of Deduction: Required. Tenant is entitled to advance notice of cleaning charges, but only if such cleaning is required as a result of tenant's negligence and is not part of the landlord's cyclical cleaning program.

Deadline for Landlord to Itemize and Return Deposit: 30 days; 10 days if no deductions.

Nebraska

Neb. Rev. Stat. § 76-1416

Limit: One month's rent (no pets); one and one-quarter months' rent (pets).

Advance Notice of Deduction: Not required.

Deadline for Landlord to Itemize and Return Deposit: 14 days.

Nevada

Nev. Rev. Stat. §§ 118A.240 to 118A.250

Exemption: Security deposit rules do not apply to the following, among others: (1) Occupancy under a contract of sale of a dwelling unit or the property of which it is a part, if the occupant is the purchaser or a person who succeeds to the purchaser's interest; (2) Occupancy by an employee of a landlord whose right to occupancy is conditional upon employment

State Security Deposit Rules (continued)

in and about the premises; (3) Occupancy by a person who is guilty of a forcible entry or forcible detainer.

Limit: Three months' rent; if both landlord and tenant agree, tenant may use a surety bond for all or part of the deposit.

Disclosure or Requirement: Lease or rental agreement must explain the conditions under which the landlord will refund the deposit.

Advance Notice of Deduction: Not required.

Deadline for Landlord to Itemize and Return Deposit: 30 days.

New Hampshire

N.H. Rev. Stat. §§ 540-A:5 to 540-A:8; 540-B:10

Exemption: Entire security deposit law does not apply to landlord who leases a single-family residence and owns no other rental property, or landlord who leases rental units in an owner-occupied building of five units or fewer (exemption does not apply to any individual unit in owner-occupied building that is occupied by a person 60 years of age or older).

Limit: One month's rent or $100, whichever is greater; when landlord and tenant share facilities, no statutory limit.

Disclosure or Requirement: Unless tenant has paid the deposit by personal or bank check, or by a check issued by a government agency, landlord must provide a receipt stating the amount of the deposit and the institution where it will be held. Regardless of whether a receipt is required, landlord must inform tenant that if tenant finds any conditions in the rental in need of repair, tenant may note them on the receipt or other written instrument, and return either within five days.

Separate Account: Required. Upon request, landlord must disclose the account number, the amount on deposit, and the interest rate. Landlord may post a bond covering all deposits instead of putting deposits in a separate account.

Interest Payment: Landlord who holds a security deposit for a year or longer must pay interest at a rate equal to the rate paid on regular savings accounts in the New Hampshire bank, savings & loan, or credit union where it's deposited. If a landlord mingles security deposits in a single account, the landlord must pay the actual interest earned proportionately to each tenant. A tenant may request the interest accrued every three years, 30 days before that year's tenancy expires. The landlord must comply with the request within 15 days of the expiration of that year's tenancy.

Advance Notice of Deduction: Not required.

Deadline for Landlord to Itemize and Return Deposit: 30 days; for shared facilities, if the deposit is more than 30 days' rent, landlord must provide written agreement acknowledging receipt and specifying when deposit will be returned—if no written agreement, 20 days after tenant vacates.

New Jersey

N.J. Stat. §§ 46:8-19 to 46:8-26

Exemption: Security deposit law does not apply to owner-occupied buildings with not more than two rental units where the tenant has failed to provide 30 days' written notice to the landlord invoking the law.

Separate Account: Required. Within 30 days of receiving the deposit and every time the landlord pays the tenant interest, landlord must disclose the name and address of the banking organization where the deposit is being held, the type of account, current rate of interest, and the amount of the deposit.

Interest Payment: Landlord with 10 or more units must invest deposits as specified by statute or place deposit in an insured money market fund account, or in another account that pays quarterly interest at a rate comparable to the money market fund. Landlords with fewer than 10 units may place deposit in an interest-bearing account in any New Jersey financial institution insured by the FDIC. All landlords may pay tenants interest earned on account annually or credit toward payment of rent due.

Advance Notice of Deduction: Not required.

Deadline for Landlord to Itemize and Return Deposit: 30 days; within five days if tenant has to move out due to fire, flood, condemnation, or evacuation.

State Security Deposit Rules (continued)

New Mexico

N.M. Stat. § 47-8-18

Exemption: Security deposit rules do not apply to the following, among others: (1) Occupancy under a contract of sale of a dwelling unit or the property of which it is a part, if the occupant is the purchaser or a person who succeeds to the purchaser's interest; (2) Occupancy by an employee of an owner pursuant to a written rental or employment agreement that specifies that the employee's right to occupancy is conditional upon employment in and about the premises.

Limit: One month's rent (for rental agreement of less than one year); no limit for leases of one year or more.

Interest Payment: Landlord who collects a deposit larger than than one month's rent on a year's lease must pay interest, on an annual basis, equal to the passbook interest.

Advance Notice of Deduction: Not required.

Deadline for Landlord to Itemize and Return Deposit: 30 days.

New York

N.Y. Gen. Oblig. Law §§ 7-103 to 7-108

Limit: One month's limit for units other than those subject to the City Rent and Rehabilitation Law or the Emergency Housing Rent Control Law.

Disclosure or Requirement: If deposit is placed in a bank, landlord must disclose the name and address of the banking organization where the deposit is being held, and the amount of such deposit.

Separate Account: Required. Statute requires that deposits not be commingled with landlord's personal assets, but does not explicitly require placement in a banking institution (however, deposits collected in buildings of six or more units must be placed in New York bank accounts).

Interest Payment: Landlord who rents out non-regulated units in buildings with five or fewer units need not pay interest. Interest must be paid at the prevailing rate on deposits received from tenants who rent units in buildings containing six or more units. The landlord in every rental situation may retain an administrative fee of 1% per year on the sum deposited. Interest can be subtracted from the rent, paid at the end of the year, or paid at the end of the tenancy according to the tenant's choice.

Advance Notice of Deduction: Required.

Deadline for Landlord to Itemize and Return Deposit: 14 days.

North Carolina

N.C. Gen. Stat. §§ 42-50 to 42-56

Exemption: Not applicable to rentals of single rooms.

Limit: One and one-half months' rent for month-to-month rental agreements; two months' rent if term is longer than two months; may also charge a reasonable, nonrefundable pet deposit.

Disclosure or Requirement: Within 30 days of the beginning of the lease term, landlord must disclose the name and address of the banking institution where the deposit is located or the name of the insurance company providing the bond.

Separate Account: Required. The landlord may choose to furnish a bond from an insurance company licensed to do business in N.C. rather than deposit the security deposit in a trust account.

Advance Notice of Deduction: Not required.

Deadline for Landlord to Itemize and Return Deposit: 30 days; if landlord's claim against the deposit cannot be finalized within that time, landlord may send an interim accounting and a final accounting within 60 days of the tenancy's termination.

North Dakota

N.D. Cent. Code § 47-16-07.1

Limit: One month's rent. If tenant has a pet, an additional pet deposit of up to $2,500 or two months' rent, whichever is greater. To encourage renting to persons with records of felony convictions, landlords may charge these applicants up to two months' rent as security. Applicants who have had court judgments entered against them "for violating the terms of a

State Security Deposit Rules (continued)

previous rental agreement" can also be charged up to two months' rent (this appears to refer to prior evictions and might not apply to evictions based on conduct not prohibited by the rental agreement).

Separate Account: Required.

Interest Payment: Landlord must pay interest if the period of occupancy is at least nine months. Money must be held in a federally insured interest-bearing savings or checking account for benefit of the tenant. Interest must be paid upon termination of the lease.

Advance Notice of Deduction: Not required.

Deadline for Landlord to Itemize and Return Deposit: 30 days.

Ohio

Ohio Rev. Code § 5321.16

Limit: No statutory limit.

Interest Payment: Any deposit in excess of $50 or one month's rent, whichever is greater, must bear interest on the excess at the rate of 5% per annum if the tenant stays for six months or more. Interest must be paid annually and upon termination of tenancy.

Advance Notice of Deduction: Not required.

Deadline for Landlord to Itemize and Return Deposit: 30 days.

Oklahoma

Okla. Stat. tit. 41, § 115

Limit: No statutory limit.

Separate Account: Required.

Advance Notice of Deduction: Not required.

Deadline for Landlord to Itemize and Return Deposit: 45 days.

Oregon

Or. Rev. Stat. § 90.300

Exemption: Security deposit rules do not apply to the following, among others: (1) Occupancy of a unit for no more than 90 days by a purchaser prior to the scheduled closing of a real estate sale or by a seller following the closing of a sale, in either case

as permitted under the terms of an agreement for sale of a dwelling unit or the property of which it is a part (a tenant who holds but has not exercised an option to purchase the unit does not qualify for this exemption); (2) Vacation occupancy; (3) Occupancy by an employee of a landlord whose right to occupancy is conditional upon employment in and about the premises.

Limit: No statutory limit. Landlord may not impose or increase deposit within first year unless parties agree to modify the rental agreement to allow for a pet or other cause, and the imposition or increase relates to that modification.

Disclosure or Requirement: Landlord must provide a receipt for any security deposit the tenant pays.

Advance Notice of Deduction: Not required.

Deadline for Landlord to Itemize and Return Deposit: 31 days.

Pennsylvania

68 Pa. Cons. Stat. §§ 250.511a to 250.512

Limit: Two months' rent for first year of renting; one month's rent during second and subsequent years of renting.

Disclosure or Requirement: For deposits over $100, landlord must deposit them in a federally or state-regulated institution, and give tenant the name and address of the banking institution and the amount of the deposit.

Separate Account: Required. Instead of placing deposits in a separate account, landlord may purchase a bond issued by a bonding company authorized to do business in the state.

Interest Payment: Tenant who occupies rental unit for two or more years is entitled to interest beginning with the 25th month of occupancy. Landlord must pay tenant interest (minus 1% fee) at the end of the third and subsequent years of the tenancy.

Advance Notice of Deduction: Not required.

Deadline for Landlord to Itemize and Return Deposit: 30 days.

State Security Deposit Rules (continued)

Rhode Island

R.I. Gen. Laws § 34-18-19

Exemption: Security deposit rules do not apply to the following, among others: (1) Occupancy under a contract of sale of a dwelling unit or the property of which it is a part, if the occupant is the purchaser or a person who succeeds to the purchaser's interest; (2) Occupancy by a paid employee of a landlord, whose right to occupancy is conditional upon employment substantially for services, maintenance, or repair of premises containing more than 11 units.

Limit: One month's rent (unfurnished); if furnished, separate furniture security deposit up to one month's rent if furnishings' replacement value at the start of the tenancy is $5,000 or more.

Advance Notice of Deduction: Not required.

Deadline for Landlord to Itemize and Return Deposit: 20 days.

South Carolina

S.C. Code § 27-40-410

Exemption: Security deposit rules do not apply to the following, among others: (1) Occupancy under a contract of sale of a dwelling unit or the property of which it is a part, if the occupant is the purchaser or a person who succeeds to the purchaser's interest; (2) Occupancy by an employee of a landlord whose right to occupancy is conditional upon employment in and about the premises; (3) Certain vacation rentals.

Limit: No statutory limit.

Advance Notice of Deduction: Not required.

Deadline for Landlord to Itemize and Return Deposit: 30 days.

South Dakota

S.D. Codified Laws §§ 43.32-6.1, 43-32-24

Limit: One month's rent (higher deposit may be charged if special conditions pose a danger to maintenance of the premises).

Advance Notice of Deduction: Not required.

Deadline for Landlord to Itemize and Return Deposit: Two weeks, and must supply reasons for withholding any portion; 45 days for a written, itemized accounting, if tenant requests it.

Tennessee

Tenn. Code § 66-28-301

Limit: No statutory limit.

Separate Account: Required. Orally or in writing, landlord must disclose the location of the separate account (but not the account number) used by landlord for the deposit.

Advance Notice of Deduction: Required.

Deadline for Landlord to Itemize and Return Deposit: No statutory deadline.

Texas

Tex. Prop. Code §§ 92.101 to 92.111

Limit: No statutory limit. Landlord may choose to offer the tenant the option to pay a nonrefundable fee in lieu of a security deposit. See Tex. Prop. Code § 92.111.

Disclosure or Requirement: If a security deposit isn't required by the lease or rental agreement, but the tenant is liable for damage or rent when they leave, the landlord must notify the tenant in writing about the claim before reporting the claim. Landlords who don't provide notice forfeit the right to collect damages and charges from the tenant.

Advance Notice of Deduction: Not required.

Deadline for Landlord to Itemize and Return Deposit: 30 days. Landlord need not refund deposit until the tenant gives the landlord a forwarding address. If landlord wants to condition the refund of the security deposit on the tenant's giving advance notice of surrender, landlord must put this condition in the lease, and it must be either underlined or printed in conspicuous bold print.

Utah

Utah Code §§ 57-17-1 to 57-17-5

Limit: No statutory limit.

Disclosure or Requirement: For written leases or rental agreements only, if part of the deposit is nonrefundable, landlord must disclose this feature.

State Security Deposit Rules (continued)

Advance Notice of Deduction: Not required.

Deadline for Landlord to Itemize and Return Deposit: 30 days.

Vermont

Vt. Stat. tit. 9, § 4461

Exemption: Security deposit rules do not apply to the following, among others: (1) Occupancy under a contract of sale of a dwelling unit or the property of which it is a part, if the occupant is the purchaser or a person who succeeds to the purchaser's interest; (2) Occupancy of a dwelling unit without right or permission by a person who is not a tenant.

Limit: No statutory limit.

Advance Notice of Deduction: Not required.

Deadline for Landlord to Itemize and Return Deposit: 14 days; 60 days if the rental is seasonal and not intended as the tenant's primary residence.

Virginia

Va. Code §§ 55.1-1204, 55.1-1206, 55.1-1208, 55.1-1226

Limit: Two months' rent. Alternatively, landlord may permit a tenant to provide damage insurance coverage in an amount not more than two months' rent in lieu of the payment of a security deposit. The damage insurance coverage must meet the requirements listed in Virginia Code Annotated sections 55.1-1226(I)-(K).

Advance Notice of Deduction: Not required.

Deadline for Landlord to Itemize and Return Deposit: 45 days after termination date or the date the tenant vacates, whichever occurs last; 30 days to itemize any deductions to be made during the course of the tenancy (45 days if the deductions exceed the amount of the security deposit). Lease can provide for expedited processing at the end of the tenancy and specify an administrative fee for such processing, which will apply only if tenant requests it with a separate written document. Landlord must give tenant written notice of tenant's right to be present at a final inspection.

Washington

Wash. Rev. Code §§ 59.18.260 to 59.18.285; 59.18.610; 59.18.670

Limit: Landlords must allow tenants to pay the deposit and fees in installments (does not apply if the deposit and any nonrefundable fees are less than 25% of the monthly rent, or the landlord has not demanded the last month's rent). Tenants with tenancies of three months or more may pay in three equal and consecutive installments, beginning at the start of the tenancy; two installments for shorter tenancies. Installment schedules must be written and signed. Does not apply to holding deposits (which may not be more than 25% of the first month's rent). Landlord may offer to waive the security deposit and instead collect a monthly fee, but cannot require tenant to opt for the fee. Landlord cannot consider tenants choice when deciding whether to approve or deny tenants rental application. Tenant may opt to pay a deposit during the tenancy. Various written disclosures concerning insurance and tenant's liability for damage must be made.

Disclosure or Requirement: In the lease, landlord must disclose the circumstances under which all or part of the deposit may be withheld. No deposit may be collected unless the rental agreement is in writing and a written checklist or statement specifically describing the condition and cleanliness of or existing damages to the premises and furnishings is provided to the tenant at the start of the tenancy.

The landlord must provide tenant with a written receipt for the deposit and provide the name, address, and location of where the deposit will be kept; if location changes, landlord must notify tenant. Nonrefundable fees must be identified as such in a written rental agreement. If landlords fail to provide a written agreement, tenants are entitled to the return of the fee. If the written agreement does not specify that the fee is refundable, it must be treated as a refundable deposit.

State Security Deposit Rules (continued)

Separate Account: Required.

Advance Notice of Deduction: Not required.

Deadline for Landlord to Itemize and Return Deposit: 21 days.

West Virginia

W.Va. Code §§ 37-6A-1 to 37-6A-6

Exemption: Agreements for the payment of security deposits entered into before June 10, 2011.

Limit: No statutory limit.

Deadline for Landlord to Itemize and Return Deposit: 60 days from the date the tenancy has terminated, or within 45 days of the occupancy of a subsequent tenant, whichever is shorter. If the damage exceeds the amount of the security deposit and the landlord has to hire a contractor to fix it, the notice period is extended 15 days.

Wisconsin

Wis. Admin. Code ATCP 134.04, 134.06; Wis. Stat. § 704.28

Exemption: Security deposit rules do not apply to the following, among others: (1) A dwelling unit occupied, under a contract of sale, by the purchaser of the dwelling unit or the purchaser's successor in interest; (2) A dwelling unit which the landlord provides free of charge to any person; (3) A dwelling unit that the landlord provides as consideration to a person whom the landlord currently employs to operate or maintain the premises.

Limit: No statutory limit.

Disclosure or Requirement: Before accepting the deposit, landlord must inform tenant of tenant's inspection rights, disclose all habitability defects and show tenant any outstanding building and housing code violations, inform tenant of the means by which shared utilities will be billed, and inform tenant if utilities are not paid for by landlord.

Advance Notice of Deduction: Not required.

Deadline for Landlord to Itemize and Return Deposit: 21 days.

Wyoming

Wyo. Stat. §§ 1-21-1207, 1-21-1208

Limit: No statutory limit.

Disclosure or Requirement: Lease or rental agreement must state whether any portion of a deposit is nonrefundable, and landlord must give tenant written notice of this fact when collecting the deposit.

Advance Notice of Deduction: Not required.

Deadline for Landlord to Itemize and Return Deposit: 30 days, when applying it to unpaid rent (or within 15 days of receiving tenant's forwarding address, whichever is later); additional 30 days allowed for deductions due to damage.

Required Landlord Disclosures

Many states require landlords to inform tenants of important state laws or individual landlord policies, either in the lease or rental agreement or in another writing. Common disclosures include a landlord's imposition of nonrefundable fees (where permitted), tenants' rights to move-in checklists, and the identity of the landlord or landlord's agent or manager. Disclosures concerning the security deposit are in the chart, "State Security Deposit Rules."

Also, keep in mind that landlords in *all* states must disclose information about lead-based paint to tenants if the building they are renting was built before 1978. See Chapter 1, "Lead Disclosures," for details.

Alabama

Ala. Code § 35-9A-202

Owner or agent identity: Landlord must disclose to the tenant in writing at or before the commencement of the tenancy the name and address of the person authorized to manage the premises, and an owner of the premises or a person authorized to act for and on behalf of the owner for the purpose of service of process and for the purpose of receiving notices and demands. (Exception: does not apply to resident purchaser under a contract of sale (but does apply to a resident who has an option to buy), nor to the continuation of occupancy by the seller or a member of the seller's family for a period of not more than 36 months after the sale of a dwelling unit or the property of which it is a part.)

Alaska

Alaska Stat. §§ 34.03.080, 34.03.150

Owner or agent identity: Landlord must disclose to the tenant in writing at or before the commencement of the tenancy the name and address of the person authorized to manage the premises, and an owner of the premises or a person authorized to act for and on behalf of the owner for the purpose of service of process and for the purpose of receiving notices and demands. (Alaska Stat. § 34.03.080)

Extended absence: The rental agreement must require that the tenant notify the landlord of an anticipated extended absence from the premises in excess of seven days; however, the notice maybe given as soon as reasonably possible after the tenant knows the absence will exceed seven days. (Alaska Stat. § 34.03.150)

Arizona

Ariz. Rev. Stat. Ann. §§ 33-1314, 33-1314.01,33-1319, 33-1321, 33-1322, 36-1637

Nonrefundable fees permitted? Yes. The purpose of all nonrefundable fees or deposits must be stated in writing. Any fee or deposit not designated as nonrefundable is refundable. (Ariz. Rev. Stat. Ann. § 33-1321)

Move-in checklist required? Yes. Tenants also have the right to be present at a move-out inspection. (Ariz. Rev. Stat. Ann. § 33-1321)

Separate utility charges: If landlord charges separately for gas, water, wastewater, solid waste removal, or electricity by installing a submetering system, landlord may recover the charges imposed on the landlord by the utility provider, plus an administrative fee for the landlord for actual administrative costs only, and must disclose separate billing and fee in the rental agreement. If landlord uses a ratio utility billing system, the rental agreement must contain a specific description of the ratio utility billing method used to allocate utility costs. (Ariz. Rev. Stat. Ann. § 33-1314.01)

Owner or agent identity: Landlord must disclose to the tenant in writing at or before the commencement of the tenancy the name and address of the person authorized to manage the premises, and an owner of the premises or a person authorized to act for and on behalf of the owner for the purpose of service of process and for the purpose of receiving notices and demands. (Ariz. Rev. Stat. Ann. § 33-1322)

Business tax pass-through: If the landlord pays a local tax based on rent and that tax increases, landlord may pass through the increase by increasing the rent upon 30 days' notice (but not before the new tax is effective), but only if the landlord's right to adjust the rent is disclosed in the rental agreement. (Ariz. Rev. Stat. Ann. § 33-1314)

Required Landlord Disclosures (continued)

Availability of landlord and tenant act: Landlord must inform tenant in writing that the Residential Landlord and Tenant Act is available on the Arizona Department of Housing's website. (Ariz. Rev. Stat. Ann. § 33-1322)

Bed bug information: Landlords must provide existing and new tenants with educational materials on bed bugs, including information and physical descriptions, prevention and control measures, behavioral attraction risk factors, information from federal, state, and local centers for disease control and prevention, health or housing agencies, nonprofit housing organizations, or information developed by the landlord. (Ariz. Rev. Stat. Ann. § 33-1319)

Smoke detectors: Landlords must install smoke detectors and give tenant written notification of tenant's responsibilities (tenant must maintain it unless tenant gives written notification to the landlord of its malfunction, at which point landlord must maintain it). (Ariz. Rev. Stat. Ann. § 36-1637)

Arkansas

Ark. Code Ann. § 18-17-502

Move-in checklist required? Yes.

Must checklist rights be stated in the lease? No.

Checklist: To show compliance with the law of implied warranty of habitability, landlord must provide tenant with a written form in which the tenant can note any habitability-related defects. The landlord is deemed to be in compliance if the tenant signs and returns the form without noting any defects or fails to return the form within two business days. Applies to leases and rental agreements entered into or renewed after November 1, 2021.

California

Cal. Civ. Code §§ 1710.2, 1940.6, 1940.7, 1940.8, 1940.9, 1946.2, 1947.5, 1947.12, 1950.5(m), 1954.603, 2079.10a; Cal. Bus. & Prof. Code § 8538; Cal. Health & Safety Code §§ 25400.28, 26147, 26148; Cal. Gov't. Code § 8589.45

Nonrefundable fees permitted? No. (Cal. Civ. Code § 1950.5(m))

Move-in checklist required? No.

Registered sexual offender database: Landlords must include this notice in every lease or rental agreement: "Notice: Pursuant to Section 290.46 of the Penal Code, information about specified registered sex offenders is made available to the public via an Internet Web site maintained by the Department of Justice at www.meganslaw.ca.gov. Depending on an offender's criminal history, this information will include either the address at which the offender resides or the community of residence and ZIP Code in which the offender resides." (Cal. Civ. Code § 2079.10a)

Tenant paying for others' utilities: Prior to signing a rental agreement, landlord must disclose whether gas or electric service to tenant's unit also serves other areas, and must disclose the manner by which costs will be fairly allocated. (Cal. Civ. Code § 1940.9)

Ordnance locations: Prior to signing a lease, landlord must disclose known locations of former federal or state ordnance in the neighborhood (within one mile of rental). (Cal. Civ. Code § 1940.7)

Mold: Prior to signing a rental agreement, landlord must provide written disclosure when landlord knows, or has reason to know, that mold exceeds permissible exposure limits or poses a health threat. Landlords must distribute a consumer handbook, developed by the State Department of Health Services, describing the potential health risks from mold. (Cal. Health & Safety Code §§ 26147, 26148)

Pest control service: When the rental agreement is signed, landlord must provide tenant with any pest control company disclosure landlord has received, which describes the pest to be controlled, pesticides used and their active ingredients, a warning that pesticides are toxic, and the frequency of treatment under any contract for periodic service. (Cal. Civ. Code § 1940.8; Cal. Bus. & Prof. Code § 8538)

Intention to demolish rental unit: Landlords or their agents who have applied for a permit to demolish a rental unit must give written notice of this fact to prospective tenants, before accepting any deposits or screening fees. (Cal. Civ. Code § 1940.6)

Required Landlord Disclosures (continued)

No-smoking policy: For leases and rental agreements signed after January 1, 2012: If the landlord prohibits or limits the smoking of tobacco products on the rental property, the lease or rental agreement must include a clause describing the areas where smoking is limited or prohibited (does not apply if the tenant has previously occupied the dwelling unit). For leases and rental agreements signed before January 1, 2012: A newly adopted policy limiting or prohibiting smoking is a change in the terms of the tenancy (will not apply to lease-holding tenants until they renew their leases; tenants renting month-to-month must be given 30 days' written notice). Does not preempt any local ordinances prohibiting smoking in effect on January 1, 2012. (Cal. Civ. Code § 1947.5)

Flooding: In leases or rental agreements signed after July 1, 2018, landlord must disclose, in at least eight-point type, that the property is in a special flood hazard area or an area of potential flooding if the landlord has actual knowledge of this fact. Actual knowledge includes receipt from a public agency so identifying the property; the fact that the owner carries flood insurance; or that the property is in an area in which the owner's mortgage holder requires the owner to carry flood insurance. Disclosure must advise tenant that additional information can be had at the Office of Emergency Services' website, and must include the internet address for the MYHazards tool maintained by the Office. Disclosure must advise tenant that owner's insurance will not cover loss to tenant's property, and must recommend that tenant consider purchasing renters' insurance that will cover loss due to fire, flood, or other risk of loss. Disclosure must note that the owner is not required to provide additional information. (Cal. Gov't. Code § 8589.45)

Bed bug information: Before signing a lease or rental agreement, landlord must give potential tenants information about bed bugs, including information about their behavior and biology, the importance of cooperation for prevention and treatment, and the importance of prompt written reporting of suspected infestations to the landlord. (Cal. Civ. Code § 1954.603)

Methamphetamine or Fentanyl: If a property has been contaminated and is subject to a remediation order, landlord must provide written notice of and a copy of the order to all prospective tenants who have submitted an application. The tenant has to acknowledge receipt of the notice in writing before signing a rental agreement, and the landlord must attach the notice to the rental agreement. If a landlord fails to provide this notice, the prospective tenant can void the rental agreement.

For the rental of mobile homes and manufactured homes, the landlord must notify prospective tenants, in writing, of all methamphetamine or fentanyl laboratory activities that have taken place in the mobile home or manufactured home, and any remediation of the home or vehicle, and the property can't be rented until the prospective tenant is provided with a copy of the order. If there is already a tenant, the landlord must attach the notice and order to the rental agreement. (Cal. Health & Safety Code § 25400.28)

Death on the premises within the past three years: If an occupant died on the property within three years of the landlord's offer to rent, the landlord must disclose this fact. Landlords are not required to disclose that an occupant of that property was living with human immunodeficiency virus (HIV) or died from AIDS-related complications. (Cal. Civ. Code § 1710.2)

Single-family tenancy subject to the Tenant Protection Act of 2019: Landlords of single-family rentals that are not subject to the Tenant Protection Act of 2019 must put the following notice in the lease or rental agreement: "This property is not subject to the rent limits imposed by Section 1947.12 of the Civil Code and is not subject to the just cause requirements of Section 1946.2 of the Civil Code. This property meets the requirements of Sections 1947.12 (d)(5) and 1946.2 (e)(8) of the Civil Code and the owner is not any of the following: (1) a real estate investment trust, as defined by Section 856 of the Internal Revenue Code; (2) a corporation; or (3) a limited liability company in which at least one member is a corporation." (Cal. Civ. Code §§ 1946.2(e)(8), 1947.12)

Required Landlord Disclosures (continued)

Single-family tenancy subject to the Tenant Protection Act of 2019, owner move-in: For tenancies subject to the Tenant Protection Act, landlord may terminate the lease in order to move in the owner or the owners spouse, domestic partner, children, grandchildren, parents, or grandparents. If the lease was entered into on or after July 1, 2020, though, the landlord can terminate the lease for this reason only when the tenant agrees in writing OR when the lease specifies that the owner can terminate the lease for this reason. (Cal. Civ. Code § 1946.2(b)(2)(A))

Tenancies subject to the Tenant Protection Act of 2019: Owners of rentals subject to the Tenant Protection Act of 2019 must provide the following as a written notice to tenants or include it in the written lease or rental agreement: "California law limits the amount your rent can be increased. See Section 1947.12 of the Civil Code for more information. California law also provides that after all of the tenants have continuously and lawfully occupied the property for 12 months or more or at least one of the tenants has continuously and lawfully occupied the property for 24 months or more, a landlord must provide a statement of cause in any notice to terminate a tenancy. See Section 1946.2 of the Civil Code for more information." The notice must be in at least 12-point type. (Cal. Civ. Code § 1946.2(f))

Colorado

Colo. Rev. Stat. Ann. §§ 38-12-801, 38-12-903, 38-12-904, 38-12-1005

Disclosure of landlord: Written rental agreements and leases must include a statement of the name and address of the person who is the landlord or the landlord's authorized agent. If this person's identity changes, the tenants must be notified of the new contact person within one business day after the change, and the landlord must post the identity of the new landlord or authorized agent in a conspicuous location on the rental premises. (Colo. Rev. Stat. Ann. § 38-12-801)

Bed bugs: Upon request from prospective tenants, landlords must disclose whether the unit for rent contained bed bugs within the previous eight months. If requested, landlords must also disclose the last date (if any) the unit being rented was inspected for, and found to be free of, bed bugs. (Colo. Rev. Stat. Ann. § 38-12-1005)

Rental application fee: Landlords who collect a rental application fee must disclose the anticipated expenses for which the fee will be used or itemize the actual expenses incurred. When landlords charge application fees based on the average cost of processing rental applications, they must explain how they determined the average rental application fee. (Colo. Rev. Stat. Ann. § 38-12-903)

Rental application denial: Landlords who deny rental applications must give rejected applicants a written notice of the denial that states the reasons for the denial. If a landlord cannot site the specific screening criteria because of the use of a proprietary screening system, the landlord must instead provide the rejected applicant with a copy of the report from the screening company. Landlords can provide electronic versions of the denial notice, but must provide a paper denial notice upon request. Landlords must make a good-faith effort to provide the notice within 20 calendar days of the denial. (Colo. Rev. Stat. Ann. § 38-12-904)

Connecticut

Conn. Gen. Stat. Ann. §§ 47a-3e, 47a-3f, 47a-6, 47a-7a

Common interest community: When rental is in a common interest community, landlord must give tenant written notice before signing a lease. (Conn. Gen. Stat. Ann. § 47a-3e)

Owner or agent identity: Before the beginning of the tenancy, landlord must disclose the name and address of the person authorized to manage the premises and the person who is authorized to receive all notices, demands, and service of process. (Conn. Gen. Stat. Ann. § 47a-6)

Required Landlord Disclosures (continued)

Bed bug information: Landlords may not advertise a unit that the landlord knows or reasonably suspects is infested with bed bugs. Before signing a lease, landlords must tell prospective tenants whether the unit (or any contiguous unit owned or subleased by the landlord) is infested. If asked by tenants or prospective tenants, landlords must disclose the last date on which the rental unit was inspected for bed bugs and found to be free of any infestation. (Conn. Stat. Ann. § 47a-7a)

Fire system information: When renting a dwelling unit in a building required to be equipped with a fire sprinkler system pursuant to any statute or regulation, the landlord of such dwelling unit must include notice in the rental agreement as to the existence or nonexistence of an operative fire sprinkler system in such building, and such notice shall be printed in not less than twelve-point boldface type of uniform font. If there is an operative fire sprinkler system in the building, the rental agreement will also state the last date of maintenance and inspection, in not less than twelve-point boldface type of uniform font. (Conn. Stat. Ann. § 47a-3f)

Well water testing: If the premises uses water from a private or semi-private well constructed after October 1, 2022, landlord must submit water quality tests to the Department of Public Health and tell applicants about the availability of literature on the Departments website. Tenants leasing agent or landlord (if tenant has no agent) must give tenant copies of the Departments recommendations for testing. (Conn. Stat. Ann. § 19a-37)

Delaware

Stoltz Management Co. v. Phillip, 593 A.2d 583 (1990); *Del. Code Ann. tit. 25, §§ 5105, 5311, 5312, 5317, 5318*

Nonrefundable fees permitted? No, except for an optional service fee for actual services rendered, such as a pool fee or tennis court fee. Tenant may elect, subject to the landlord's acceptance, to purchase an optional surety bond instead of or in combination with a security deposit. (*Stoltz Management Co. v.*

Phillip, 593 A.2d 583 (1990); Del. Code Ann. tit. 25, § 5311)

Owner or agent identity: On each written rental agreement, the landlord must prominently disclose the names and usual business addresses of all persons who are owners of the rental unit or the property of which the rental unit is a part, or the names and business addresses of their appointed resident agents. (25 Del. Code § 5105)

Summary of landlord-tenant law: A summary of the Landlord-Tenant Code, as prepared by the Consumer Protection Unit of the Attorney General's Office or its successor agency, must be given to the new tenant at the beginning of the rental term. If the landlord fails to provide the summary, the tenant may plead ignorance of the law as a defense. (25 Del. Code § 5118)

Bed bug information: Before showing or renting a unit, landlords must inspect rentals for evidence of bed bugs and may not show or rent units that the landlord knows or has reason to know are infested. Landlords must tell prospective tenants whether adjacent units are infested with or are being treated for an infestation. (25 Del. Code § 5317)

Separate utility metering: Landlords may install meters for the purposes of separately charging individual units for utility services, but can only bill tenants according to these measurements if the rental agreement discloses the existence and use of meters. (25 Del. Code § 5312)

District of Columbia

D.C. Code Ann. §§ 42-3502.22, 42-3505.31; DC ST §§ 42-3502.22, 42-3531.01 and following; 12 D.C. Mun. Regs. § PM-704G; 14 D.C. Mun. Regs. § 300

Nonrefundable fees permitted? Yes. (D.C. Code Ann. § 42-3502.22

General disclosures: Upon receiving a rental application, landlords must provide on a disclosure form published by the Rent Administrator (or in another suitable format until a form is published) along with supporting documents each of the following : (a) the units rental rate; (b) any pending

Required Landlord Disclosures (continued)

petitions filed that could affect the rental unit, including petitions for rent increases during the following 12 months; (c) any surcharges on the rent (including capital improvement surcharges) and the date they expire; (d) the frequency of possible rent increases; (e) the rent-controlled or exempt status of the rental, its business license, and a copy of the registration or claim of exemption (and any recent related filings) ; (f) all copies of code violation reports for the rental within the last 12 months, or previously issued reports for violations which have not been abated; (g) the Rent Administrators pamphlet that explains rent increases and petitions that can be filed; (h) the amount of any nonrefundable application fee; (i) the amount of the security deposit, the interest rate on the security deposit, and how the security deposit will be returned when the tenant vacates the unit; (j) ownership information; (k) information about the presence of mold in the rental unit or common areas in the previous three years, unless the mold has been remediated by certified and licensed indoor mold remediation professional; (l) the voter registration packet developed by the D.C. Board of Elections (this packet should be part of the Rent Administrators disclosure form, but if it has not been included in the form, the landlord should provide the packet if one exists); and (m) a copy of the current Tenant Bill of Rights published by the Office of the Tenant Advocate.

Landlords must give written notice to each tenant, on a form published by the Rent Administrator (or in another suitable format until a form is published), that the disclosure forms and documents for the tenants rental unit are available for inspection. The written notice must include the location of the disclosure forms and a table of contents laying out the categories of information included in the disclosure forms.

Upon a tenant's written request not more than once per calendar year, the landlord, within 10 business days of the request, must also disclose the amount of, and the basis for, each rent increase for the prior three years. If applicable, the disclosure

must identify any substantially identical rental unit on which a vacancy increase was based. (D.C. Code § 42-3502.22)

Rental regulations: At the start of every new tenancy, landlord must give tenant a copy of the District of Columbia Municipal Regulations, CDCR Title 14, Housing, Chapter 3, Landlord and Tenant; and a copy of Title 14, Housing, Chapter 1, § 101 (Civil Enforcement Policy) and Chapter 1, § 106 (Notification of Tenants Concerning Violations). (14 D.C. Mun. Regs. § 300))

Late fees: Landlords can charge late rent fees only if the maximum amount of the late fee that may be charged is disclosed in the written lease or rental agreement. (D.C. Code § 42-3505.31)

Fire alarms: In buildings with four or more rental, rooming, or sleeping units (including condominium or cooperative units), owners must conspicuously post (and give to each tenant) written information on the following: How to operate manual alarm boxes, how to respond when smoke detectors activate (including abandoning the dwelling unit, closing its door, and activating the nearest alarm box), information on whether the building is monitored by a supervising station, and instructions on calling 911. (12 D.C. Mun. Regs. § PM-704G)

Fees and data: Before requesting information or fees from applicants, landlords must disclose amount and purpose of fees or deposits, whether mandatory or voluntary, and whether refundable. Must describe the types of information requested, the landlords automatic and optional denial criteria, and the tenants right to specified information about any credit or consumer report. Landlords must furnish data on the number of units that will become available over a specified time (or, if such data is not available, the number of units available over the prior fiscal year). Must tell applicants that the landlord will approve or deny their application within a stated number of days after receiving it. Tenants must be told of their right to dispute a decision allegedly based on inaccurate information or the landlords use of prohibited criteria (landlords must respond); and

Required Landlord Disclosures (continued)

of their right to file a complaint with the Office of Human Rights or the Superior Court, if they think the landlord has violated these provisions. (D.C. Code § 42-3505.10)

Must fee policy be stated in rental agreement? Yes.

Bed bug information: Landlords may not offer rentals that they know or have reason to know contain bed bugs. If the building has had an infestation within the previous 120 days, before signing a rental agreement the landlord must give tenants the Department of Buildings form, on which specified information must be disclosed. (D.C. Code § 42-3551.02)

Florida

Fla. Stat. Ann. §§ 83.50, 404.056

Nonrefundable fees permitted? Yes, no statute directly on point, but by custom, nonrefundable fees are allowed.

Landlord identity: The landlord, or a person authorized to enter into a rental agreement on the landlord's behalf, must disclose in writing to the tenant, at or before the commencement of the tenancy, the name and address of the landlord or a person authorized to receive notices and demands on the landlord's behalf. (Fla. Stat. Ann. § 83.50)

Radon: In all leases, landlord must include this warning: "RADON GAS: Radon is a naturally occurring radioactive gas that, when it has accumulated in a building in sufficient quantities, may present health risks to persons who are exposed to it over time. Levels of radon that exceed federal and state guidelines have been found in buildings in Florida. Additional information regarding radon and radon testing may be obtained from your county health department." (Fla. Stat. Ann. § 404.056)

Georgia

Ga. Code Ann. §§ 44-1-16, 44-7-3, 44-7-20, 44-7-30, 44-7-33

Nonrefundable fees permitted? Yes. Landlord and tenant may agree that certain prepaid sums, covering future rent or services or utilities supplied to the tenant, will not be returned to the tenant at the end of the tenancy. (Ga. Code Ann. § 44-7-30)

Move-in checklist required? Yes. Landlords cannot collect a security deposit unless they have given tenants a list of preexisting damages. Landlord must provide tenant with a comprehensive list of any existing damage to the premises before the tenant gives landlord a security deposit. (Ga. Code Ann. § 44-7-33)

Flooding: Before signing a lease, if the living space or attachments have been damaged by flooding three or more times within the past five years, landlord must so disclose in writing. (Ga. Code Ann. § 44-7-20)

Owner or agent identity: When or before a tenancy begins, landlord must disclose in writing the names and addresses of the owner of record (or a person authorized to act for the owner) for purposes of service of process and receiving and receipting demands and notices; and the person authorized to manage the premises. If such information changes during the tenancy, landlord must advise tenant within 30 days in writing or by posting a notice in a conspicuous place. (Ga. Code Ann. § 44-7-3)

Former residents, crimes: Unless asked by a prospective tenant, landlord does not have to disclose whether the rental was the site of a homicide or other felony, or a suicide or a death by accidental or natural causes; or whether it was occupied by a person who was infected with a virus or any other disease that has been determined by medical evidence as being highly unlikely to be transmitted through the occupancy of a dwelling place presently or previously occupied by such an infected person. However, if a prospective tenant asks about any of these things, landlord must answer truthfully to the best of the landlord's individual knowledge. (Ga. Code Ann. § 44-1-16)

Hawaii

Haw. Rev. Stat. §§ 521-42, 521-43

Nonrefundable fees permitted? No.

Must fee policy be stated in the rental agreement? No.

Other fees: The landlord may not require or receive from or on behalf of a tenant at the beginning of a rental agreement any money other than the money for the first month's rent and a security deposit as provided in this section.

Required Landlord Disclosures (continued)

Move-in checklist required? Yes. (Haw. Rev. Stat. § 521-42)

Owner or agent identity: Landlord must disclose name of owner or agent; if owner lives in another state or on another island, landlord must disclose name of agent on the island. (Haw. Rev. Stat. § 521-43)

Tax excise number: Landlord must furnish its tax excise number so that tenant can file for a low-income tax credit. (Haw. Rev. Stat. § 521-43)

Idaho

No disclosure statutes.

Illinois

Utilities: *765 Ill. Comp. Stat. § 740/5*
Rent concessions: *765 Ill. Comp. Stat. §§ 730/0.01 to 730/6*
Radon: *720 Ill. Comp. Stat. §§ 46/15, 46/25*
Smoke detectors: *425 Ill. Comp. Stat. § 60/3(d)*
Carbon monoxide alarms: *430 Ill. Comp. Stat. § 135/10(c)*

Utilities: Where tenant pays a portion of a master metered utility, landlord must give tenant a copy in writing either as part of the lease or another written agreement of the formula used by the landlord for allocating the public utility payments among the tenants. (765 Ill. Comp. Stat. § 740/5)

Rent concessions: Any rent concessions must be described in the lease, in letters not less than one-half inch in height consisting of the words "Concession Granted," including a memorandum on the margin or across the face of the lease stating the amount or extent and nature of each such concession. Failure to comply is a misdemeanor. (765 Ill. Comp. Stat. §§ 730/0.01 to 730/6)

Radon: Landlords are not required to test for radon, but if the landlord tests and learns that a radon hazard is present in the dwelling unit, landlord must disclose this information to current and prospective tenants. If a tenant notifies a landlord that a radon test indicates the existence of a radon hazard in the rental unit, landlord must disclose that risk to any prospective tenant of that unit, unless a subsequent test by the landlord shows that a radon hazard does not exist. Requirements do not apply if the dwelling unit is on the third or higher story above ground level, or when the landlord has undertaken mitigation work and a subsequent test shows that a radon hazard does not exist. (720 Ill. Comp. Stat. §§ 46/15, 46/25)

Smoke detectors: Landlord must give one tenant per dwelling written information about smoke detector testing and maintenance. (425 Ill. Comp. Stat. § 60/3(d))

Carbon monoxide alarms: Landlord must give one tenant per dwelling written information regarding CO alarm testing and maintenance. (430 Ill. Comp. Stat. § 135/10(c))

Indiana

Ind. Code Ann. § 8-1-2-1.2, 32-31-1-21, 32-31-3-18, 32-31-5-7

Agent identity: Landlord's agent must disclose in writing the name and address of a person living in Indiana who is authorized to manage the property and to act as the owner's agent. (Ind. Code Ann. § 32-31-3-18)

Smoke detectors: Landlord must require the tenant to acknowledge in writing that the rental unit is equipped with a functional smoke detector. (Ind. Code Ann. § 32-31-5-7)

Floodplain disclosure: If the lowest floor of a rental structure (including a basement) is at or below the 100-year frequency flood elevation, the landlord must disclose in the lease that the structure is located in a floodplain. (Ind. Code Ann. § 32-31-1-21)

Water or sewage disposal services: A landlord who pays for water, sewage disposal, or both, and who passes the costs on to tenants must describe the following in the lease, the tenants' first bill, or in a writing before signing the lease: A description of the water or sewage disposal services to be provided, and an itemized statement of the fees that will be charged. The disclosure must be printed using a font that is at least as large as the largest font used in the document in which the disclosure is included. The disclosure must include a description of the water or sewage disposal services to be provided, an itemized statement of the fees that will be charged, and this statement: "If you believe you are being charged in violation of this disclosure or if you believe you are

Required Landlord Disclosures (continued)

being billed in excess of the utility services provided to you as described in this disclosure, you have a right under Indiana law to file a complaint with the Indiana Utility Regulatory Commission. You may contact the Commission at (insert phone number for the tenant to contact the Commission)." (Ind. Code Ann. § 8-1-2-1.2)

Iowa

Iowa Code § 562A.13

Owner or agent identity: Landlord must disclose to the tenant in writing at or before the commencement of the tenancy the name and address of the person authorized to manage the premises, and an owner of the premises or a person authorized to act for and on behalf of the owner for the purpose of service of process and for the purpose of receiving notices and demands. (Iowa Code § 562A.13)

Utilities: For shared utilities, landlord must fully explain utility rates, charges, and services to the prospective tenant before the rental agreement is signed. (Iowa Code § 562A.13)

Contamination: The landlord or a person authorized to enter into a rental agreement on behalf of the landlord must disclose to each tenant, in writing before the commencement of the tenancy, whether the property is listed in the comprehensive environmental response compensation and liability information system maintained by the federal Environmental Protection Agency. (Iowa Code § 562A.13)

Kansas

Kan. Stat. Ann. §§ 58-2548, 58-2551

Move-in checklist required? Yes. Within 5 days of move-in, landlord and tenant must jointly inventory the rental. (Kan. Stat. Ann. § 58-2548)

Owner or agent identity: Landlord must disclose to the tenant in writing at or before the commencement of the tenancy the name and address of the person authorized to manage the premises, and an owner of the premises or a person authorized to act for and on behalf of the owner for the purpose of service of process and for the purpose of receiving notices and demands. (Kan. Stat. Ann. § 58-2551)

Kentucky

Ky. Rev. Stat. Ann. §§ 224.1-410, 383.580, 383.585, 902 Ky. Admin. Regs. 47:200

Move-in checklist required? Yes. Landlord and tenant must complete a checklist before landlord can collect a security deposit. (Ky. Rev. Stat. Ann. § 383.580)

Must checklist rights be stated in the lease? No.

Owner or agent identity: Landlord must disclose to the tenant in writing at or before the commencement of the tenancy the name and address of the person authorized to manage the premises, and an owner of the premises or a person authorized to act for and on behalf of the owner for the purpose of service of process and for the purpose of receiving notices and demands. (Ky. Rev. Stat. Ann. § 383.585)

Methamphetamine contamination disclosure: An owner of contaminated property who rents a property where the local health department has posted a methamphetamine contamination notice must disclose in writing to potential tenants that the property is contaminated and has not been decontaminated pursuant to the state's requirements. The disclosure must contain the physical address of the property, the location within the posted property that was used in the production of methamphetamine, and a copy of the Notice of Methamphetamine Contamination. If a prospective tenant asks, the owner must provide a copy of any documents related to the methamphetamine contamination provided to the owner by law enforcement, the Energy and Environment Cabinet, the Department for Public Health, or the local health department. (Ky. Rev. Stat. Ann. § 224.1-410; 902 Ky. Admin. Regs. 47:200)

Louisiana

La. Rev. Stat. Ann. §§ 9:3258.1, 9:3260.1

Application fee: Landlords can't charge an application fee unless they give applicants a written notice of (1) the amount of the fee (2) whether the landlord will consider credit scores, employment history, criminal history, or eviction records in deciding whether to rent to the applicant; and (3)

Required Landlord Disclosures (continued)

permission for the applicant to provide a statement of 200 words or less explaining that the applicant has experienced financial hardship resulting from a state or federally declared disaster or emergency and how that hardship impacted the applicant's credit, employment, or rental history (the landlord must reference COVID-19 and hurricanes). (La. Rev. Stat. Ann. § 9:3258.1)

Foreclosure: Before entering into a lease or rental agreement, landlord must disclose to potential tenants their right to receive notification of any future foreclosure action. If the premises are currently subject to a foreclosure action, landlord must also disclose this in writing. (La. Rev. Stat. Ann. § 9:3260.1)

Maine

Me. Rev. Stat. Ann. tit. 14, §§ 6021-A, 6024, 6030-C, 6030-D, 6030-E

Utilities: No landlord may lease or offer to lease a dwelling unit in a multiunit residential building where the expense of furnishing electricity to the common areas or other area not within the unit is the sole responsibility of the tenant in that unit, unless both parties to the lease have agreed in writing that the tenant will pay for such costs in return for a stated reduction in rent or other specified fair consideration that approximates the actual cost of electricity to the common areas. (Me. Rev. Stat. Ann. tit. 14, § 6024)

Energy efficiency: Landlord must provide to potential tenants who will pay for energy costs (or upon request from others) a residential energy efficiency disclosure statement in accordance with Title 35-A, section 10006, subsection 1 that includes, but is not limited to, information about the energy efficiency of the property. Before a tenant enters into a contract or pays a deposit to rent or lease a property, the landlord must provide the statement to the tenant, obtain the tenant's signature on the statement, and sign the statement. The landlord must retain the signed statement for at least 3 years. Alternatively, the landlord may include in the application for the residential property the name of each supplier of energy that previously supplied the unit, if known, and

the following statement: "You have the right to obtain a 12-month history of energy consumption and the cost of that consumption from the energy supplier." (Me. Rev. Stat. Ann. tit. 14, § 6030-C)

Radon: Unless a mitigation system has been installed, starting in 2014 and every 10 years after when requested by a tenant, the landlord shall test for radon in the rental. If the building was constructed after March 1, 2014, the landlord shall test for radon within 12 months of the occupancy of the building by a tenant. Within 30 days of receiving test results, the landlord shall provide written notice to existing tenants that includes the date of the test, the results, whether mitigation has been performed, the risk associated with radon, and notice that the tenant has the right to conduct a test. The same written notice must also be given to any new tenants before they sign a lease or pay a deposit to rent. The notice must include an acknowledgment that the tenant has received the disclosure. (Me. Rev. Stat. Ann. tit. 14, § 6030-D)

Bed bugs: Before renting a dwelling unit, landlord must disclose to a prospective tenant if an adjacent unit or units are currently infested with or are being treated for bed bugs. Upon request from a tenant or prospective tenant, landlord must disclose the last date that the dwelling unit the landlord seeks to rent or an adjacent unit or units were inspected for a bed bug infestation and found to be free of a bed bug infestation. (Me. Rev. Stat. Ann. tit. 14, § 6021-A)

Smoking policy: Landlord must give tenant written disclosure stating whether smoking is prohibited on the premises, allowed on the entire premises, or allowed in limited areas of the premises. If the landlord allows smoking in limited areas on the premises, the notice must identify the areas on the premises where smoking is allowed. Disclosure must be in the lease or a separate written notice, and landlord must disclose before tenant signs a lease or pays a deposit and must obtain a written acknowledgment of notification from the tenant. (Me. Rev. Stat. Ann. tit. 14, § 6030-E)

Required Landlord Disclosures (continued)

Maryland

Md. Code Real Prop., § 8-203.1

Habitation: *Md. Code Real Prop., § 8-208*

Owner disclosure: *Md. Code Real Prop., § 8-210*

Reusable tenant screening reports: *Md. Code Real Prop., § 8-218*

RUBS: *Md. Code Real Prop., § 8-212.4*

Move-in checklist required? Yes. Before collecting a deposit, landlord must supply a receipt with details on move-in and move-out inspections, and the receipt must be part of the lease. (Md. Code Ann., [Real Prop.], § 8-203.1)

Must checklist rights be stated in the lease? No.

Habitation: A lease must include a statement that the premises will be made available in a condition permitting habitation, with reasonable safety, if that is the agreement, or if that is not the agreement, a statement of the agreement concerning the condition of the premises; and the landlord's and the tenant's specific obligations as to heat, gas, electricity, water, and repair of the premises. (Md. Code Real Prop., § 8-208)

Owner or agent identity: The landlord must include in a lease or post the name and address of the landlord; or the person, if any, authorized to accept notice or service of process on behalf of the landlord. (Md. Code Real Prop., § 8-210)

Montgomery County: Before a prospective tenant signs a lease for 125 days or more, the landlord of a rental within a condominium or development must provide to the prospective tenant, if applicable, a copy of the rules, declaration, and recorded covenants and restrictions that limit or affect the use and occupancy of the property or common areas and to which the owner of the rental is obligated. The written lease must, if applicable, include a statement that the obligations of the owner that limit or affect the use and occupancy of the property are enforceable against the tenant. (Md. Code Real Prop., § 8-210)

Reusable tenant screening reports: Landlords must notify prospective tenants about whether the landlord accepts reusable tenant screening reports (reports generated by a consumer reporting agency within the previous 30 days that the tenant provides to the landlord and for which the landlord doesn't charge an additional fee). Notice must be made in writing or by posting in a conspicuous manner. (Md. Code Real Prop., § 8-218)

Ratio billing systems: Landlords who use a "ratio billing system" must disclose to prospective tenants the utilities that are covered, the landlords method of allocation, and any administrative fees; and copies of the last two statements for each utility and average monthly usage information. Landlords must tell tenants of their rights to inspect records and provide them with a citation to this legal rule. Failure to disclose as required makes the lease unenforceable. (Md. Code Real Prop., § 8-212.4)

Massachusetts

Mass. Gen. Laws ch. 186, §§ 15B(2)(c), 15C, 21, 22(f)

Move-in checklist required? Yes, if landlord collects a security deposit. (Mass. Gen. Laws ch. 186, § 15B(2)(c))

Insurance: Upon tenant's request and within 15 days, landlord must furnish the name of the company insuring the property against loss or damage by fire and the amount of insurance provided by each such company and the name of any person who would receive payment for a loss covered by such insurance. (Mass. Gen. Laws ch. 186, § 21)

Tax escalation: If real estate taxes increase, landlord may pass on a proportionate share of the increase to the tenant only if the lease discloses that in the event of an increase, the tenant will be required to pay only the proportion of the increase as the tenant's leased unit bears to the property being taxed (that proportion must be disclosed in the lease). In addition, the lease must state that if the landlord receives a tax abatement, landlord will refund a proportionate share of the abatement, minus reasonable attorneys' fees. (Mass. Gen. Laws ch. 186, § 15C))

Utilities: Landlord may not charge for water unless the lease specifies the charge and the details of the water submetering and billing arrangement. (Mass. Gen. Laws ch. 186, § 22(f))

Required Landlord Disclosures (continued)

Michigan

Stutelberg v. Practical Management Co., *245 N.W.2d 737 (1976); Mich. Comp. Laws §§ 554.601b, 554.608, 554.634*

Nonrefundable fees permitted? Yes. (*Stutelberg v. Practical Management Co., 245 N.W.2d 737 (1976)*)

Move-in checklist required? Yes. However, the requirement does not need to be included in the rental agreement. (Mich. Comp. Laws § 554.608)

Owner or agent identity: A rental agreement must include the name and address at which notice can be given to the landlord. (Mich. Comp. Laws § 554.634)

Truth in Renting Act: A rental agreement must also state in a prominent place in type not smaller than the size of 12-point type, or in legible print with letters not smaller than 1/8 inch, a notice in substantially the following form:

"NOTICE: Michigan law establishes rights and obligations for parties to rental agreements. This agreement is required to comply with the Truth in Renting Act. If you have a question about the interpretation or legality of a provision of this agreement, you may want to seek assistance from a lawyer or other qualified person." (Mich. Comp. Laws § 554.634)

Rights of domestic violence victims: A rental agreement or lease may contain a provision stating, "A tenant who has a reasonable apprehension of present danger to him or her or his or her child from domestic violence, sexual assault, or stalking may have special statutory rights to seek a release of rental obligation under MCL 554.601b." If the rental agreement or lease does not contain such a provision, the landlord must post an identical written notice visible to a reasonable person in the landlord's property management office, or deliver written notice to the tenant when the lease or rental agreement is signed. (Mich. Comp. Laws § 554.601b)

Minnesota

Minn. Stat. Ann. §§ 504B.151, 504B.171, 504B.173, 504B.181, 504B.195

Owner or agent identity: Landlord must disclose to the tenant in writing at or before the commencement of the tenancy the name and address of the person authorized to manage the premises, and an owner of the premises or a person authorized to act for and on behalf of the owner for the purpose of service of process and for the purpose of receiving notices and demands. (Minn. Stat. Ann. § 504B.181)

Outstanding inspection orders, condemnation orders, or declarations that the property is unfit: The landlord must disclose the existence of any such orders or declarations before the tenant signs a lease or pays a security deposit. (Minn. Stat. Ann. § 504B.195)

Buildings in financial distress: Once a landlord has received notice of a deed cancellation or notice of foreclosure, landlord may not enter into a periodic tenancy where the tenancy term is more than two months, or a lease where the lease extends beyond the redemption period (other restrictions may apply). (Minn. Stat. Ann. § 504B.151)

Landlord and tenant mutual promises: This mutual promise must appear in every lease or rental agreement: "Landlord and tenant promise that neither will unlawfully allow within the premises, common areas, or curtilage of the premises (property boundaries): controlled substances, prostitution or prostitution-related activity; stolen property or property obtained by robbery; or an act of domestic abuse, criminal sexual conduct, or harassment, as defined by MN Statute Section 504B.206(1)(a), against a tenant, licensee, or any authorized occupant. They further promise that the aforementioned areas will not be used by themselves or anyone acting under their control to manufacture, sell, give away, barter, deliver, exchange, distribute, purchase, or possess a controlled substance in violation of any criminal provision of chapter 152." (Minn. Stat. Ann. § 504B.171)

Screening fee: Before accepting an applicant's screening fee, landlords must disclose in writing: The name, address, and phone number of the tenant screening service (if landlord uses such a service), and the landlord's acceptance criteria. Landlords must notify rejected applicants within 14 days, identifying the criteria the applicant did not meet. (Minn. Stat. Ann. § 504B.173)

Mississippi

No disclosure statutes.

Missouri

Mo. Rev. Stat. §§ 441.236, 442.055, 535.185

Methamphetamine contamination: Landlord who knows that the premises were used to produce methamphetamine must disclose this fact to prospective tenants, regardless of whether the people involved in the production were convicted for such production. (Mo. Rev. Stat. § 441.236)

Owner or agent identity: Landlord must disclose to the tenant in writing at or before the commencement of the tenancy the name and address of the person authorized to manage the premises, and an owner of the premises or a person authorized to act for and on behalf of the owner for the purpose of service of process and for the purpose of receiving notices and demands. (Mo. Rev. Stat. § 535.185)

Radioactive or hazardous material: Landlords who know that the rental property is or was contaminated with radioactive or other hazardous material must disclose this fact to prospective tenants. Landlords have knowledge when they've received a report stating that the property is or was contaminated. Failure to disclose when required is a Class A misdemeanor. (Mo. Rev. Stat. § 442.055)

Montana

Mont. Code Ann. §§ 70-16-703, 70-24-301, 70-25-101(4), 70-25-206, 75-10-1305

Nonrefundable fees permitted? No. A fee or charge for cleaning and damages, no matter how designated, is presumed to be a security deposit. (Not a clear statement that such a fee isn't nonrefundable, but by implication it must be.) (Mont. Code Ann. § 70-25-101(4))

Move-in checklists required? Yes, checklists are required when landlords collect a security deposit. (Mont. Code Ann. § 70-25-206)

Owner or agent identity: Landlords or people authorized to enter into a rental agreement on their behalf shall disclose to the tenant in writing at or before the commencement of the tenancy the name and address of the person authorized to manage the premises; and the owner of the premises or a person authorized to act for the owner for the purpose of service of process and receiving notices and demands. (Mont. Code Ann. § 70-24-301)

Mold: Before signing a lease, if a landlord has knowledge that mold is present in the rental, the landlord must disclose its presence; and if the landlord knows that the building has been tested for mold, the landlord must advise the tenant that testing has occurred and provide a copy of the results (if available), as well as any evidence of subsequent treatment. Landlords can avoid liability for damages resulting from mold if they comply with these rules, provide tenants with a mold disclosure statement in the form prescribed by statute, and obtain the tenants' written acknowledgment of receipt of the statement. (Mont. Code Ann. § 70-16-703)

Methamphetamine contamination: Before signing a lease or rental agreement, a landlord who knows that the property has been contaminated from smoke from the use of meth or was used as a meth lab must disclose this history to a potential tenant. Disclosure is not required if the property has been remediated to the states standards by a contractor who is certified by the state. Landlords who themselves did not cause the contamination, and who have obtained documentation of decontamination that they have provided to tenants, will not be liable in a tenant's lawsuit for damages. (Mont. Code Ann. § 75-10-1305)

Nebraska

Neb. Rev. Stat. § 76-1417

Owner or agent identity: The landlord or any person authorized to enter into a rental agreement on his or her behalf must disclose to the tenant in writing at or before the commencement of the tenancy the name and address of the person authorized to manage the

Required Landlord Disclosures (continued)

premises, and an owner of the premises or a person authorized to act for and on behalf of the owner for the purpose of service of process and receiving notices and demands.

Nevada

Nev. Rev. Stat. Ann. §§ 118A.200, 118A.275

Nonrefundable fees permitted? Yes. Lease must explain fees that are required and the purposes for which they are required. (Nev. Rev. Stat. Ann. § 118A.200)

Move-in checklist required? Yes. Lease must include tenants' rights to a checklist and a signed record of the inventory and condition of the premises under the exclusive custody and control of the tenant. (Nev. Rev. Stat. Ann. § 118A.200)

Nuisance and flying the flag: Lease must include a summary of the provisions of NRS 202.470 (penalties for permitting or maintaining a nuisance); information regarding the procedure a tenant may use to report to the appropriate authorities a nuisance, a violation of a building, safety, or health code or regulation; and information regarding the right of the tenant to engage in the display of the flag of the United States, as set forth in NRS 118A.325. (Nev. Rev. Stat. Ann. § 118A.200)

Foreclosure proceedings: Landlord must disclose to any prospective tenant, in writing, whether the premises to be rented is the subject of a foreclosure proceeding (disclosure need not be in the lease). (Nev. Rev. Stat. Ann. § 118A.275)

Lease signed by an agent of the landlord who does not hold a property management permit: In single-family rentals only, unless the lease is signed by an authorized agent of the landlord who holds a current property management permit, the top of the first page of the lease must state, in font that is at least twice the size of any other size in the agreement, that the tenant might not have valid occupancy unless the lease is notarized or signed by an authorized agent of the owner who holds a management permit. The notice must give the current address and phone number of the landlord. In addition, it must state

that even if the foregoing has not been provided, the agreement is enforceable against the landlord. (Nev. Rev. Stat. Ann. § 118A.200)

New Hampshire

N.H. Rev. Stat. Ann. § 477:4-g, 540-A:6

Move-in checklist required? Yes. Landlord must inform tenant that if tenant finds any conditions in the rental in need of repair, tenant may note them on the security deposit receipt or other writing. Not a true checklist. (N.H. Rev. Stat. Ann. § 540-A:6)

Must checklist rights be stated in the lease? No.

Methamphetamine disclosure: If methamphetamine was produced on a property and the department of environmental sciences has not determined that the property meets remediation cleanup standards, the landlord must disclose in writing to the tenant that methamphetamine production has occurred. (N.H. Rev. Stat. § 477:4-g)

New Jersey

N.J. Stat. Ann. §§ 46:8-44, 46:8-45, 46:8-46, 46:8-50, 46:8-55, 55:13A-7.14, 55:13A-7.18, 55:13A-7.19, N.J. Admin. Code §§ 5:10-27.1, 5:10-27 App. 27A

Flood zone: Prior to move-in, landlord must inform tenant if rental is in a flood zone or area (does not apply to properties containing two or fewer dwelling units, or to owner-occupied properties of three or fewer units). (N.J. Stat. Ann. § 46:8-50)

Truth in Renting Act: Except in buildings of two or fewer units, and owner-occupied premises of three or fewer units, landlord must distribute to new tenants at or prior to move-in the Department of Community Affairs' statement of legal rights and responsibilities of tenants and landlords of rental dwelling units (Spanish also). (N.J. Stat. Ann. §§ 46:8-44, 46:8-45, 46:8-46)

Child protection window guards: Landlords of multi-family properties must include information in the lease about tenants' rights to request window guards. The Legislature's Model Lease and Notice clause reads as follows: "The owner (landlord) is required by law to provide, install and maintain window guards in the apartment if a child or children

Required Landlord Disclosures (continued)

10 years of age or younger is, or will be, living in the apartment or is, or will be, regularly present there for a substantial period of time if the tenant gives the owner (landlord) a written request that the window guards be installed. The owner (landlord) is also required, upon the written request of the tenant, to provide, install and maintain window guards in the hallways to which persons in the tenant's unit have access without having to go out of the building. If the building is a condominium, cooperative or mutual housing building, the owner (landlord) of the apartment is responsible for installing and maintaining window guards in the apartment and the association is responsible for installing and maintaining window guards in hallway windows. Window guards are only required to be provided in first floor windows where the window sill is more than six feet above grade or there are other hazardous conditions that make installation of window guards necessary to protect the safety of children." The notice must be conspicuous and in boldface type. (N.J. Stat. Ann. § 55:13A-7.14; N.J. Admin. Code §§ 5:10-27.1, 5:10-27 App. 27A)

Water quality: Owners of multifamily properties who must prepare a Consumer Confidence Report, or who receive such a report from a public community water system, must post the report in every routinely used common area (if the property has no such area, owners must give copies to each rental unit). Owners of multifamily properties who supply water, who are not required to prepare a Consumer Confidence Report, but who must test its water, must post a chart containing the results of the tests. Charts must be posted in every routinely used common area (if the property has no such area, owners must give copies to each rental unit). (N.J. Stat. Ann. § 55:13A-7.18)

Application fee: Landlords cannot collect application fees without first disclosing in writing to the applicant whether the landlord will review and consider criminal history and a statement that the applicant may provide evidence demonstrating inaccuracies

within the applicant's criminal record or evidence of rehabilitation or other mitigating factors. (N.J. Stat. Ann. § 46:8-55)

Postings in multiple dwellings: Landlords of tenant-occupied multiple dwellings must post in a conspicuous area where likely to be seen by tenants the following information in both English and Spanish: (1) emergency contact info for the owner or managing agent (2)instructions on how to access and use the comprehensive social services information toll-free telephone hotline. The information must also be posted on the website of any management company that manages a tenant-occupied multiple dwelling. (N.J. Stat. Ann. § 55:13A-7.19(1)(a))

Multiple dwellings lease disclosure: Every lease offered to a tenant in a multiple dwelling must include in both English and Spanish: (1) the website address of the management company and (2) instructions on how to access and use the comprehensive social services information toll-free telephone hotline. (N.J. Stat. Ann. § 55:13A-7.19(1)(b))

New Mexico

N.M. Stat. Ann. § 47-8-19, N.M. Admin. Code § 20.4.5.13

Owner or agent identity: Landlord must disclose to the tenant in writing at or before the commencement of the tenancy the name and address of the person authorized to manage the premises, and an owner of the premises or a person authorized to act for and on behalf of the owner for the purpose of service of process and for the purpose of receiving notices and demands. (N.M. Stat. Ann. § 47-8-19)

Illegal drug lab on premises: Landlord cannot rent a property where controlled substances were manufactured or located unless landlord provides written notice to tenant of these facts. The tenant must acknowledge receipt of the notice in writing, and the landlord must provide a copy of the notice and acknowledgment to the New Mexico environment department. (N.M. Admin. Code § 20.4.5.13)

Required Landlord Disclosures (continued)

New York

N.Y. Gen. Oblig. Laws § 7-108, N.Y. Envtl. Conserv. Law § 27-2405, 9 NYCRR § 4665.15, N.Y. Real Prop. Law § 231-b, § 235-bb, N.Y. Mult. Res. Law §§ 4, 15, N.Y. Exec. Law § 170-d

Refundable fees: No, not needed to be stated in rental agreement. (N.Y. Gen. Oblig. Laws § 7-108)

Move-in checklist: Yes, rights not needed to be stated in lease (N.Y. Gen. Oblig. Laws § 7-108)

Checklists, other details: Tenants are entitled to a pre-move-out inspection unless tenant terminates with less than two weeks' notice.

Air contamination: Landlord who receives a government report showing that air in the building has, or may have, concentrations of volatile organic compounds (VOCs) that exceed governmental guidelines must give written notice to prospective and current tenants. The notice must appear in at least 12-point bold face type on the first page of the lease or rental agreement. It must read as follows: "NOTIFICATION OF TEST RESULTS The property has been tested, for contamination of indoor air: test results and additional information are available upon request." (N.Y. Envtl. Conserv. Law § 27-2405)

Certificate of occupancy: In structures with three or fewer dwelling units, where a certificate of occupancy is required by law, landlords must provide prospective tenants proof of a current certificate prior to signing a lease or rental agreement. Landlords may provide prospective tenants with a copy of the actual certificate, or provide notice of said certificate in bold face type. Waivers of this requirement are void. (N.Y. Real Prop. Law § 235-bb)

Smoke detectors: In multifamily buildings of three or more units, condominiums, and cooperatives located in towns, villages, and cities with populations less than 325,000, landlord must notify tenants in writing, individually or by posting a notice in a common area, of owners' and tenants' duties regarding smoke detectors. (N.Y. Mult. Res. Law §§ 4, 15)

Reasonable accommodation: Landlords must give all tenants and prospective tenants a written notice of their right to request reasonable modifications and accommodations for their disability. The notice must be posted in all vacant available rentals and given to all current tenants within 30 days of the beginning of their tenancy. The law, 9 NYCRR Section 4665.15(e), provides the wording for the required notice, which landlords may copy and distribute.

Flood disclosures: Every lease must disclose whether any or all of the premises are within a FEMA flood plain, a Special Flood Hazard Area or 100-year flood-plain, a Moderate Risk Flood Hazard Area or 500-year floodplain, and whether the premises has been flooded due to a natural flood event. The lease must include this notice: "Flood insurance is available to renters through the Federal Emergency Management Agency's (FEMA's) National Flood Insurance Program (NFIP) to cover your personal property and contents in the event of a flood. A standard renter's insurance policy does not typically cover flood damage. You are encouraged to examine your policy to determine whether you are covered." (N.Y. Real Prop. Law § 231-b)

North Carolina

N.C. Gen. Stat. Ann. § 42-46

Nonrefundable fees permitted? Landlord may collect only one of the following, when specific conditions are met: Complaint filing fee, court appearance fee, and second trial fee. Failure to pay the fees cannot support a termination notice. (N.C. Gen. Stat. Ann. § 42-46)

Eviction fees: If landlords wish to collect fees relating to eviction, they must specify certain types of fees in a written lease. Landlords must disclose their right to collect reasonable attorneys' fees, which cannot exceed 15% of the amount owed by the tenant, or 15% of the monthly rent stated in the lease if the eviction is based on a default other than the nonpayment of rent. Landlords must also disclose the fees they will charge for filing a complaint, to appear in court, and for their second trial (landlord can charge and retain only one of these fees). (N.C. Gen. Stat. Ann. § 42-46)

Required Landlord Disclosures (continued)

Attorneys' fees and costs: Landlords cannot charge tenants for attorneys' fees and costs without making certain disclosures. See "State Laws on Attorneys' Fees and Court Costs Clauses" chart in this appendix. (N.C. Gen. Stat. Ann. § 42-46)

North Dakota

N.D. Cent. Code § 47-16-07.2

Move-in checklist required? Yes. Landlord must give tenant a statement describing the condition of the premises when tenant signs the rental agreement. Both parties must sign the statement. (N.D. Cent. Code § 47-16-07.2)

Ohio

Ohio Rev. Code Ann. § 5321.18

Owner or agent identity: Every written rental agreement must contain the name and address of the owner and the name and address of the owner's agent, if any. If the owner or the owner's agent is a corporation, partnership, limited partnership, association, trust, or other entity, the address must be the principal place of business in the county in which the residential property is situated. If there is no place of business in such county, then its principal place of business in this state must be disclosed, including the name of the person in charge thereof.

Oklahoma

Okla. Stat. Ann. tit. 41, §§ 113a, 116, 118, and Okla. Stat. Ann. tit. 74, § 324.11a

Flooding: If the premises to be rented has been flooded within the past five (5) years and such fact is known to the landlord, the landlord shall include such information prominently and in writing as part of any written rental agreements. (Okla. Stat. Ann. tit. 41, § 113a)

Owner information: As a part of any rental agreement the lessor shall prominently and in writing identify what person at what address is entitled to accept service or notice under this act. Landlord must disclose to the tenant in writing at or before the commencement of the tenancy the name and address of the person authorized to manage the premises, and an owner of the premises or a person authorized to act for and on behalf of the owner for the purpose of service of process and receiving notices and demands. (Okla. Stat. Ann. tit. 41, § 116)

Smoke detectors: Landlord must explain to tenant how to test the smoke detector to ensure that it is in working order. (Okla. Stat. Ann. tit. 74, § 324.11a)

Methamphetamine disclosure: Before signing a rental agreement, if the landlord knows or has reason to know that the unit or any part of the premises was used in the manufacture of methamphetamine, the landlord must disclose this information to a prospective tenant. Does not apply when the landlord has tested the unit or premises and the results show that the level of contamination is less than 0.1 mcg per 100cm^2 of surface materials in the affected part. (Okla. Stat. Ann. tit. 41, § 118)

Tenant repairs, maintenance, alterations, or remodeling: When landlord and tenant agree that the tenant will perform specified repairs, maintenance tasks, alterations, or remodeling, they must put this agreement in writing, independent of the rental agreement, and presented in a manner that will make it hard to overlook (using ample font size, for example). (Okla. Stat. Ann. tit. 41, § 118)

Oregon

Or. Rev. Stat. Ann. §§ 90.220, 90.222, 90.228, 90.295, 90.302, 90.305, 90.310, 90.315, 90.316, 90.317, 90.318, 90.367, 479.270

Nonrefundable fees permitted? No. Landlords' written rules may not provide for tenant fees, except for specified events as they arise, including a late rent payment; tenant's late payment of a utility or service charge; a dishonored check, pursuant to Or. Rev. Stat. Ann. § 30.701(5); failure to clean up pet waste in areas other than tenant's unit; failure to clean up garbage and rubbish (outside tenant's dwelling unit); failure to clean pet waste of a service or companion animal from areas other than the dwelling unit; parking violations and improper use of vehicles within the premises; smoking in a designated nonsmoking area; keeping

Required Landlord Disclosures (continued)

an unauthorized pet capable of inflicting damage on persons or property; tampering or disabling a smoke detector. (Or. Rev. Stat. Ann. § 90.302)

Must fee policy be stated in rental agreement? Yes.

Owner or agent identity: Landlord must disclose to the tenant in writing at or before the commencement of the tenancy the name and address of the person authorized to manage the premises, and an owner of the premises or a person authorized to act for and on behalf of the owner for the purpose of service of process and for the purpose of receiving notices and demands. (Or. Rev. Stat. Ann. § 90.305)

Legal proceedings: If at the time of the execution of a rental agreement for a dwelling unit in premises containing no more than four dwelling units the premises are subject to any of the following circumstances, the landlord must disclose that circumstance to the tenant in writing before the execution of the rental agreement: (a) Any outstanding notice of default under a trust deed, mortgage, or contract of sale, or notice of trustee's sale under a trust deed; (b) Any pending suit to foreclose a mortgage, trust deed, or vendor's lien under a contract of sale; (c) Any pending declaration of forfeiture or suit for specific performance of a contract of sale; or (d) Any pending proceeding to foreclose a tax lien. (Or. Rev. Stat. Ann. § 90.310)

Utilities: The landlord must disclose to the tenant in writing at or before the commencement of the tenancy any utility or service that the tenant pays directly to a utility or service provider that directly benefits the landlord or other tenants. A tenant's payment for a given utility or service benefits the landlord or other tenants if the utility or service is delivered to any area other than the tenant's dwelling unit.

A landlord may require a tenant to pay to the landlord a utility or service charge that has been billed by a utility or service provider to the landlord for utility or service provided directly to the tenant's dwelling unit or to a common area available to the tenant as part of the tenancy. A utility or service charge that shall be assessed to a tenant for a

common area must be described in the written rental agreement separately and distinctly from such a charge for the tenant's dwelling unit. Unless the method of allocating the charges to the tenant is described in the tenant's written rental agreement, the tenant may require that the landlord give the tenant a copy of the provider's bill as a condition of paying the charges. (Or. Rev. Stat. Ann. § 90.315)

Recycling: In a city or the county within the urban growth boundary of a city that has implemented multifamily recycling service, a landlord who has five or more residential dwelling units on a single premises must notify new tenants at the time of entering into a rental agreement of the opportunity to recycle. (Or. Rev. Stat. Ann. § 90.318)

Smoking policy: Landlord must disclose the smoking policy for the premises, by stating whether smoking is prohibited on the premises, allowed on the entire premises, or allowed in limited areas. If landlord allows smoking in limited areas, the disclosure must identify those areas. (Or. Rev. Stat. Ann. § 90.220)

Carbon monoxide alarm instructions: If rental contains a CO source (a heater, fireplace, appliance, or cooking source that uses coal, kerosene, petroleum products, wood, or other fuels that emit carbon monoxide as a by product of combustion; or an attached garage with an opening that communicates directly with a living space), landlord must install one or more CO monitors and give tenant written instructions for testing the alarm(s), before tenant takes possession. (Or. Rev. Stat. Ann. §§ 90.316, 90.317)

Smoke alarm or smoke detector: When tenant moves in, landlord must give tenant written instructions for testing smoke alarms and smoke detectors. (Or. Rev. Stat. Ann. § 479.270)

Floodplain: If a dwelling unit is located in a 100-year flood plain, the landlord must provide notice in the dwelling unit rental agreement that the dwelling unit is located within the flood plain. If a landlord fails to provide a notice as required under this section, and the tenant of the dwelling unit suffers an uninsured loss due to flooding, the tenant may recover from

Required Landlord Disclosures (continued)

the landlord the lesser of the actual damages for the uninsured loss or two months' rent. (Or. Rev. Stat. Ann. § 90.228)

Renters' insurance: Landlord may require tenants to maintain liability insurance (certain low-income and subsidized tenancies excepted), but only if the landlord obtains and maintains comparable liability insurance and provides documentation to any tenant who requests the documentation, orally or in writing. The landlord may provide documentation to a tenant in person, by mail, or by posting in a common area or office. The documentation may consist of a current certificate of coverage. Any landlord who requires tenants to obtain renters' insurance must disclose the requirement and amount in writing prior to entering into a new tenancy, and may require the tenant to provide documentation before the tenancy begins. (Or. Rev. Stat. Ann. § 90.222)

Homeowner assessments: If landlord wants to pass on homeowners' association assessments that are imposed on anyone moving into or out of the unit, the written rental agreement must include this requirement. Landlord must give tenants a copy of each assessment before charging the tenant. (Or. Rev. Stat. Ann. § 90.302)

Applicant screening fees: Before accepting application fees, landlords must, among other things, disclose in writing to the applicant (1) the amount of the screening charge (2) the landlord's criteria for selection (3) the screening process and considerations (4) the applicant's right to dispute information in a screening report (5) required nondiscrimination policies (6) the amount of rent and deposits, and (7) whether the landlord requires renters' insurance (and how much). (Or. Rev. Stat. Ann. § 90.295)

Pennsylvania

No disclosure statutes.

Rhode Island

R.I. Gen. Laws §§ 34-18-20, 34-18-22, 34-18-22.1

Owner disclosure: Landlord must disclose to the tenant in writing at or before the commencement

of the tenancy the name and address of the person authorized to manage the premises, and an owner of the premises or a person authorized to act for and on behalf of the owner for the purpose of service of process and for the purpose of receiving notices and demands. (R.I. Gen. Laws § 34-18-20)

Code violations: Before entering into any residential rental agreement, landlord must inform a prospective tenant of any outstanding minimum housing code violations that exist on the building that is the subject of the rental agreement. (R.I. Gen. Laws § 34-18-22.1)

Notice of foreclosure: A landlord who becomes delinquent on a mortgage securing real estate upon which the rental is located for a period of 120 days must notify the tenant that the property may be subject to foreclosure; and until the foreclosure occurs, the tenant must continue to pay rent to the landlord as provided under the rental agreement. (R.I. Gen. Laws § 34-18-20)

General liability insurance policy: Landlords must provide a copy of the declaration page from the landlord's general liability policy with the lease, and must provide tenants with a new copy each time the policy is renewed. (R.I. Gen. Laws § 34-18-22)

South Carolina

S.C. Code Ann. §§ 5-25-1330, 27-40-410, 27-40-420

Owner or agent identity: Landlord must disclose to the tenant in writing at or before the commencement of the tenancy the name and address of the person authorized to manage the premises, and an owner of the premises or a person authorized to act for and on behalf of the owner for the purpose of service of process and for the purpose of receiving notices and demands. (S.C. Code Ann. § 27-40-420)

Unequal security deposits: If landlord rents five or more adjoining units on the premises, and imposes different standards for calculating deposits required of tenants, landlord must, before a tenancy begins, post in a conspicuous place a statement explaining the standards by which the various deposits are calculated (or, landlord may give the tenant the written statement). (S.C. Code Ann. § 27-40-410)

Required Landlord Disclosures (continued)

Smoke detectors: When tenant moves in, owner must give tenant written or verbal instructions, or both, for testing the detectors and replacing batteries in battery-powered detectors. (S.C. Code Ann. § 5-25-1330)

South Dakota

S.D. Codified Laws Ann. § 43-32-30

Methamphetamine contamination: andlord who has actual knowledge of the existence of any prior manufacturing of methamphetamines on the premises must disclose that information to any lessee or any person who may become a lessee. If the residential premises consists of two or more housing units, the disclosure requirements apply only to the unit where there is knowledge of the existence of any prior manufacturing of methamphetamines. (S.D. Codified Laws Ann. § 43-32-30)

Tennessee

Tenn. Code Ann. § 66-28-302, 66-28-403

Owner or agent identity: The landlord or any person authorized to enter into a rental agreement on the landlord's behalf must disclose to the tenant in writing at or before the commencement of the tenancy the name and address of the agent authorized to manage the premises, and an owner of the premises or a person or agent authorized to act for and on behalf of the owner for the acceptance of service of process and for receipt of notices and demands. (Tenn. Code Ann. § 66-28-302)

Showing rental to prospective tenants: Landlord may enter to show the premises to prospective renters during the final 30 days of a tenancy (with 24 hours' notice), but only if this right of access is set forth in the rental agreement or lease. (Tenn. Code Ann. § 66-28-403)

Texas

Tex. Prop. Code Ann. §§ 92.008, 92.016, 92.019, 92.020, 92.056, 92.103, 92.111, 92.159, 92.201, 92.0131, 92.0135, 92.3515

Nonrefundable fees permitted? Yes. Landlords cannot collect late fees unless notice of the fee is included in a written lease. *(Tex. Prop. Code Ann.*

§ 92.019; Holmes v. Canlen Management Corp., 542 S.W.2d 199 (1976))

Owner or agent identity: In the lease, other writing, or posted on the property, landlord must disclose the name and address of the property's owner and, if an entity located off-site from the dwelling is primarily responsible for managing the dwelling, the name and street address of the management company. (Tex. Prop. Code Ann. § 92.201)

Emergency contact information: Landlords must provide tenants with an emergency phone number to call when there is a condition affecting physical health or safety of tenant. (Tex. Prop. Code Ann. § 92.020)

Security device requests: If landlord wants tenant requests concerning security devices to be in writing, this requirement must be in the lease in boldface type or underlined. (Tex. Prop. Code Ann. § 92.159)

Return of security deposit: A requirement that a tenant give advance notice of moving out as a condition for refunding the security deposit is effective only if the requirement is in the lease, underlined or printed in conspicuous bold print. (Tex. Prop. Code Ann. § 92.103)

Domestic violence victims' rights: Victims of sexual abuse or assault on the premises may break a lease, after complying with specified procedures, without responsibility for future rent. Tenants will be responsible for any unpaid back rent, but only if the lease includes the following statement, or one substantially like it: "Tenants may have special statutory rights to terminate the lease early in certain situations involving family violence or a military deployment or transfer." (Tex. Prop. Code Ann. § 92.016)

Tenant's rights when landlord fails to repair: A lease must contain language in underlined or bold print that informs the tenant of the remedies available when the landlord fails to repair a problem that materially affects the physical health or safety of an ordinary tenant. These rights include the right to: repair and deduct; terminate the lease; and obtain

Required Landlord Disclosures (continued)

a judicial order that the landlord make the repair, reduce the rent, pay the tenant damages (including a civil penalty), and pay the tenant's court and attorneys' fees. (Tex. Prop. Code Ann. § 92.056)

Landlord's towing or parking rules and policies: For tenants in multiunit properties, if the landlord has vehicle towing or parking rules or policies that apply to the tenant, the landlord must give the tenant a copy of the rules or policies before the lease agreement is signed. The copy must be signed by the tenant, included in the lease or rental agreement, or be made an attachment to either. If included, the clause must be titled "Parking" or "Parking Rules" and be capitalized, underlined, or printed in bold print.) (Tex. Prop. Code Ann. § 92.0131.)

Electric service interruption: Landlord who submeters electric service, or who allocates master metered electricity according to a prorated system, may interrupt tenant's electricity service if tenant fails to pay the bill, but only after specific notice and according to a complex procedure. Exceptions for ill tenants and during extreme weather. (Tex. Prop. Code Ann. § 92.008(h))

Selection criteria for applicants: At the time landlords provide prospective tenants with applications, they must also provide printed notice of their tenant selection criteria, including reasons why applications may be denied. The notice must contain certain acknowledgment language that the applicant must sign. (Tex. Prop. Code Ann. § 92.3515)

Floodplain disclosure: Landlords must provide tenants with written notice stating the substantial equivalent of: "Landlord ( ) is or ( ) is not aware that the dwelling you are renting is located in a 100-year floodplain. If neither box is checked, you should assume the dwelling is in a 100-year floodplain. Even if the dwelling is not in a 100-year floodplain, the dwelling may still be susceptible to flooding. The Federal Emergency Management Agency (FEMA) maintains a flood map on its Internet website that is searchable by address, at no cost, to determine if a dwelling is located in a flood hazard area. Most

tenant insurance policies do not cover damages or loss incurred in a flood. You should seek insurance coverage that would cover losses caused by a flood." If the landlord knows that flooding has damaged any portion of a dwelling at least once during the five-year period immediately preceding the effective date of the lease, the landlord shall provide a written notice to tenant that's substantially equivalent to: "Landlord ( ) is or ( ) is not aware that the dwelling you are renting has flooded at least once within the last five years." These notices must be given to the tenant in a separate written document at or before the execution of the lease. (Tex. Prop. Code Ann. § 92.0135)

Utah

Utah Code Ann. §§ 57-17-2, 57-22-4, 57-27-201

Must fee policy be stated in the rental agreement?: Yes. All fees, fines, assessments, interest, or other costs must be included in the lease or rental agreement, unless the rental agreement is on a month-to-month basis and the landlord provides the renter a 15-day notice of the charge. (Utah Code Ann. § 57-22-4)

Move-in checklists required? Yes. Landlords must give prospective renters a written inventory of the condition of the residential rental unit, excluding ordinary wear and tear; give the renter a form to document the condition of the residential rental and allow the resident a reasonable time after the renter's occupancy of the unit to complete and return the form; or provide the prospective renter an opportunity to conduct a walk-through inspection of the rental. (Utah Code Ann. § 57-22-4)

Nonrefundable fees permitted? Yes. If there is a written agreement and if any part of the deposit is to be made non-refundable, it must be so stated in writing to the renter at the time the deposit is taken. (Utah Code Ann. § 57-17-2)

Applicant disclosures: Before accepting an application fee or any other payment from a prospective renter, the landlord must disclose in writing: (1) a good faith estimate of the rent and

Required Landlord Disclosures (continued)

each fixed, non-rent expense that's part of the lease or rental agreement (2) the type of each use-based, non-rent expense that's part of the lease or rental agreement (3) the day that the rental will be available (4) the criteria the landlord will use to determine whether to rent to the applicant; and (5) how the applicant can recover any payments made if the good-faith rent or expense estimates were incorrect. (Utah Code Ann. § 57-22-4)

Disclosure of Management: Before the tenancy begins, the landlord must disclose in writing the owner's name, address, and telephone number or the name, address, and telephone number of any person authorized to manage the rental or act on behalf of the owner and receive notices. (Utah Code Ann. § 57-22-4)

Disclosure of rules: Before the tenancy begins, the landlord must provide the renter with a copy of any rules and regulations applicable to the rental. The landlord must also provide a signed copy of the written lease or rental agreement. (Utah Code Ann. § 57-22-4)

Methamphetamine contamination: If landlord has actual knowledge that the property is currently contaminated from the use, storage, or manufacture of methamphetamine, the landlord must disclose that the property is contaminated in the lease. (Utah Code Ann. § 57-27-201)

Vermont

No disclosure statutes.

Virginia

Va. Code Ann. §§ 55.1-1204, 55.1-1206, 55.1-1212, 55.1-1214 to 1219, 55.1-1223

Move-in checklist required? Yes. Within five days of move-in, landlord or tenant or both together must prepare a written report detailing the condition of the premises. Landlord must disclose within this report the known presence of mold. (Va. Code Ann. § 55.1-1214)

Tenant rights and responsibilities: Landlords shall offer prospective tenants a written lease or rental agreement that contains the terms of the tenancy

and provide with it the statement of tenant rights and responsibilities developed by the Department of Housing and Community Development. (Va. Code Ann. § 55.1-1204)

Renters' insurance: If the lease or rental agreement doesn't require the tenant to obtain renters' insurance, the landlord must provide a written notice to the tenant before signing the lease or rental agreement stating that (1) the landlord isn't responsible for the tenant's personal property (2) the landlord's insurance doesn't cover the tenant's personal property (3) if the tenant wishes to protect personal property, the tenant should purchase renter's insurance; and (4) that any renter's insurance obtained by tenant won't cover flood damage and the renter should find out whether the property is in a special flood hazard area. (Va. Code Ann. § 55.1-1206)

Owner or agent identity: Landlord must disclose to the tenant in writing at or before the commencement of the tenancy the name and address of the person authorized to manage the premises, and an owner of the premises or a person authorized to act for and on behalf of the owner for the purpose of service of process and for the purpose of receiving notices and demands. (Va. Code Ann. § 55.1-1216)

Sale plans: In the event of the sale of the premises, the landlord must notify tenants of the sale and disclose to tenants the name and address of the purchaser and a telephone number for contacting the purchaser. (Va. Code Ann. § 55.1-1216)

Miltary zone: The landlord of property in any locality in which a military air installation is located, or any person authorized to enter into a rental agreement on landlord's behalf, must provide to a prospective tenant a written disclosure that the property is located in a noise zone or accident potential zone, or both, as designated by the locality on its official zoning map. (Va. Code Ann. § 55.1-1217)

Mold: Move-in inspection report must include whether there is any visible evidence of mold (deemed correct unless tenant objects within five days); if evidence is present, tenant may terminate

Required Landlord Disclosures (continued)

or not move in. If tenant stays, landlord must remediate the mold condition within five business days, reinspect, and issue a new report indicating that there is no evidence of mold. (Va. Code Ann. § 55.1-1215)

Ratio utility billing: Landlords who use a ratio utility billing service or who intend to collect monthly billing and other administrative and late fees, must disclose these fees in a written rental agreement. (Va. Code Ann. § 55.1-1212)

Condominium plans: If an application for registration as a condominium or cooperative has been filed with the Real Estate Board, or if there is within six months an existing plan for tenant displacement resulting from demolition or substantial rehabilitation of the property, or conversion of the rental property to office, hotel, or motel use or planned unit development, the landlord or any person authorized to enter into a rental agreement on his behalf must disclose that information in writing to any prospective tenant. (Va. Code Ann. § 55.1-1216)

Defective drywall: Landlords who know of the presence of unrepaired defective drywall in the rental must disclose this before the tenant signs a lease or rental agreement. (Va. Code Ann. § 55.1-1218)

Methamphetamine disclosure: When the landlord knows that the unit was used to manufacture methamphetamine, landlord must give the tenant a written disclosure of this use before the tenant signs a lease, if the unit hasn't been mitigated as required by law. (Va. Code Ann. § 55.1-1219)

Insecticide/pesticide application: Landlords must give tenants written notice no less than 48 hours prior to applying an insecticide or pesticide in the tenant's dwelling unit unless the tenant agrees to a shorter notification period. If a tenant requests the application of the insecticide or pesticide, the 48-hour notice is not required. Tenants who have concerns about specific insecticides or pesticides must notify the landlord in writing no less than 24 hours before the scheduled insecticide or pesticide application.

The tenant shall prepare the dwelling unit for the application of insecticides or pesticides in accordance with any written instructions of the landlord and, if insects or pests are found to be present, follow any written instructions of the landlord to eliminate the insects or pests following the application of insecticides or pesticides. In addition, landlords must post notice of all insecticide or pesticide applications in areas of the rental other than the dwelling units. Such notice shall consist of conspicuous signs placed in or upon the rental where the insecticide or pesticide will be applied at least 48 hours prior to the application. (Va. Code Ann. § 55.1-1223)

Washington

Wash. Rev. Code Ann. §§ 59.18.060, 59.18.253, 59.18.257, 59.18.260, 59.18.285

Move-in checklists required? Checklists are required when landlords collect a security deposit. If landlord fails to provide checklist, landlord is liable to the tenant for the amount of the deposit. (Wash. Rev. Code Ann. § 59.18.260)

Nonrefundable fees permitted? Yes. If landlord collects a nonrefundable fee, the rental document must clearly specify that it is nonrefundable. Landlords cannot collect fees to put a prospective tenant on a wait list for a rental. (Wash. Rev. Code Ann. § 59.18.285)

Fire protection: At the time the lease is signed, landlord must provide fire protection and safety information, including whether the building has a smoking policy, an emergency notification plan, or an evacuation plan. (Wash. Rev. Code Ann. § 59.18.060)

Owner or agent identity: In the rental document or posted conspicuously on the premises, landlord must designate to the tenant the name and address of the person who is the landlord by a statement on the rental agreement or by a notice conspicuously posted on the premises. If the person designated does not reside in Washington, landlord must also designate a person who resides in the county to act as an agent for the purposes of service of notices and process. (Wash. Rev. Code Ann. § 59.18.060)

Required Landlord Disclosures (continued)

Mold: At the time the lease is signed, landlord must provide tenant with information provided or approved by the department of health about the health hazards associated with exposure to indoor mold. (Wash. Rev. Code Ann. § 59.18.060)

Screening criteria: Before obtaining any information about an applicant, landlord must provide (in writing or by posting) the type of information to be accessed, criteria to be used to evaluate the application, and (for consumer reports) the name and address of the consumer reporting agency to be used, including the applicant's rights to obtain a free copy of the report and dispute its accuracy. Landlord must advise tenants whether landlord will accept a comprehensive reusable tenant screening report done by a consumer reporting agency (in which case the landlord may not charge the tenant a fee for a screening report). If landlord maintains a website that advertises residential rentals, the home page must include this information. (Wash. Rev. Code Ann. § 59.18.257)

Tenant screening fee: Landlords who do their own screening may charge a fee for time and costs to obtain background information, but only if they provide the information explained in "Screening criteria," above. (Wash. Rev. Code Ann. § 59.18.257)

Holding deposits: Fees or deposits to hold a rental cannot exceed 25% of the first month's rent. Upon receipt of the fee or deposit, landlords must issue a receipt and a written statement of the conditions, if any, under which the fee or deposit may be retained. (Wash. Rev. Code Ann. § 59.18.253)

West Virginia

W.Va. Code §§ 15A-10-12; W.Va. Code R. §§ 64-92-6, 64-92-7, 37-6A-1(14)

Nonrefundable fees permitted? Nonrefundable fee must be expressly agreed to in writing. (W.Va. Code § 37-6A-1(14))

Carbon monoxide (CO): Anyone who installs a CO detector in a rental unit must inform either the owner, landlord, or resident of the dangers of CO poisoning, and must supply instructions on how to operate the detector. When landlords work on fuel-burning heating or cooking equipment or a units venting system, they must inform tenants of the dangers of CO poisoning and recommend the purchase of a CO detector.

Any landlord who performs repair or maintenance work on a fuel-burning heating or cooking source or a venting system in a rental unit must inform the tenant of the dangers of carbon monoxide poisoning and recommend the installation of a carbon monoxide detector. (W.Va. Code § 15A-10-12)

Methamphetamine contamination: Landlord who has received a remediation completion certificate from the West Virginia Department of Health and Human Resources must disclose it to prospective tenants. If work is ongoing, landlord must disclose the location of the drug lab, remediation plans, and law enforcement actions. (W. Va. Code R. § 64-92-7)

Wisconsin

Wis. Admin. Code §§ 134.04-.06, 134.09, Wis. Stat. Ann. §§ 704.05, 704.07, 704.14, 704.08 ;. § 704.07(2) (bm); § 704.05(5))

Move-in checklist required? Yes. Tenant has a right to inspect the rental and give landlord a list of defects, and to receive a list of damages charged to the prior tenant. Tenant has seven days after start of the tenancy to return the list to the landlord. (Wis. Admin. Code § 134.06; Wis. Stat. Ann. § 704.08)

Must checklist rights be stated in the lease? No.

Owner or agent identity: Landlord must disclose to the tenant in writing, at or before the time a rental agreement is signed, the name and address of: the person or persons authorized to collect or receive rent and manage and maintain the premises, and who can readily be contacted by the tenant; and the owner of the premises or other person authorized to accept service of legal process and other notices and demands on behalf of the owner. The address must be an address within the state at which service of process can be made in person. (Wis. Admin. Code § 134.04)

Required Landlord Disclosures (continued)

Nonstandard rental provisions: If landlord wants to enter premises for reasons not specified by law, landlord must disclose the provision in a separate written document entitled "NONSTANDARD RENTAL PROVISIONS" before the rental agreement is signed. (Wis. Admin. Code § 134.09)

Habitability deficiencies: Landlord must disclose serious problems that affect the rental unit's habitability. (Wis. Admin. Code § 134.04)

Utility charges: If charges for water, heat, or electricity are not included in the rent, the landlord must disclose this fact to the tenant before entering into a rental agreement or accepting any earnest money or security deposit from the prospective tenant. If individual dwelling units and common areas are not separately metered, and if the charges are not included in the rent, the landlord must disclose the basis on which charges for utility services will be allocated among individual dwelling units. (Wis. Admin. Code § 134.04)

Uncorrected code violations: Before signing a rental contract or accepting a security deposit, the landlord must disclose to the tenant any uncorrected code violation of which the landlord is actually aware, that affects the dwelling unit or a common area and poses a significant threat to the tenant's health or safety. "Disclosure" consists of showing prospective tenants the portions of the building affected, as well as the notices themselves. (Wis. Stat. Ann. § 704.07(2)(bm); Wis. Admin. Code § 134.04)

Disposing of abandoned property: If landlord intends to immediately dispose of any tenant property left behind after move-out, landlord must notify tenant at the time lease is signed. (But landlord must hold prescription medications and medical equipment for seven days, and must give notice before disposing of vehicles or manufactured homes to owner and any known secured party.) (Wis. Stat. Ann. § 704.05(5))

Notice of domestic abuse protections: Landlords must include the following notice in the rental agreement or in an addendum to the agreement: "NOTICE OF DOMESTIC ABUSE PROTECTIONS"

(1) As provided in section 106.50(5m)(dm) of the Wisconsin statutes, a tenant has a defense to an eviction action if the tenant can prove that the landlord knew, or should have known, the tenant is a victim of domestic abuse, sexual assault, or stalking and that the eviction action is based on conduct related to domestic abuse, sexual assault, or stalking committed by either of the following:

(a) A person who was not the tenant's invited guest.

(b) A person who was the tenant's invited guest, but the tenant has done either of the following:

1. Sought an injunction barring the person from the premises.

2. Provided a written statement to the landlord stating that the person will no longer be an invited guest of the tenant and the tenant has not subsequently invited the person to be the tenant's guest.

(2) A tenant who is a victim of domestic abuse, sexual assault, or stalking may have the right to terminate the rental agreement in certain limited situations, as provided in section 704.16 of the Wisconsin statutes. If the tenant has safety concerns, the tenant should contact a local victim service provider or law enforcement agency.

(3) A tenant is advised that this notice is only a summary of the tenant's rights and the specific language of the statutes governs in all instances." (Wis. Stat. Ann. § 704.14)

Wyoming

Wyo. Stat. Ann. § 1-21-1207

Nonrefundable fees permitted? Yes. If any portion of the deposit is not refundable, rental agreement must include this information and tenant must be told before paying a deposit.

State Laws on Landlord's Access to Rental Property									
This is a synopsis of state laws that specify circumstances when a landlord may enter rental premises and the amount of notice required for such entry.									
				Reasons Landlord May Enter					
State	State Law Citation	Amount of Notice Required in Nonemergency Situations	Form of Notice	To Deal With an Emergency	To Inspect the Premises	To Make Repairs, Alterations, or Improvements	To Show Property to Prospective Tenants or Purchasers	During Tenant's Extended Absence	When Tenant Has Abandoned the Property
Alabama	Ala. Code §§ 35-9A-303, 35-9A-423	Two days	Not specified	✓	✓	✓	✓	✓	✓
Alaska	Alaska Stat. §§ 34.03.140, 34.03.230	24 hours	Not specified	✓	✓	✓	✓	✓	✓
Arizona	Ariz. Rev. Stat. § 33-1343	Two days; notice period does not apply, and tenant's consent is assumed, if entry is pursuant to tenant's request for maintenance as prescribed in Ariz. Rev. Stat. § 33-1341, paragraph 8.	Not specified	✓	✓	✓	✓		✓
Arkansas	Ark. Code § 18-17-602	No notice specified	Not specified		✓	✓	✓		
California	Cal. Civ. Code §§ 1950.5, 1954	Reasonable notice; 24 hours is presumed reasonable (48 hours for initial move-out inspection).	Written notice required, but oral notice is sufficient if the entry is to show the property to prospective or actual purchasers, but only if the landlord has given written notice within the previous 120 days, telling the tenant that the property is for sale and such oral notice might be given (24 hours' notice is presumed reasonable; landlord must leave a note when leaving).	✓	✓	✓	✓		✓

State Laws on Landlord's Access to Rental Property (continued)

State	State Law Citation	Amount of Notice Required in Nonemergency Situations	Form of Notice	Reasons Landlord May Enter					
				To Deal With an Emergency	To Inspect the Premises	To Make Repairs, Alterations, or Improvements	To Show Property to Prospective Tenants or Purchasers	During Tenant's Extended Absence	When Tenant Has Abandoned the Property
Colorado	Colo. Rev. Stat. § 38-12-1004	Notice statute relates only to access for inspecting for or treating a bed bug infestation. 48 hours' notice required unless lease says otherwise.	Not specified, unless the access is related to a possible or actual bed bug infestation, in which case notice must be electronic or written.						
Connecticut	Conn. Gen. Stat. §§ 47a-16 to 47a-16a	Reasonable notice	Written or oral	✓	✓	✓	✓	✓	✓
Delaware	Del. Code tit. 25, §§ 5113, 5507, 5509, 5510	48 hours	Written, by giving a copy to an adult who resides at the rental unit or at the tenant's usual residence (if it's not the rental) or by mailing via registered or certified mail or first class mail as evidenced by a certificate of mailing postage-prepaid, addressed to the tenant at the rental. The notice can also be posted at the rental unit when it's combined with a return receipt of a certificate of mailing.	✓	✓	✓	✓	✓	
District of Columbia	D.C. Code Ann. § 42-3505.51	48 hours	Written and electronic (including email and mobile text messaging), but if the tenant doesn't provide an acknowlegment of the electronic notice in writing, the landlord must provide a paper notice.	✓	✓	✓	✓		

				Reasons Landlord May Enter					
State	**State Law Citation**	**Amount of Notice Required in Nonemergency Situations**	**Form of Notice**	To Deal With an Emergency	To Inspect the Premises	To Make Repairs, Alterations, or Improvements	To Show Property to Prospective Tenants or Purchasers	During Tenant's Extended Absence	When Tenant Has Abandoned the Property
Florida	Fla. Stat. § 83.53	24 hours for repairs; landlord may enter "when necessary" in an emergency, when a tenant unreasonably withholds consent, or when the tenant is gone (without notifying the landlord) for a period of time equal to one-half the time for periodic rental payments.	Not specified	✓	✓	✓	✓	✓	
Georgia	No statute								
Hawaii	Haw. Rev. Stat. §§ 521-53, 521-70(b)	Two days	Not specified	✓	✓	✓	✓	✓	✓
Idaho	No statute								
Illinois	No statute								
Indiana	Ind. Code § 32-31-5-6	Reasonable notice	Written or oral	✓	✓	✓	✓		✓
Iowa	Iowa Code §§ 562A.19, 562A.28, 562A.29	24 hours	Not specified	✓	✓	✓	✓	✓	✓
Kansas	Kan. Stat. §§ 58-2557, 58-2565	Reasonable notice	Not specified	✓	✓	✓	✓	✓	✓
Kentucky	Ky. Rev. Stat. §§ 383.615, 383.670	Two days	Not specified	✓	✓	✓	✓	✓	✓
Louisiana	La. Civ. Code art. 2693	No notice specified	Not specified			✓			
Maine	Me. Rev. Stat. tit. 14, § 6025	24 hours	Not specified	✓	✓	✓	✓		
Maryland	No statute								
Massachusetts	Mass. Gen. Laws ch. 186, § 15B(1)(a)	No notice specified	Not specified		✓	✓	✓		✓

State Laws on Landlord's Access to Rental Property (continued)

				Reasons Landlord May Enter					
State	State Law Citation	Amount of Notice Required in Nonemergency Situations	Form of Notice	To Deal With an Emergency	To Inspect the Premises	To Make Repairs, Alterations, or Improvements	To Show Property to Prospective Tenants or Purchasers	During Tenant's Extended Absence	When Tenant Has Abandoned the Property
Michigan	No statute								
Minnesota	Minn. Stat. § 504B.211	Reasonable notice	Not specified	✓	✓	✓	✓		
Mississippi	Miss. Code § 89-7-49	When a landlord believes tenant has abandoned property, and the tenant owes rent, the landlord may request the constable of the county to go onto the premises to ascertain abandonment and leave a notice.	Written notice						✓
Missouri	No statute								
Montana	Mont. Code §§ 70-24-108, 70-24-312, 70-24-426	24 hours	Email (if email is provided in the lease or rental agreement), hand delivery, mail with a certificate of mailing or by certified mail, or a post on the main entry door of the dwelling unit.	✓	✓	✓	✓	✓	✓
Nebraska	Neb. Rev. Stat. §§ 76-1423, 76-1432	24 hours	Not specified	✓	✓	✓	✓	✓	✓
Nevada	Nev. Rev. Stat. § 118A.330	24 hours	Not specified	✓	✓	✓	✓		✓
New Hampshire	N.H. Rev. Stat. § 540-A:3	Notice that is adequate under the circumstances; however, 48 hours' notice when entering after receiving notice of a bed bug infestation in an adjacent unit.	Not specified, but 48 hours when entering to evaluate a possible or actual bed bug infestation.	✓	✓	✓	✓		

				Reasons Landlord May Enter					
State	**State Law Citation**	**Amount of Notice Required in Nonemergency Situations**	**Form of Notice**	To Deal With an Emergency	To Inspect the Premises	To Make Repairs, Alterations, or Improvements	To Show Property to Prospective Tenants or Purchasers	During Tenant's Extended Absence	When Tenant Has Abandoned the Property
New Jersey	N.J. Stat. § 2A:39-1; N.J.A.C. 5:10-5.1 (for buildings with more than one unit)	In buildings with fewer than three units: Landlords can enter only when they have the tenant's permission or a court order. In buildings with three or more units: Landlords have a right to access the unit to inspect it, make repairs or perform maintenance, and deal with emergencies, but must give reasonable notice (one day under ordinary circumstances) before entering.	Not specified						
New Mexico	N.M. Stat. §§ 47-8-24, 47-8-34	24 hours	Written notice	✓	✓	✓	✓	✓	✓
New York	No statute								
North Carolina	No statute								
North Dakota	N.D. Cent. Code § 47-16-07.3	Reasonable notice	Not specified	✓	✓	✓	✓		✓
Ohio	Ohio Rev. Code §§ 5321.04(A)(8), 5321.05(B)	24 hours	Not specified	✓	✓	✓	✓		
Oklahoma	Okla. Stat. tit. 41, § 128	One day	Not specified	✓	✓	✓	✓		✓
Oregon	Or. Rev. Stat. §§ 90.322, 90.410	24 hours	Not specified	✓	✓	✓	✓	✓	✓
Pennsylvania	No statute								

State Laws on Landlord's Access to Rental Property (continued)

State Laws on Landlord's Access to Rental Property (continued)

State	State Law Citation	Amount of Notice Required in Nonemergency Situations	Form of Notice	Reasons Landlord May Enter					
				To Deal With an Emergency	To Inspect the Premises	To Make Repairs, Alterations, or Improvements	To Show Property to Prospective Tenants or Purchasers	During Tenant's Extended Absence	When Tenant Has Abandoned the Property
Rhode Island	R.I. Gen. Laws § 34-18-26	Two days	Not specified	✓	✓	✓	✓	✓	✓
South Carolina	S.C. Code §§ 27-40-530, 27-40-730	24 hours	Not specified	✓	✓	✓	✓		✓
South Dakota	No statute								
Tennessee	Tenn. Code §§ 66-28-403, 66-28-507	24 hours (applies only within the final 30 days of the rental agreement term, when landlord intends to show the premises to prospective renters and this right of access is set forth in the rental agreement).	Not specified	✓	✓	✓	✓	✓	✓
Texas	No statute								
Utah	Utah Code §§ 57-22-4, 57-22-5(2)(c)	24 hours, unless rental agreement specifies otherwise.	Not specified				✓		
Vermont	Vt. Stat. tit. 9, § 4460	48 hours	Not specified	✓	✓	✓	✓		
Virginia	Va. Code §§ 55.1-1229, 55.1-1249	For routine maintenance only: 72 hours, but no notice needed if entry follows tenant's request for maintenance	Not specified	✓	✓	✓	✓	✓	✓
Washington	Wash. Rev. Code § 59.18.150	Two days; one day to show property to actual or prospective tenants or buyers	Written notice, unless it is impracticable to do so.	✓	✓	✓	✓		✓
West Virginia	No statute								

				Reasons Landlord May Enter					
State	**State Law Citation**	**Amount of Notice Required in Nonemergency Situations**	**Form of Notice**	To Deal With an Emergency	To Inspect the Premises	To Make Repairs, Alterations, or Improvements	To Show Property to Prospective Tenants or Purchasers	During Tenant's Extended Absence	When Tenant Has Abandoned the Property
Wisconsin	Wis. Stat. § 704.05(2); Wis. Admin Code § ATCP 134.09(2)	With 12 hours' advance notice, landlords may enter at reasonable times. Landlords and tenants may sign a separate "Nonstandard Rental Provision" agreement, in which they provide for entry for reasons not enumerated in this chart.	Not specified	✓	✓	✓	✓	✓	✓
Wyoming	No statute								

State Laws on Landlord's Access to Rental Property (continued)

State Landlord-Tenant Exemption Statutes

Your state's general landlord-tenant statutes (listed in the "State Landlord-Tenant Statutes" chart above) might not apply to all types of rentals and landlord-tenant relationships: Most states define what a rental is for purposes of the statutes. Other states might not define what a rental is, but instead exempt certain types of occupancies from the general landlord-tenant statutes. Some states do both. To check whether your state's general landlord-tenant statutes apply to your situation, review the statutes listed in the "State Landlord-Tenant Statutes" chart for any definition of what your state considers a rental. Next, you'll need to find out whether your situation falls within any exemptions from the general landlord-tenant statutes. This chart provides information about the exemptions that are most relevant to readers of this book. If your state does not have an exemption statute, you'll see "No statute" written in the Exemptions column.

Alabama

Ala. Code §§ 35-9A-122, 35-9A-601

1. Occupancy under a contract of sale of a dwelling unit or the property of which it is a part, if the occupant is the purchaser or a person who succeeds to the interest of the purchaser

2. Occupancy by a member of a social organization in the portion of a structure operated for the benefit of the organization

3. Transient occupancy in a hotel, motel, or lodgings

4. Occupancy by an employee of a landlord whose right to occupancy is conditional upon employment at the premises

5. Occupancy under a rental agreement covering premises rented by the occupant primarily for agricultural purposes

6. Continuation of occupancy by the seller or a member of the seller's family for a period of not more than 36 months after the sale of a dwelling unit or the property of which it is a part; and

7. Rental agreements most recently entered into, extended, or renewed before January 1, 2007.

Alaska

Alaska Stat. §§ 34.03.330, 34.03.370

1. Occupancy under a contract of sale of a dwelling unit or the property of which it is a part if the occupant is the purchaser or a person who succeeds to the interest of a purchaser

2. Occupancy by a member of a social organization in the portion of a structure operated for the benefit of the organization

3. Transient occupancy in a hotel, motel, lodgings, or other transient facility

4. Occupancy by an employee of a landlord whose right to occupancy is conditioned upon employment substantially for services, maintenance, or repair to the premises

5. Occupancy under a rental agreement covering premises used by the occupant primarily for agricultural purposes

6. Occupancy under a rental agreement covering premises used as part of a transitional or supportive housing program that is sponsored or operated by a public corporation or by a nonprofit corporation and that provides shelter and related support services; and

7. Any rental agreement, lease, or tenancy most recently entered into, extended, or renewed before March 19, 1974.

Arizona

Ariz. Rev. Stat. § 33-1308

1. Occupancy under a contract of sale of a dwelling unit or the property of which it is a part, if the occupant is the purchaser or a person who succeeds to the purchaser's interest

2. Occupancy by a member of a social organization in the portion of a structure operated for the benefit of the organization

3. Transient occupancy in a hotel, motel or recreational lodging

State Landlord-Tenant Exemption Statutes (continued)

4. Occupancy by an employee of a landlord as a manager or custodian whose right to occupancy is conditional upon employment at the premises; and

5. Occupancy in or operation of public housing as authorized, provided or conducted under or pursuant to any federal law or regulation.

Arkansas

Ark. Code § 18-17-202

1. Occupancy under a contract of sale of a dwelling unit or the property of which it is a part, if the occupant is the purchaser or a person who succeeds to the purchaser's interest

2. Occupancy by a member of a social organization in the portion of a structure operated for the benefit of the organization

3. Transient occupancy in a hotel, motel, or other accommodations subject to any sales tax on lodging

4. Occupancy by an employee of a landlord whose right to occupancy is conditional upon employment in and about the premises

5. Occupancy under a rental agreement covering the premises used by the occupant primarily for agricultural purposes; and

6. Residence, whether temporary or not, at a public or private charitable or emergency protective shelter.

California

Cal. Civ. Code § 1940

1. Transient occupancy in a hotel, motel, residence club, or other facility; and

2. Occupancy at a hotel or motel where the innkeeper retains a right of access to and control of the dwelling unit and the hotel or motel provides or offers certain services.

Colorado

Colo. Rev. Stat. § 38-12-511

1. Occupancy under a contract of sale of a dwelling unit or the property of which it is a part, if the occupant is the purchaser, seller, or a person who succeeds to the purchaser's or seller's interest

2. Occupancy by a member of a social organization in the portion of a structure operated for the benefit of the organization

3. Transient occupancy in a hotel or motel that lasts less than 30 days

4. Occupancy by an employee or independent contractor whose right to occupancy is conditional upon performance of services for an employer or contractor

5. Occupancy in a structure that is located within an unincorporated area of a county, does not receive water, heat, and sewer services from a public entity, and is rented for recreational purposes, such as a hunting cabin, yurt, hut, or other similar structure

6. Occupancy under rental agreement covering a residential premises used by the occupant primarily for agricultural purposes; and

7. Any relationship between the owner of a mobile home park and the owner of a mobile home situated in the park.

Connecticut

Conn. Gen. Stat. § 47a-2

1. Occupancy under a contract of sale of a dwelling unit or the property of which such unit is a part, if the occupant is the purchaser or a person who succeeds to the purchaser's interest

2. Occupancy by a member of a social organization in the portion of a structure operated for the benefit of such organization

3. Transient occupancy in a hotel, motel, or similar lodging; and

4. Occupancy by a personal care assistant or other person who is employed by a person with a disability to assist and support such disabled person with daily living activities or housekeeping chores and is provided dwelling space in the personal residence of such disabled person as a benefit or condition of such employment.

State Landlord-Tenant Exemption Statutes (continued)

Delaware

Del. Code tit. 25, §§ 5101, 5102

1. Residence at an institution where such residence is merely incidental to detention or to the provision of medical, geriatric, educational, counseling, religious, or similar services

2. Residence by a member of a fraternal organization in a structure operated for the benefit of the organization

3. Residence in a hotel, motel, cubicle hotel or other similar lodgings

4. Nonrenewable rental agreements of 120 days or less for any calendar year for a dwelling located within the boundaries of Broadkill Hundred, Lewes-Rehoboth Hundred, Indian River Hundred, Baltimore Hundred and Cedar Creek Hundred; and

5. Rental agreements for ground upon which improvements were constructed or installed by the tenant and used as a dwelling, where the tenant retains ownership or title thereto, or obtains title to existing improvement on the property.

District of Columbia

D.C. Code § 42-3502.05

1. Rental units operated by a foreign government as a residence for diplomatic personnel

2. Rental units in an establishment which has as its primary purpose providing diagnostic care and treatment of diseases; and

3. Dormitories.

Also: Following a determination by the Rent Administrator, any rental intended for use as long-term temporary housing by families with 1 or more members that satisfies each of the following requirements:

  A. The rental is occupied by families that, at the time of their initial occupancy, have had incomes at or below 50% of the District median income for families of the size in question for the immediately preceding 12 months;

  B. The provider of the rental is a nonprofit charitable organization that operates the rental on a strictly not-for-profit basis; and

  C. The housing provider offers a comprehensive social services program to resident families.

Florida

Fla. Stat. § 83.42

1. Occupancy under a contract of sale of a dwelling unit or the property of which it is a part in which the buyer has paid at least 12 months' rent or in which the buyer has paid at least 1 month's rent and a deposit of at least 5% of the purchase price of the property; and

2. Transient occupancy in a hotel, condominium, motel, roominghouse, or similar public lodging, or transient occupancy in a mobile home park.

Georgia

No statute

Hawaii

Haw. Rev. Stat. § 521-7

1. Residence in a structure directly controlled and managed by:

  A. The University of Hawaii or any other university or college in the State for housing its own students or faculty or residence in a structure erected on land leased from the university or college by a nonprofit corporation for the exclusive purpose of housing students or faculty of the college or university; or

  B. A private dorm management company that offers a minimum of 50 beds to students of any college, university, or other institution of higher education in the State

2. Occupancy under a bona fide contract of sale of the dwelling unit or the property of which it is a part where the tenant is, or succeeds to the interest of, the purchaser

3. Residence by a member of a fraternal organization in a structure operated without profit for the benefit of the organization

State Landlord-Tenant Exemption Statutes (continued)

4. Transient occupancy on a day-to-day basis in a hotel or motel

5. Occupancy by an employee of the owner or landlord whose right to occupancy is conditional upon that employment for a period of up to four years, pursuant to a plan for the transfer of the dwelling unit or the property of which it is a part to the occupant

6. A lease of improved residential land for a term of 15 years or more

7. Occupancy by the prospective purchaser after an accepted offer to purchase and prior to the actual transfer of the owner's rights; and

8. Occupancy by the seller of residential real property after the transfer of the seller's ownership rights.

Idaho

No statute

Illinois

No statute

Indiana

Ind. Code § 32-31-2.9-4

1. Occupancy under a contract of sale of a rental unit or the property of which the rental unit is a part if the occupant is the purchaser or a person who succeeds to the purchaser's interest

2. Occupancy by a member of a social organization in the part of a structure operated for the benefit of the organization

3. Transient occupancy in a hotel, motel, or other lodging

4. Occupancy by an employee of a landlord whose right to occupancy is conditional upon employment at the premises; and

5. Rental agreements covering property used by the occupant primarily for agricultural purposes.

Iowa

Iowa Code §§ 562A.5, 562A.37

1. Occupancy under a contract of sale of a dwelling unit or the property of which it is a part, if the occupant is the purchaser or a person who succeeds to the purchaser's interest

2. Occupancy by a member of a social organization in the portion of a structure operated for the benefit of the organization

3. Transient occupancy in a hotel, motel, or other similar lodgings

4. Occupancy by an employee of a landlord whose right to occupancy is conditional upon employment at the premises

5. Rental agreements covering premises used by the occupant primarily for agricultural purposes; and

6. Rental agreements most recently entered into, extended, or renewed on or before January 1, 1979.

Kansas

Kan. Stat. §§ 58-2541, 58-2573

1. Occupancy under a contract of sale of a dwelling unit or the property of which it is a part, if the occupant is the purchaser or a person who succeeds to the purchaser's interest

2. Occupancy by a member of a social organization in the portion of a structure operated for the benefit of the organization

3. Transient occupancy in a hotel, motel, or rooming house

4. Occupancy by an employee of a landlord whose right to occupancy is conditional upon employment at the premises

5. Occupancy under a rental agreement covering premises used by the occupant primarily for agricultural purposes; and

6. Any rental agreement most recently entered into, extended, or modified before July 1, 1975.

Kentucky

Ky. Rev. Stat. § 383.535

1. Occupancy under a contract of sale of a dwelling unit or the property of which it is a part, if the occupant is the purchaser or a person who succeeds to the purchaser's interest

State Landlord-Tenant Exemption Statutes (continued)

2. Occupancy by a member of a social organization in the portion of a structure operated for the benefit of the organization

3. Transient occupancy in a hotel, or motel, or lodgings subject to state transient lodgings or room occupancy excise tax act

4. Occupancy by an employee of a landlord whose right to occupancy is conditional upon employment at the premises; and

5. Occupancy of a dwelling located on land devoted to the production of livestock, livestock products, poultry, poultry products, or the growing of tobacco or other crops.

Louisiana

No statute

Maine

No statute

Maryland

Md. Code Real Prop. § 8-201

Tenancies arising after the sale of owner-occupied residential property where the seller and purchaser agree that the seller may remain in possession of the property for a period of not more than 60 days after the settlement.

Massachusetts

No statute

Michigan

Mich. Comp. Laws § 554.601 // Mich. Comp. Laws § 554.632

1. Occupancy in a motel, motor home, or other tourist accommodation, when used as a temporary accommodation for guests or tourists; and

2. Premises used as the principal place of residence of the owner and rented occasionally during temporary absences.

Minnesota

No statute

Mississippi

Miss. Code § 89-8-3

1. Occupancy under a contract of sale of a dwelling unit or the property of which it is a part, if the occupant is the purchaser or a person who succeeds to the purchaser's interest

2. Occupancy by a member of a social organization in the portion of a structure operated for the benefit of the organization

3. Transient occupancy in a hotel, motel, or lodgings

4. Occupancy under a rental agreement covering premises used by the occupant primarily for agricultural purposes

5. Occupancy when the occupant is performing agricultural labor for the owner and such premises are rented for less than fair rental value; and

6. Any rental agreement entered into before July 1, 1991.

Missouri

No statute

Montana

Mont. Code § 70-24-104

1. Occupancy under a contract of sale of a dwelling unit or the property of which it is a part if the occupant is the purchaser or a person who succeeds to the purchaser's interest

2. Occupancy by a member of a social organization in the portion of a structure operated for the benefit of the organization

3. Transient occupancy in a hotel or motel

4. Occupancy under a rental agreement covering premises used by the occupant primarily for commercial or agricultural purposes

5. Occupancy by an employee of a landlord whose right to occupancy is conditional upon employment at the premises; and

6. Occupancy outside a municipality under a rental agreement that includes hunting, fishing, or agricultural privileges, along with the use of the dwelling unit.

State Landlord-Tenant Exemption Statutes (continued)

Nebraska

Neb. Rev. Stat. §§ 76-1408, 76-1448

1. Occupancy under a contract of sale of a dwelling unit or the property of which it is a part, if the occupant is the purchaser or a person who succeeds to the purchaser's interest

2. Occupancy by a member of a social organization in the portion of a structure operated for the benefit of the organization

3. Transient occupancy in a hotel or motel

4. Occupancy by an employee of a landlord whose right to occupancy is conditional upon employment at the premises

5. Occupancy under a rental agreement covering premises used by the occupant primarily for agricultural purposes

6. A lease of improved or unimproved residential land for a term of five years or more; and

7. Rental agreements most recently entered into, extended, or renewed on or before July 1, 1975.

Nevada

Nev. Rev. Stat. §§ 118A.180, 118A.530

1. Rental agreements for manufactured homes

2. Occupancy under a contract of sale of a dwelling unit or the property of which it is a part, if the occupant is the purchaser or successor to the purchaser's interest

3. Occupancy by a member of a social organization in the portion of a structure operated for the benefit of the organization

4. Occupancy in a hotel or motel for less than 30 consecutive days unless the occupant clearly manifests an intent to remain for a longer continuous period

5. Occupancy by an employee of a landlord whose right to occupancy is solely conditional upon employment at the premises

6. Occupancy under a rental agreement covering premises used by the occupant primarily for agricultural purposes

7. Occupancy by a person who is guilty of a forcible entry or forcible detainer; and

8. Rental agreements most recently entered into, extended, or renewed before July 1, 1977.

New Hampshire

N.H. Rev. Stat. § 540:1-a

1. Rooms in rooming or boarding houses that are rented to transient guests for fewer than 90 consecutive days

2. Rooms in hotels, motels, inns, tourist homes, and other dwellings rented for recreational or vacation use

3. Single-family homes in which the occupant has no lease, which is the primary and usual residence of the owner

4. Shared residential facilities (properties with separate sleeping areas for each occupant and in which each occupant has access to and shares with the owner one or more areas of the property)

5. Vacation or recreational rentals

6. Residential units leased by a member of a social organization that provides student housing for a postsecondary institution in a structure owned and operated by the social organization; and

7. Occupancies in which the occupant is hired to provide care or assistance for a person with disabilities.

New Jersey

N.J. Stat. § 46:8-9.12 // N.J. Stat. § 46:8-44

1. Seasonal rentals (does not include use or rental of living quarters for seasonal, temporary or migrant farm workers in connection with any work or place where work is being performed)

2. Dwelling units in rentals containing not more than two such units

3. Owner-occupied premises of not more than three dwelling units; and

4. Hotels, motels, or other guest houses serving transient or seasonal guests.

State Landlord-Tenant Exemption Statutes (continued)

New Mexico

N.M. Stat. §§ 47-8-9, 47-8-51

1. Occupancy under a contract of sale of a dwelling unit or the property of which it is part, if the occupant is the purchaser or a person who succeeds to the purchaser's interest

2. Occupancy by a member of a social organization in the portion of a structure operated for the benefit of the organization

3. Transient occupancy in a hotel or motel

4. Occupancy by an employee of an owner pursuant to a written rental or employment agreement that specifies that the employee's right to occupancy is conditional upon employment at the premises

5. Occupancy under a rental agreement covering premises used by the occupant primarily for agricultural purposes; and

6. Rental agreements most recently entered into, extended, or renewed on or before July 1, 1975.

New York

N.Y. Mult. Dwell. Law §§ 3, 4, 8, 9, 13, 14 // N.Y. Mult. Resid. Law §§ 3, 4, 9 // N.Y. Gen. Oblig. Law § 7-108

1. Rentals in cities with a population of less than 325,000; and

2. Rentals occupied by fewer than three families living independently of each other.

N.Y. Mult. Resid. Law §§ 3, 4, 9

1. Rentals in cities with a population equal to or greater than 325,000; and

2. Rentals occupied by fewer than three families living independently of each other.

N.Y. Gen. Oblig. Law § 7-108(1-a)(a)

Seasonal use dwelling units are exempt from the security deposit limit.

North Carolina

N.C. Gen. Stat. § 42-39

1. Transient occupancy in a hotel, motel, or similar lodging

2. Vacation rentals; and

3. Dwellings provided without charge or rent.

North Dakota

No statute

Ohio

Ohio Rev. Code § 5321.01

1. Tourist homes, hotels, motels, recreational vehicle parks, recreation camps, combined park-camps, temporary park-camps, and other similar facilities where circumstances indicate a transient occupancy

2. Farm residences furnished in connection with the rental of land of a minimum of two acres for production of agricultural products by one or more of the occupants

3. Manufactured home parks, marinas, and agricultural labor camps; and

4. Occupancy in hotels and single room occupancy facilities.

Oklahoma

Okla. Stat. tit. 41, § 104

1. Occupancy under a contract of sale or contract for deed of a dwelling unit or of the property of which it is a part, if the occupant is the purchaser or a person who succeeds to the purchaser's interest

2. Occupancy by a member of a social organization in a structure operated for the benefit of the organization

3. Transient occupancy in a hotel, motel, or other similar lodging; and

4. Occupancy under a rental agreement covering premises used by the occupant primarily for agricultural purposes.

Oregon

Or. Rev. Stat. §§ 90.110, 90.113, 90.120

1. Occupancy of a dwelling unit for no more than 90 days by a purchaser prior to the scheduled closing of a real estate sale or by a seller following

State Landlord-Tenant Exemption Statutes (continued)

the closing of a sale, in either case as permitted under the terms of an agreement for sale of the property

2. Occupancy by a member of a social organization in the portion of a structure operated for the benefit of the organization

3. Transient occupancy in a hotel or motel

4. Occupancy by a squatter

5. Vacation occupancy

6. Occupancy by an employee of a landlord whose right to occupancy is conditional upon employment at the premises; and

7. Occupancy under a rental agreement covering premises used by the occupant primarily for agricultural purposes.

Note that different rules might apply to occupancy of manufactured dwellings, floating homes, and recreational vehicles.

Pennsylvania

No statute

Rhode Island

R.I. Gen. Laws § 34-18-8

Unless the parties expressly agree to be governed by them, the following occupancies are exempted from the residential landlord-tenant statutes:

1. Occupancy under a contract of sale of a dwelling unit or the property of which it is a part, if the occupant is the purchaser or a person who succeeds to the purchaser's interest

2. Occupancy by a member of a social organization in the portion of a structure operated for the benefit of the organization

3. Transient occupancy in a hotel, motel, or other lodging

4. Occupancy by a paid employee of a landlord, whose right to occupancy is conditional upon employment substantially for services, maintenance, or repair of premises containing more than eleven units; and

5. Residence at a transitional housing facility.

South Carolina

S.C. Code § 27-40-120

1. Occupancy under a contract of sale of a dwelling unit or the property of which it is a part, if the occupant is the purchaser or a person who succeeds to the purchaser's interest

2. Occupancy by a member of a social organization in the portion of a structure operated for the benefit of the organization

3. Transient occupancy in a hotel, motel, or other accommodations subject to the sales tax on accommodations

4. Occupancy by an employee of a landlord whose right to occupancy is conditional upon employment at the premises

5. Occupancy under a rental agreement covering the premises used by the occupant primarily for agricultural purposes; and

6. Occupancy under a rental agreement for a vacation time share.

South Dakota

No statute

Tennessee

Tenn. Code § 66-28-102

1. Rentals in counties with a population of less than 75,000, according to the 2010 federal census or any subsequent federal census

2. Rental agreements most recently entered into, extended, or renewed before July 1, 1975

3. Occupancy under a contract of sale of a dwelling unit or the property of which it is a part, if the occupant is the purchaser or a person who succeeds to the purchaser's interest

4. Transient occupancy in a hotel, motel, or lodgings subject to city, state, or transient lodgings laws; and

5. Occupancy under a rental agreement covering premises used by the occupant primarily for agricultural purposes.

State Landlord-Tenant Exemption Statutes (continued)

Texas

No statute

Utah

Utah Code § 57-22-2

1. Boarding houses or similar facilities

2. Mobile home lots; and

3. Recreational properties rented on an occasional basis.

Vermont

Vt. Stat. tit. 9, § 4452

1. Occupancy under a contract of sale of a dwelling unit or the property of which it is a part, if the occupant is the purchaser or a person who succeeds to the purchaser's interest

2. Occupancy by a member of a social or religious organization in the portion of a building operated for the benefit of the organization

3. Transient occupancy in a hotel or motel

4. Rental of a mobile home lot

5. Transient residence in seasonal or short-term vacation or recreational properties; and

6. Occupancy of a dwelling unit without right or permission by a person who is not a tenant.

Virginia

Va. Code § 55.1-1201

1. Occupancy by a member of a social organization in the portion of a structure operated for the benefit of the organization

2. Occupancy in a campground

3. Occupancy by a tenant who pays no rent pursuant to a rental agreement

4. Occupancy by an employee of a landlord whose right to occupancy in a multifamily dwelling unit is conditioned upon employment at the premises or a former employee whose occupancy continues less than 60 days

5. Occupancy under a contract of sale of a dwelling unit or the property of which it is a part, if the occupant is the purchaser or a person who succeeds to the purchaser's interest; and

6. Occupancy in a hotel, motel, extended stay facility, vacation residential facility, timeshare, boardinghouse, or similar transient lodging when the occupancy is not the resident's primary residence, or when the resident uses it as a primary residence for less than 90 days.

Washington

Wash. Rev. Code §§ 59.18.040, 59.18.415, 59.18.430, 59.18.435

1. Occupancy under a bona fide earnest money agreement to purchase or contract of sale of the dwelling unit or the property of which it is a part, where the tenant is, or stands in the place of, the purchaser

2. Residence in a hotel, motel, or other transient lodging

3. Rental agreements for the use of any single-family residence which are incidental to leases or rentals entered into in connection with a lease of land to be used primarily for agricultural purposes

4. Rental agreements providing housing for seasonal agricultural employees while provided in conjunction with such employment

5. Rental agreements with the state of Washington, department of natural resources, on public lands

6. Occupancy by an employee of a landlord whose right to occupy is conditioned upon employment at the premises

7. Leases of single-family dwellings for a period of a year or more or leases of a single-family dwelling containing a bona fide option to purchase by the tenant (but an attorney for the tenant must approve on the face of the agreement any lease exempted from these laws); and

8. Leases entered into before July 16, 1973.

West Virginia

No statute

State Landlord-Tenant Exemption Statutes (continued)

Wisconsin

Wis. Admin. Code ATCP 134.01

1. Occupancy by a member of a fraternal or social organization which operates that dwelling unit

2. Occupancy under a contract of sale, by the purchaser of the dwelling unit or the purchaser's successor in interest

3. Occupancy by tourist or transient occupants

4. Occupancy that the landlord provides free of charge to any person, or that the landlord provides as consideration to a person whom the landlord currently employs to operate or maintain the premises; and

5. Occupancy by a tenant who is engaged in commercial agricultural operations on the premises.

Wyoming

No statute

How to Use the Downloadable Forms on the Nolo Website

This book comes with forms that you can download online at:

www.nolo.com/back-of-book/LEAR.html

To use the files, your computer must have specific software programs installed. Here is a list of types of files provided by this book, as well as the software programs you'll need to access them.

- **RTF.** You can open, edit, print, and save these RTF (Rich Text Format) form files with most word processing programs such as Microsoft *Word*, Windows *WordPad*, and recent versions of *WordPerfect*. On a Mac, you can use Apple *TextEdit* or Apple *Pages*. You can also work with the forms through a word processing app such as Google Docs (www.docs.google.com).

- **PDF.** You can view these files with Adobe *Reader*, free software from www.adobe.com. Unless you have a pdf editing tool or software, you must print out our PDFs and complete them by hand.

Editing RTFs

Here are some general instructions about editing RTF forms in your word processing program. Refer to the book's instructions and sample agreements for help about what should go in each blank.

- **Underlines.** Underlines indicate where to enter information. Replace the blank/underlined section with the needed text.

- **Bracketed and italicized text.** Bracketed and italicized text indicates instructions. Be sure to remove all instructional text before you finalize your document.

- **Optional text.** Optional text gives you the choice to include or exclude it. Delete any optional text you don't want to use. Renumber numbered items, if necessary.

- **Alternative text.** Alternative text gives you the choice between two or more text options. Delete those options you don't want to use. Renumber numbered items, if necessary.

- **Signature lines.** Signature lines should appear on a page with at least some text from the document itself.

Every word processing program uses its own commands to open, format, save, and print documents, so refer to your software's help documents for help using your program. Nolo cannot provide technical support for questions about how to use your computer or your software.

CAUTION

In accordance with U.S. copyright laws, the forms provided by this book are for your personal use only.

List of Forms Available on the Nolo Website

Use the tables below to find the file name for each form. All forms listed are available for download at: **www.nolo.com/back-of-book/LEAR.html**

Forms in RTF Format	
Form Title	**File Name**
Notice of Conditional Acceptance Based on Credit Report or Other Information	Acceptance.rtf
Rental Application	Application.rtf
Consent to Contact References and Perform Credit Check	CheckConsent.rtf
Landlord-Tenant Checklist	Checklist.rtf
Notice of Denial Based on Credit Report or Other Information	Denial.rtf
Fixed-Term Residential Lease	FixedLease.rtf
Fixed-Term Residential Lease (Spanish Version)	PlazoFijo.rtf
Month-to-Month Residential Rental Agreement	MonthToMonth.rtf
Month-to-Month Residential Rental Agreement (Spanish Version)	Mensual.rtf
Move-In Letter	MoveIn.rtf
Move-Out Letter	MoveOut.rtf
Tenant's Notice of Intent to Move Out	MoveNotice.rtf
Tenant References	References.rtf

Forms in PDF Format	
Form Title	**File Name**
Rental Application	Application.pdf
Tenant's Notice of Intent to Move Out	MoveNotice.pdf
Protect Your Family From Lead in Your Home Pamphlet	leadpdfe.pdf
Protect Your Family From Lead in Your Home Pamphlet (Spanish Version)	leadpdfs.pdf
Disclosure of Information on Lead-Based Paint or Lead-Based Paint Hazards	lesr_eng.pdf
Disclosure of Information on Lead-Based Paint or Lead-Based Paint Hazards (Spanish Version)	spanless.pdf
IRS Schedule E (Form 1040)	f1040se.pdf

Index

**NOLO**

More from Nolo

Nolo.com offers a large library of legal solutions and forms, created by Nolo's in-house legal editors. These reliable documents can be prepared in minutes.

Create a Document Online

Incorporation. Incorporate your business in any state.

LLC Formation. Gain asset protection and pass-through tax status in any state.

Will. Nolo has helped people make over 2 million wills. Is it time to make or revise yours?

Living Trust (avoid probate). Plan now to save your family the cost, delays, and hassle of probate.

Download Useful Legal Forms

Nolo.com has hundreds of top quality legal forms available for download:

- bill of sale
- promissory note
- nondisclosure agreement
- LLC operating agreement
- corporate minutes
- commercial lease and sublease
- motor vehicle bill of sale
- consignment agreement
- and many more.

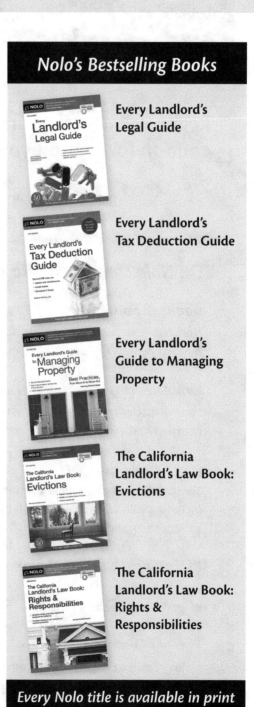

Nolo's Bestselling Books

Every Landlord's Legal Guide

Every Landlord's Tax Deduction Guide

Every Landlord's Guide to Managing Property

The California Landlord's Law Book: Evictions

The California Landlord's Law Book: Rights & Responsibilities

Every Nolo title is available in print and for download at Nolo.com.

www.nolo.com

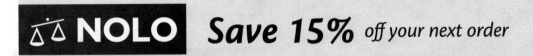

NOLO Save 15% off your next order

Register your Nolo purchase, and we'll send you a **coupon for 15% off** your next Nolo.com order!

On Nolo.com you'll also find:

Books & Software

Nolo publishes hundreds of great books and software programs for consumers and business owners. Order a copy, or download an ebook version instantly, at Nolo.com.

Online Forms

You can quickly and easily make a will or living trust, form an LLC or corporation, or make hundreds of other forms—online.

Free Legal Information

Thousands of articles answer common questions about everyday legal issues, including wills, bankruptcy, small business formation, divorce, patents, employment, and much more.

Plain-English Legal Dictionary

Stumped by jargon? Look it up in America's most up-to-date source for definitions of legal terms, free at Nolo.com.

Lawyer Directory

Nolo's consumer-friendly lawyer directory provides in-depth profiles of lawyers all over America. You'll find information you need to choose the right lawyer.

LEAR15